YES, AND...

Yes, and...
daily
meditations

RICHARD ROHR

Franciscan
MEDIA
Cincinnati, Ohio

Scripture passages are the author's own translation.

Cover image: Two Doors, Mont St. Michel, France,
©William Clift 1997

Book design by Mark Sullivan

Library of Congress Cataloging-in-Publication Data
Rohr, Richard.
Yes, and? : daily meditations / Richard Rohr.
pages cm
Includes bibliographical references.
ISBN 978-1-61636-644-5 (alk. paper)
1. Meditations. I. Title.
BV4832.3.R64 2013
242'.2—dc23
2013009745

Published by Franciscan Media
28 W. Liberty St.
Cincinnati, OH 45202
www.FranciscanMedia.org
www.AmericanCatholic.org

Printed in the United States of America.
Printed on recycled paper.
13 14 15 16 17 5 4 3 2 1

CONTENTS

FOREWORD
David G. Benner, Ph.D.

Every season of life offers special gifts and this wonderful collection of daily meditations clearly reveals that as he turns seventy, Richard Rohr is busy unwrapping important stage-of-life gifts. And what a blessing that is to the rest of us!

I have been reading Fr. Rohr for the past twenty years and eagerly look forward to each of his new books. This collection of meditations will be a gift to anyone who reads it but is, I think, a particularly special gift to those of us who have been journeying with him for a while. The reason for that is that the book is organized around the seven underlying themes of his life and teaching.

Erik Erikson describes the developmental challenge of the eighth stage of a successfully lived life as involving a movement from generativity to ego integrity. No one familiar with his prodigious output of books, webcasts, conferences, and newsletters could ever doubt that Fr. Rohr has achieved the generativity that Erikson suggests is the core developmental challenge of midlife. However, the contentment, fulfillment, and wisdom that are the core of maturity in late adulthood do not come from productivity or creativity. The challenge of the eighth stage of life is to avoid despair by reflecting on one's life and understanding its meaning and significance.

Such reflection was the inner work out of which this collection of meditations was born. And this is what makes this book so much more than a mere compendium of musings. The author's articulation of the seven big themes is itself worth the price of this book. But these are more than simply the themes that have organized his life's work; they are the fundamental issues that any serious Christian must engage in to develop a healthy and holistic spiritual worldview.

The result is a set of daily meditations that offers meat for chewing, not warm milk to make you feel good. And chewing—that is, pondering—is exactly what I have been doing since reading these meditations. The wonderful thing about this format is that the meat is nicely cut up into small pieces so there is no worry about choking! But what makes them worth pondering is that they are the result of a life well-lived.

So, prepare yourself for a treat. Settle back and read this book slowly. And make space in your day to chew on what you are reading. Doing so will deepen your life.

David G. Benner, Ph.D., is a transformational architect and cartographer of the human spirit and soul. His most recent books have included *Spirituality and the Awakening Self* (2012), *Soulful Spirituality* (2011), and *Opening to God* (2010). He can be found online at www.drdavidgbenner.ca and on Twitter @drdavidgbenner.

INTRODUCTION
"By What Authority?" (Luke 20:2)

This might seem like a short but heavy introduction to a book of meditations, but I want to be clear from the beginning about where I get the authority and confidence to talk the way I do. I do not want you to think the meditations in this book are just *my personal ideas and opinions*. Yes, my ongoing love and my ongoing education have largely been based in the Judeo-Christian Scriptures, and I have preached and taught from them for over forty years. I have often struggled with how much damage the Bible has done in human history, and I have often been amazed at how much good the Bible has done, too! There has to be a way to maximize these inherent possibilities for the good, the true, and the beautiful. I hope I can do that here, even if you are not a reader of the Scriptures yourself. They have a kind of natural and inherent authority, even if you are not a religious person as such.

You deserve to know my science for interpreting sacred texts. It is called a "hermeneutic." Without an honest and declared hermeneutic, we have no consistency or authority in our interpretation of the Bible. My methodology is very simple; *I will try to interpret Scripture the way that Jesus did.* This is precisely what Christians should mean when we speak of interpreting the Old Testament in the light of Christ. Ironically, then, it is no longer old at all, but always fresh and contemporary! If Jesus himself is our interpretive key, it will allow you to take Jewish texts and history more seriously than ever before, and to appreciate the honest context from which Jesus spoke.

To take the Scriptures seriously *is not to take them literally.*. Literalism is invariably *the lowest and least level of meaning.* Most Biblical authors understood this, which is why they felt totally free to take so many obvious liberties with what we would call "facts." In many ways, we have moved backwards in our ability to read spiritual and transformative texts, especially after the Enlightenment of the seventeenth and eighteenth centuries when religious people got on the defensive and lost their own unique vantage point. *Serious* reading of Scripture will allow you to find an ever-new spiritual meaning for the liberation of history, the liberation of the soul, and the liberation of God in every generation. Then the text is true on many levels, instead of trying to prove it is true on just the one simple, factual level. Sacred texts always maximize your possibilities for life and love, which is why we call them sacred. I am afraid we have for too long used the Bible merely to prove various church positions, which largely narrows their range and depth. Instead of transforming people, the Biblical texts became utilitarian and handy ammunition.

Biblical messages often proceed from historical events, but they do not depend upon communicating those events with perfect accuracy. That is never the point in writing, unless you are a contemporary journalist afraid of lawsuits or loss of reputation. Fortunately, Moses, Jeremiah, and the prophets did not share those concerns. Our Jewish ancestors sometimes called this deeper approach *midrash*, or extrapolating from *the mere story* to find its actual message. We all do the same when we read anything today, but Jesus and his Jewish people were much more honest and up front about this. Even more than telling us exactly *what to see* in the Scriptures, Jesus taught us *how to see, what to emphasize*, and also *what could be de-emphasized, or even ignored.* Jesus is himself our hermeneutic, and he was in no way a fundamentalist or literalist. He was a man of the Spirit. Just watch him, and watch how he does it (which means you must have some knowledge of *his* Scriptures!).

Jesus consistently ignored or even denied exclusionary, punitive, and triumphalistic texts in his own Jewish Bible in favor of passages that emphasized inclusion, mercy, and honesty. That becomes self-evident once you are told and begin to look for yourself.

He had a deeper and wider eye that knew what passages were creating a highway for God and which passages were merely cultural, self-serving, and legalistic additions. When Christians pretend that every line in the Bible is of equal importance and inspiration, they are being very *unlike* Jesus.

He read his own inspired Scriptures in a spiritual and highly selective way, absolutely ignoring and even rejecting some parts of it in favor of inclusive and helpful messages and parables. *Jesus read the inspired text in an inspired way*, which is precisely why he was accused of "teaching with authority and not like our scribes" (Matthew 7:29). He then accused fervent and pious "teachers of the law" of largely missing the point; "You understand neither the Scriptures nor the power of God" (Mark 12:24), he told them (Mark 12:24). We cannot make the same mistake all over again—and now in his name.

We must be honest and admit that the New Testament was largely written in Greek—a language which Jesus did not speak or understand—and even this was done thirty to seventy years after his death and centuries before the age of digital recorders. We can only conclude that *the exact words of Jesus were apparently not that important for the Holy Spirit—or for us.* We have only a few snippets of Jesus's exact words in his native Aramaic. This should keep us all humble and searching for our own experience of the Risen Christ—now—instead of arguing over Greek verbs and tenses.

Finally, our very inclusion of the Jewish Bible into the official canon of our Christian Bible is forever *a standing statement about inclusivity itself.* Our Bible structurally admits that the Jewish Bible and Jewish religion, and their painful history, was indeed inspired and led by God, long before Jesus. It is amazing that we were ever able to miss such a central point. Abraham, Moses, and Sarah were fully justified before God without ever knowing Jesus—by the words of our own Christian Scriptures. Our Bible is an inclusive text, which already builds on pre-Jewish history, pagan roots and language, intertestamental literature, and clear Greek influences. That is much of its genius and puts us on a good trajectory for always finding the sacred in what first seems secular.

So I thank you for your courage and humility in opening this book. I pray that each time you close it, you will be wiser, holier, more compassionate, and more able to love our suffering world.

Richard Rohr
February 2013

METHODOLOGY

Scripture as validated by experience and experience as validated by tradition are good scales for one's spiritual worldview.

INTRODUCTION

This first theme is in great part what philosophers would call *epistemology*: *How* do we know what we think we know? How and why do I, Richard Rohr, say the things I say with any kind of authority or confidence? Why should you trust these writings? How do you know that these are not just *my* ideas? Or merely one biased opinion? They are certainly expressed in my limited culture, understanding, and vocabulary. How could they not be? You have no basis for trusting these words unless I am living within and drawing from the entire Force Field of the Holy Spirit which we Catholics would also call "the communion of saints."

I am first saying a deep *Yes* to that force field, and I am just adding an *And!* This is not to disagree with the mainline orthodoxy at all, but to simply add what every generation must add "to bind you together in love and to stir your minds, so that your understanding may come to full development, until you really know God's secret in which all the jewels of wisdom and knowledge are hidden" (Colossians 2:2–3). I thank Paul for giving me that verse. I would never have had the courage to say it on my own.

I have to risk writing, as every spiritual writer does, and I must be willing to be judged wrong by others more intelligent, wiser, and holier than I. But this is the leap that I and all others must also make in order to communicate that bit of the Great Truth of the Gospel to which we each have our own access. Paul also reassures me when he said that this Body of Christ is "groaning forward in one great act of giving birth" (Romans 8:22). Should we call it evolutionary Christianity? There is no other kind if the Spirit is still active and speaking.

John the Baptist did it early on with his daring and new river ritual and with no temple priesthood to support him. Paul did it with his independent letters, when there was no apostolic authority to assure or reassure him. In fact, they even fought him. Jesus did it with the Judaism of his time and place. This is the only pattern available to us in the humble and willingly fallible world of faith, and yet it is how we each tentatively contribute our little part to the great truth of God. Only future history will know whether ours was good or bad teaching. That is how we all live in the faith of our own moment in time, and must hand ourselves over to God's always larger future, just as Jesus did in Gethsemane.

I am, of course, trusting and hoping that what is contained here is much more than a bit of truth, precisely because I have found some serious validation in the Judeo-Christian Scriptures, plus a clear consistency with enough of the connecting dots of the Great Tradition: two thousand years of Jewish interpretation and two thousand years of Christian interpretation, mystics, saints, Church councils, friends of God, theologians and philosophers of the ecumenical Body of Christ. This is *the force field of the Holy Spirit* that you and I continue to be a part of whenever we are living, writing, and praying in loving union with God and God's work in this world.

I pray and hope that all I say and teach in these meditations comes from this place of loving union. Antagonism evokes a mirror image of the same. To paraphrase St. Joan of Arc, I also want to say, "If I am in your truth, God keep me there. If I am not, God put me there."

FOUNDATIONAL AUTHORITIES

Since the Reformation in the sixteenth century, much Christian infighting and misunderstanding has occurred over the Catholic and Orthodox emphasis on Tradition (which usually got confused with small cultural traditions) versus the new Protestant emphasis on Scripture, even "Scripture alone!" (Which gradually devolved into each group choosing among the Scriptures it would emphasize and the ones it would ignore.)

Both currents have now shown their weaknesses, their blind spots, and their biases. They lacked the dynamic third principle of *God Experience*: personal experience that is processed and held accountable by both Scripture and Tradition, and by solid spiritual direction and counseling. This will be our *trilateral* principle at the Rohr Institute's Living School of Action and Contemplation. (I am aware of John Wesley's later named "quadrilateral method" which also included reason as a fourth principle. I see the use of reason as precisely our ability to use Scripture, Tradition, and experience in a consistent, balanced, and reasonable way. But I do not want to give reason the importance of a fourth principle, because it now tends to trump the other three).

John the Baptist let his personal God experience trump both Scripture (which he hardly ever quotes directly) and his own Tradition (which is why this son of the priestly class had to move his own ritual down to the riverside). Jesus and Paul also clearly use and respect their own Scriptures and Jewish Tradition, yet courageously interpret them both in light of their personal experience of God. There is an essential message here from our central biblical figures.

A DIFFERENT KIND OF KNOWING

The essential religious experience is that you are being known through more than knowing anything in particular yourself. Yet despite this difference, it will feel like true knowing. This new way of knowing can be called contemplation, non-dualistic thinking or third-eye seeing. Such prayer, such seeing, takes away your anxiety about figuring it all out fully for yourself, or needing to be right about your formulations. Thomas Aquinas called this "connatural knowledge" and John Duns Scotus called it "intuitive cognition." It is a more integrated knowing than mere reason alone.

With this access point, God becomes more a verb than a noun, more a process than a conclusion, more an experience than a dogma, more a personal relationship than an idea. There is Someone dancing with you, and you no longer need to prove to anyone that you are right, nor are you afraid of making mistakes. Another word for that is *faith*.

+Adapted from *The Naked Now: Learning to See as the Mystics See,* p. 23

PRAYER

"Everything exposed to the light itself becomes light," says Ephesians 5:13. In prayer, we merely keep returning the divine gaze, and we become its reflection, almost in spite of ourselves (2 Corinthians 3:18). The word *prayer* has often been trivialized by making it into a way of getting what we want. But I use *prayer* as the umbrella word for any *interior journeys or practices that allow you to experience faith, hope, and love within yourself.* It is not a technique for getting things, a pious exercise that somehow makes God happy, or a requirement for entry into heaven. It is much more like practicing heaven now.

+Adapted from *The Naked Now: Learning to See as the Mystics See,* pp. 22–23

SELF-KNOWLEDGE AND GOD KNOWLEDGE

Our operative God image is often a subtle combination of our mom and our dad or any other significant authority figures. Once we begin an inner life of prayer and in-depth study of sacred texts, we slowly begin to grow and move beyond childhood conditioning, and from then on, it only gets better. Grace does its work and creates a unique "work of art" (Ephesians 2:10). Much religion is merely early conditioning, not yet God experience for oneself.

Early "God talk"—without self-knowledge and inner journey—is largely a sincere pretense, even to the person who consciously believes the language (read the teachings of Socrates, Teresa of Avila, and Carl Jung). The miracle of grace and true prayer is that they invade the *unconscious* mind and heart (where our real truth lies)—and thus really change us! They invade them so much that the love of God and the love of self invariably proceed forward together. On the practical level, they are experienced as the same thing!

+Adapted from *Things Hidden: Scripture as Spirituality*, pp. 162–163

NOT TO PROVE ANYTHING
BUT TO EXPERIENCE SOMEONE

I'd like to invite you to look at Scripture in a new way. In my book *Wondrous Encounters*, you will find many Scripture readings for the season of Lent. Using the Scripture readings of the season, I would like to teach you *how* to use Scripture. How can we put the Old Testament or Hebrew Scriptures together with the Christian Scriptures? I do not want to just share information or data or facts about Jesus, or the history of the Hebrews. I want to help you to experience an encounter with God.

I am going to repeat a phrase three times because I don't want it to just be a throwaway phrase. I want to lay a foundation with this mantra because I think this is why good theology, good Scripture, and a good approach to Scripture and to spirituality are so crucially important. The phrase is:

Your image of God creates you.

Your image of God creates you.

Your image of God creates you.

+Adapted from the webcast *A Teaching on Wondrous Encounters*
(CD, DVD, MP3)

BASIC CONVERSION MUST PRECEDE STUDY

The sacred texts of the Bible are filled with absolute breakthroughs, epiphanies, and manifestations of the highest level of encounter, conversion, transformation, and Spirit. The Bible also contains texts that are punitive, petty, tribal, and idiotic. A person can prove *anything* he or she wants from a single line of the Bible. To tell you the truth, the Bible says just about everything you might want to hear—somewhere! This is a sad and humiliating recognition. But you can relearn your way of reading Scripture in a prayerful, calm, skillful, and mature way. Then you can hear with head and heart and Spirit working as one, and not just engage in a search for quick answers.

Maybe one of the biggest mistakes in the history of Christianity is that we have separated spirituality from theology and Scripture study. In other words, we put the Scriptures (and theology) in the hands of very immature and unconverted people, even clergy. We put the Scriptures in the hands of people who are still at the egocentric level, who still think, "It's all about me," and who use the Bible in a very willful way. It is all dualistic win *or* lose for them. The egocentric will still dominates: the need to be right, the need to be first, the need to think I am saved and other people are not. This is the lowest level of human consciousness, and God cannot be heard from that heady place or be met at that level.

+Adapted from the webcast *A Teaching on Wondrous Encounters*
(CD, DVD, MP3)

BOTH GROUPS USED (OR IGNORED) SCRIPTURE
INSIDE OF A SMALL SELF

Thomas Merton said it was actually dangerous to put the Scriptures in the hands of people whose inner self is not yet sufficiently awakened to encounter the Spirit, because they will try to use God for their own egocentric purposes. (This is why religion is so subject to corruption!) Now, if we are going to talk about *conversion and penance*, let me apply that to the two major groups that have occupied Western Christianity—Catholics and Protestants. Neither one has really let the Word of God guide their lives.

Catholics need to be *converted* to giving the Scriptures some actual authority in their lives. Luther wasn't wrong when he said that most Catholics did not read the Bible. Most Catholics are still not that interested in the Bible. (For most of history they did not have the printing press nor could most people read, so you can't blame them entirely.) I have been a priest for forty-two years now, and I would say, sadly, that most Catholics would rather hear quotes from saints, popes and bishops, the current news, or funny stories, if they are to pay attention. If I quote strongly from the Sermon on the Mount, they are almost throwaway lines. I can see Catholics glaze over because they have never read the New Testament, much less studied it, or been guided by it. I am very sad to have to admit this. It is the Achilles' heel of much of the Catholic world, priests included. (The only good thing about it is that they never fight you like Protestants do about Scripture. They are easily duped, and the hierarchy has been able to take advantage of this.)

If Catholics need to be converted, Protestants need to do *penance*. Their shout of *"sola Scriptura"* ("only Scripture") has left them at the mercy of their own cultures, their own limited education, their own prejudices, and their own selective reading of some texts while avoiding others. Partly as a result, slavery, racism, sexism, classism, xenophobia, and homophobia have lasted authoritatively into our time—by people who claim to love Jesus! I think they need to do penance for what many of them have done with the Bible!

They largely interpreted the Bible in a very individualistic and other-worldly way. It was "an evacuation plan for the next world" to use Brian McLaren's phrase—and just for their group. Most of Evangelical Protestantism has no cosmic message, no social message, and little sense of social justice or care for the outsider. Both Catholics and Protestants (Orthodox too!) found a way to do their own thing while posturing friend-ship with Jesus.

+Adapted from the webcast *A Teaching on Wondrous Encounters* (CD, DVD, MP3)

FUNDAMENTALISM MISSES THE FUNDAMENTAL

My dear friend Dr. Gerald May made a distinction years ago that I have found myself using frequently. He says spirituality is not to encourage *willfulness*, but in fact *willingness*. Spirituality creates willing people who let go of their need to be first, to be right, to be saved, to be superior, and to define themselves as better than other people. That game is over and gone; and if you haven't come to the willing level—"not my will but Thy will be done" as Jesus says (Matthew 26:39)—then I think the Bible will almost always be misused.

I would like to say that the goal in general is to be *serious* about the Scriptures. We have often substituted being *literal* with being *serious*, and they are not the same! (Read that a second time, please). The point I would like to make is that literalism is not to take the text seriously at all! Pure literalism, in fact, avoids the real impact, the real message. Literalism is the lowest and least level of meaning in a spiritual text. Willful people use Scripture literally when it serves their purposes, and they use it figuratively when it gets in the way of their cultural biases; willing people let the Scriptures change them instead of using them to change others.

+Adapted from the webcast *A Teaching on Wondrous Encounters*
(CD, DVD, MP3)

THE BIBLE HUMBLES US BEFORE IT ENLIGHTENS US

How can we look at the biblical text in a manner that will convert or change us? I am going to define the Bible in a new way for some of you. *The Bible is an honest conversation with humanity about where power really is.* All spiritual texts, including the Bible, are books whose primary focus lies outside of themselves, in the Holy Mystery.

The Bible illuminates your human experience through struggling with it. It is not a substitute for human experience. It is an invitation into the struggle itself: You are supposed to be bothered by some of the texts. Human beings come to consciousness by struggle, and most especially struggle with God and sacred texts. We remain largely unconscious if we avoid all conflicts, dilemmas, paradoxes, inconsistencies, or contradictions.

The Bible is a book filled with conflicts and paradoxes and historical inaccuracies. It is filled with contradictions and it is precisely in learning to struggle with these seeming paradoxes that we grow up—not by avoiding them with a glib one-sentence answer that a sixteen-year-old can memorize. If I had settled for the mostly one-line answers to everything from *Fr. McGuire's Baltimore Catechism*, my spiritual journey would have been over in the third grade. And for many people, otherwise educated in other fields, that is exactly what happened. We created people who have quick answers instead of humble searchers for God and truth. God and truth never just fall into your lap, but are given as gifts only to those who really want them and desire them.

+Adapted from the webcast *A Teaching on Wondrous Encounters* (CD, DVD, MP3)

TO LOVE IS TO ALLOW SOMETHING
TO FLOW THROUGH US

Jesus *commanded* us to love; so we know love is not just a feeling, since we cannot command feelings. Love is mostly a decision.

Jesus did not say:

When you get healed, love;

When you grow up, love;

When you feel loving, love;

When you get it together and have dealt with all your mother/father/ husband/children wounds, then you must love.

No, the commandment for all of us is to *love* now, and thus fill the tragic gaps of every moment.

I think we know the love of God much more when we ourselves can "do love" than when people tell us we are loveable. (That just feels good!) We can always disbelieve the second, but the first is an unexplainable power from beyond ourselves. We know we are being used, and the "Living Water" is flowing through us (John 7:38).

+Adapted from *Letting Go: A Spirituality of Subtraction*

DOCTRINES ARE FOR THE SAKE OF EXPERIENCE

Christians speak of the "paschal mystery," the process of loss and renewal that was lived and personified in the death and raising up of Jesus. We can affirm that belief in song and ritual, as some Christians do in the Eucharist. However, until we have personally lost our own foundation and ground and then experienced God upholding us so that we come out even more alive on the other side, the expression "paschal mystery" is little understood and not essentially transformative. It is a mere theological affirmation or liturgical acclamation.

"Cross and resurrection" is a doctrine to which most Christians would probably intellectually assent, but it is not yet the very cornerstone of their own life philosophy. That is the difference between mere belief systems and a living faith. We move from one to the other only through actual encounter, surrender, trust and an inner experience of presence and power. Then it is our secret discovery too, and not just a church theology.

+From *Things Hidden: Scripture as Spirituality*, pp. 62, 63

FREEDOM FOR LOVE

Mystical moments may be described as a kind of emancipation. If it isn't an experience of newfound freedom, I don't think it is an authentic God experience. God is always bigger than you imagined or expected or even hoped for. When you see people going to church and becoming smaller instead of larger, you have every reason to question whether the practices or sermons or sacraments or liturgies are opening them to an authentic God experience.

On a practical level, such experiences will feel like a new freedom to love, and you wonder where it comes from. Why do I have this new desire, this new capacity to love new people, to love the old people better, maybe to enter into some kind of new love for the world? I will find that even my thoughts are more immediately loving, patient, and compassionate.

Clearly, you are participating in a Love that's being given to you. You are not creating this. You are not generating this. It is being generated through you and in you and for you. You are *participating* in something larger than yourself, and you are just allowing it and trusting it for the pure gift that it is.

+Adapted from *Following the Mystics through the Narrow Gate....*
Seeing God in All Things (CD, DVD, MP3)

MORALISM INSTEAD OF MYSTICISM

God always entices us through love.

Most of us were taught that God would love us *if* and *when* we changed. In fact, God loves you so that you *can* change. What empowers change, what makes you desirous of change, is the experience of love and acceptance itself. This is the engine of change. If the mystics say that one way, they say it a thousand ways. But because most of our common religion has not been at the mystical level, we've been given an inferior message—that God loves you *when* you change (moralism). It puts it all back on you, which is the opposite of being saved. Moralism leads you back to navel-gazing, and you can never succeed at that level. You are never holy enough, pure enough, refined enough, or loving enough. Whereas, when you fall into God's mercy, when you fall into God's great generosity, you find, seemingly from nowhere, this capacity to change. No one is more surprised than you are. You know it is a total gift.

+Adapted from *Following the Mystics through the Narrow Gate….*
Seeing God in All Things (CD, DVD, MP3)

POSSIBILITY AND PERMISSION

If you keep listening to the love, if you keep receiving the love, trusting the love—even with all your limitations, with all your unworthiness, with all your limited intellect or whatever you feel holds you back—you start to experience within yourself a sense of *possibility*. Whatever life is inviting you into, you have this sense that it is still okay and, even better, that you can do it! As Mother Teresa loved to say, "The only real success is faithfulness." To be faithful to this inner love is in itself the greatest success. It is of itself the major possibility. No outer successes are henceforth necessary to be happy.

This is what makes the mystics sort of dangerous: It's not just possibility they experience—but *permission*. It's permission to color outside the lines. It's permission to be who they really are. It's not just gay people who have to come out of their closets.

We're all in our closets. The gay rights movement has just given us a good metaphor for what we all have to do. We're all afraid to come out of our various closets. This liberation is not a need to be outrageous or rebellious. It's so much better than that. *It is permission to be the image and likeness of God that you already are!* We each are unlike any other image or likeness. God is saying to each of us, "All I want is for you to return to the Sender who you really are!" Ironically, it takes most of our lives to find that True Self, to accept it, and to return it to the Manufacturer—now with our own signature attached.

+Adapted from *Following the Mystics through the Narrow Gate....*
Seeing God in All Things (CD, DVD, MP3)

THE FEMININE HAS A HEAD START

Historically speaking, in most cultures the role of men has been to create, to make new things, to fix broken things, and to defend us from things that could hurt us. All these are wonderful and necessary roles for the preservation of the human race.

However, most children saw their mothers in a different way. She was not a creator, a fixer, or a defender, but rather a transformer. Once a woman has carried her baby inside of her body for nine months and brought it forth through the pain of childbirth and into the world, she knows the mystery of transformation at a cellular level. She knows it intuitively; yet she usually cannot verbalize it, nor does she need to. She just holds it at a deeper level of consciousness. She knows something about mystery, about miracles, and about transformation that men will never know (which is why males have to be initiated!). Women who are not mothers often learn it by simply being in the community of women.

The feminine body can be seen as a cauldron of transformation. Her body turns things into other things—her body turns an act of love into a perfect little child. Yet, in her heart, she knows *she* did not do it. All she had to do was to wait and eat well, to believe and to hope for nine months. This gives a woman a very special access to understanding spirituality as transformation—if she is able to listen to her own experience and her own body. Admittedly, not all women do.

+Adapted from *On Transformation: Collected Talks, Volume 1: The Maternal Face of God* (CD). Also, read *Adam's Return* on the concept of male initiation, and why women did not need initiation in the classic sense.

MALE AND FEMALE KNOWING

Sara Ruddick, in her book *Maternal Thinking: Toward a Politics of Peace*, speaks of the *attentive* love of a mother. In summary, Ruddick says mothers are characterized by attentive love. They have to keep watching this new life; they have to keep listening and adjusting to the needs of the child. It is necessary to recognize a new agenda with the growth of the child. If the mother cannot transform herself into attentive love, she quite simply cannot be a mother. She has to learn early on that life is about change, not about standing her ground, which is not going to help a child. All growth is about changing and adjusting to what is needed *at this moment, with these tears, and by this child.* The mother cannot run to abstract truths. Philosophy and theology courses at this point in her life might be boring to her, but many men might love them! In fact, that is what seminaries have been all about.

I cannot help but think that the present persecution of the religious sisters by the Vatican reflects this difference. The sisters, by and large, went toward human need and pain with attentive love. The clergy, I being one of them, can easily stay in abstract theories, ideologies, and theologies and never get to any concrete or attentive love at all. Immature males often prefer to know everything from above, whereas wise women also know each thing from below. Of course, in the end there is a place for both.

+Adapted from *On Transformation: Collected Talks, Volume 1:*
The Maternal Face of God (CD)

MIRROR NEURONS

Much of what we find in the eyes of Jesus must first have been in the eyes of Mary. The mother's vision is powerfully communicated to her children. Mary had to be his first spiritual director, the one who humanly gave a life vision to Jesus, who taught Jesus *how* to believe, and how to feel his feelings. What was in Jesus's eyes was somehow first in hers. (We now know this to be true scientifically from our new understanding of mirror neurons.) In both of their eyes is what they both believed about God, and it was a co-believing!

The Eternal Feminine holds us naked at each end of life: the Madonna first brings us into life, and then the grief-stricken mother of the *Pietá* hands us over to death. She expands our capacity to feel, to enter the compassion and the pain of being human. She holds joy deeply, where death cannot get to it. Jesus learns by watching her, and he protects her motherhood in some of his very last words from the cross (John 19:26–27), just as she protected his sonship.

Not a word is spoken by Mary in either place, at his birth or at his death. Did you ever think about that? Mary simply trusts and experiences deeply. She is simply and fully present. *Faith is not first of all for overcoming obstacles; it is for experiencing them—all the way through!*

+Adapted from *Radical Grace: Daily Meditations*, pp. 153–154

KNOWING THROUGH ART

I remember once seeing a painting, in a European art museum, of the ascension. It was rather huge, and at the very top, right beneath the frame, were the bare feet of Jesus as he ascended into heaven. It felt almost comical. Most of the painting was of the apostles looking up in various poses of fear, confusion, disbelief, and awe. It struck me that the ascension was the final stage of Jesus's human life, and every human life—when the material world is reunited to its spiritual Source. At least that is what the artist seemed to be saying, and the various poses of the apostles illustrated our various stances toward eternal life and divine union.

The ascension is about the final reunion of what appeared to be separated for a while: earth and heaven, human and divine, matter and Spirit, feet and freedom. They are again one in the end, and it was important, the artist seemed to say, that we see ordinary human feet going into heaven! If the Christ is the archetype of the full human journey, now we know how it all resolves itself in the end. "So that where I am, you also will be" (John 14:3).

THEME OF THEMES

Any way we receive the Spirit is just as real and just as good as any other. God meets us where we are and makes a healing and expanding presence known to us in the exact way we are most ready to experience it. God fills our hearts in whatever measure we are open to the Spirit, just like any true Lover might desire to do.

And when grace does happen, we know that we did nothing to deserve it. It is God's pure graciousness "or grace would not be grace at all" (Romans 11:6). It is what makes people fall in love with God. So be open to surrendering to such "radical grace." God's love is never determined by the worthy or unworthy object of love, but only by being true to who God is in himself. "We may be unfaithful, but God is always faithful, for he cannot disown his own self" (2 Timothy 2:13).

+Adapted from *Great Themes of Scripture*, pp. 90–91

RITUAL AS KNOWING

The ritual of Eucharist clarifies and delineates Christianity from among the other religions of the world. We have many things in common, but Christianity is the only religion that says that God became a human body, and we are going to continue to promote embodiment as the way of knowing. God became *flesh*, as John's Gospel puts it (1:14), and Eucharist continues that mystery in space and time. The theological word for that is *incarnation* or *enfleshment*.

Yet *it seems that it is much easier for God to convince bread of what it really is than for God to convince us*. We alone balk, rebel, and analyze. Let's be honest and admit that "eat my body and drink my blood" is scandalous talk (John 6:64–66) that has stopped scandalizing us! And so we miss the point. Eucharist is intentionally shocking. It is cannibalistic, intimate, invasive, and sexual! Jesus did not say, "Think about this," "Fight about this," "Stare at this." He just said, "Eat this" and "Do this." Eucharist is a dynamic, interactive event that makes one out of two, just as sexual union does when two lovers want to be inside each other.

If we did not have the Eucharist, we would have to create it, the ritual is so perfect. Sometimes it seems that outsiders can appreciate this more than Christians. As Gandhi said, "There are so many hungry people in the world that God could only come into the world in the form of food." It is marvelous that God would enter our lives not just in the form of sermons or Bibles, but as ingested food and drink. Jesus comes to feed us more than just to teach us. Lovers can understand that. Others will make high liturgy and abstruse theology out of it.

+Adapted from *Eucharist as Touchstone* (CD, MP3)

PERENNIAL WISDOM

I can't believe that God expects all human beings to start from zero and to reinvent the wheel of life in their own small lifetimes. We must build on the common "communion of saints" throughout the ages. This is the inherited fruit and gift that is sometimes called the "wisdom tradition." It is not always inherited simply by belonging to one group or religion. It largely depends on how informed, mature, and experienced your particular teachers are. Most seminaries, I am afraid, merely exposed ministers to their own denomination's conclusions and did not have time for much native, interfaith, or ecumenical education, which broadens the field from "my religion, which has the whole truth," to "universal wisdom, which my religion teaches in this way." If it is true, then it has to be true everywhere.

There have been many generations of sincere seekers who've gone through the same human journey and there is plenty of collective and common wisdom to be had. It is often called "the perennial tradition" or the "perennial philosophy" because it keeps recurring in different religions and with different metaphors. But the foundational wisdom is usually the same.

WE COME TO CONSCIOUSNESS BY STRUGGLING WITH INHERENT TENSIONS

All of the stories of healing, transformation, awareness, and enlightenment that we find in the Bible come to people moving beyond the usual definitions of power (such as false power, temporary power, dominative power, or cultural power) to discover their deeper soul and their true spiritual power. The Bible and all spiritual books are books whose primary focus lies outside of themselves. Sacred texts are not an end in themselves, but they must insert you into new and larger realities—through a necessary struggle with your present level of consciousness (Faith holds onto you during that time!) Religious texts and rituals are not a substitute for human experience. They are meant to invite you into a helpful struggle, and in a certain way, they actually create a conflict or dissonance for you! If you resolve that tension too quickly by glib belief, you actually learn nothing new and go to no new place.

Let me give you an example. When Jesus says the last will be first and the first will be last (Matthew 20:16), you can glibly say "Yes, I agree with that. Jesus said it, so it is true." In fact, you don't really agree with it, you don't even understand it until you eventually struggle with it and finally admit that you don't know if you agree with it: "How is that true? I don't know that I even agree with it." Maybe this struggle will last years before it finally becomes inner experience. So to say you believe it yet avoid its often inherent unreasonability, contradictions, dilemmas, and tensions is to not really understand its purpose and message at all. It will have no transformative effect on you.

+Adapted from the webcast *A Teaching on Wondrous Encounters*
(CD, DVD, MP3)

TWO STEPS BACKWARD OFTEN PRECEDES ANY THREE STEPS FORWARD

There is a necessary and inherent dissonance in many of the texts in the Bible (such as Jesus calling a woman "a dog" in Mark 7:27). We largely remain *unwise* if we avoid these conflicts, dilemmas, paradoxes, inconsistencies, or contradictions; and I want to say those contradictions are in the biblical text itself and presented to you for serious consideration—until you get the point. This is the real meaning of what we call *Lectio Divina*, or spiritual reading of a text. You are supposed to struggle with spiritual texts, but when you make the Bible into a quick answer book, you largely remain at your present level of awareness. There are groups who would describe the Bible as an answer book for all of life's problems. *The Bible is actually a conflict book.* It is filled with seeming contradictions or paradoxes, and if you read it honestly and humbly it should actually create problems for you!

The way you struggle with the fragmentation of the Bible is the way you *probably* struggle with your own fragmentation and the fragmentation of everything else. The Bible offers you a mirror that reflects back to you how you live life in general. There are very high levels of consciousness and holiness in the biblical text, and texts which are frankly hateful, selfish, and punitive. You need to recognize them as such. As Wendell Berry says, "the mind that is not baffled is not employed." The Bible mirrors our own human fragmentation, your own two steps backward and your own occasional three steps forward. Your spiritual eyes will eventually be trained to see which way you—and the text—are going (see 1 Corinthians 2:10–16).

+Adapted from the webcast *A Teaching on Wondrous Encounters*
(CD, DVD, MP3)

GOOD POWER

In past meditations we have defined the Bible as an honest conversation between humanity and God but never for a moment do we deny divine inspiration, a guided conversation going *both* ways between God and the soul and *where real power really is*. This leads to the question: "What are some reasons that those who claim to be Christians are afraid of power or the power they can have for good?"

The Bible is a conversation about power. It is not saying that all power is bad. We have become so mistrustful of power and have seen how often it has been misused even in the Bible that we tend to think all power is bad. However, in the Acts of the Apostles the very word applied to the Holy Spirit is *dunamis* or "power" (Acts 1:8). So power cannot be bad. There has to be a good meaning to power.

Power in the hands of a truly converted person, a person who is not egocentric, is necessary and good. Mother Teresa was powerful. Too often, even in our own Roman Catholic tradition, we have aligned our power with the power of the state, with the power of money, with the power of control, with the power of authority, or with the power of ambition, and as a result, we have distorted and even avoided the true meaning of *spiritual* power.

+Adapted from the webcast *A Teaching on Wondrous Encounters*
(CD, DVD, MP3)

THE METHODOLOGY OF PRAYER

I would like to offer you a form of prayer to practice letting go and to practice what seems like losing but is actually finding.

The "Welcoming Prayer" encourages you to identify in your life, now or in the past, a hurt or an offense or someone who has done you wrong or let you down.

Feel the pain of the offense the way you first felt it or are feeling it in this moment, and feel the hurt in your body. (Why is this important? Because if you move it to your mind, you will go back to dualistic thinking and judgments: good guy/bad guy, win/lose, either/or.)

Feel the pain, grief, and anger, but do not create the usual win/lose scenario. Identify yourself with the suffering side of life, how much it hurts to hurt. How abandoned you felt if you were abandoned. Hold this in your heart space, your body space, instead of processing it mentally, or creating a story line.

Once you can move to that place and know how much it hurts to hurt, it will not be possible for you to want that experience for anybody else.

This might take a few minutes. Welcome the experience and it can move you to the Great Compassion. Don't fight it! Don't split and blame! Welcome the grief and anger in all of its heaviness. Now it will become a great teacher.

If you can do this, you will see that welcoming the pain and letting go of all of your oppositional energy against suffering will actually free you from it! It is like reversing your engines. Who would have thought this? *It is our resistance to things as they are that causes most of our unhappiness*—at least I know it is so for me.

+Adapted from *The Art of Letting Go: Living the Wisdom of Saint Francis* (CD)

LETTING GO AS CLEANING THE LENS OF SEEING

I don't understand the physics of this, but it is said that the reason a bird sitting on a hot wire does not get electrocuted is quite simply because it does not touch the ground to give the electricity a pathway. That is what the "Welcoming Prayer" is doing, and that is what I am asking you to do. Stay like a bird, sitting on the hot wire, holding the creative tension, but do not ground it in a bad way by thinking of it, by critiquing it, by analyzing it. Actually welcome it in a positive way. Hold on to it. As a Christian, I think that is what Jesus was doing on the cross. He was holding all the pain of the world, at least symbolically or archetypically; and though the world had come to hate Jesus, he refused to hate back.

Jesus revealed to us how to bear the pain of the world instead of handing on the pain to those around us. When you stop resisting suffering, when you can really do something so foolish as to welcome the pain, it leads you into a broad and spacious place where you live out of the abundance of Divine Love. I can't promise you it will leave quickly or easily. To forgive is not the same as to forget.

Forgiveness has the power to lead you to your True Self in God. Because the hurts of life are so great, you cannot let go of the pain on your own. At that point, you need to draw from a Larger Source. What you are doing with forgiveness is changing your egoic investment in your own painful story—which too often has become your ticket to sympathy and sometimes your very identity. Forgiveness is one of the most radically free things a human being can do. When we forgive, we have to let go of our own feelings, our own ego, our own offended identity, and find our identity at a completely different level—the divine level. I even wonder if it is possible to know God at all—outside of the mystery of forgiveness (Luke 1:77).

+Adapted from *The Art of Letting Go: Living the Wisdom of Saint Francis* (CD)

SILENCE IS ALMOST TOO SIMPLE

The simplest spiritual discipline is some degree of solitude and silence. But it's the hardest, because none of us want to be with someone we don't love. Besides that, we invariably feel bored with ourselves, and all of our loneliness comes to the surface.

We won't have the courage to go into that terrifying place without Love to protect us and lead us, without the light and love of God overriding our own self-doubt. Such silence is the most spacious and empowering technique in the world, yet it's not a technique at all. It's precisely the refusal of all technique.

+Adapted from *Radical Grace: Daily Meditations*, p. 106

SPIRITUAL THINGS MUST BE TASTED
MORE THAN UNDERSTOOD

St. Bernard of Clairvaux (1090–1153), the founder of the Cistercian Order, set the gold standard for mystical writing in his *Commentary on the Song of Songs*. All he could make use of was the one erotic book in the Bible to communicate what is happening between God and the soul. And many followed him for centuries to come.

Bernard said that we are the mutual food of one another, just as lovers are. Jesus gives us himself as food in the Eucharist, and the willing soul offers itself for God to eat in return: "If I eat and am not eaten, it will seem that God is in me, but I am not yet in God" (*Commentary* 71:5). I must both eat God and be eaten by God, Bernard says. Now this is the language of mystical theology, which is upsetting to the rational mind but utterly delightful and consoling to anyone who knows the experience.

The mystic sits in the silence of such language until it silences him into the experience itself.

+A reflection on the feast of St. Bernard of Clairvaux

FULL LIBERATION

The term *liberation theology* has a negative connotation in the minds of some people. It sounds like something heretical, leftist, or Marxist, and certainly not biblical. In fact, it is at the heart of the Judeo-Christian tradition and marks its very beginning. It is amazing that much of Christianity has been able to avoid the obvious for so long.

We see the beginnings of liberation theology as early as twelve hundred years before Christ with the Exodus experience of the Jewish people. Something divine happened that allowed an enslaved group of Semitic people in Egypt to experience many levels of liberation from slavery to a promised land and to confront the pharaoh to let the people go! The burning bush experience quickly becomes a momentous act of civil disobedience. The Exodus was both an inner journey and an outer journey—and then the basic template and metaphor for the whole Bible. If the inner journey does not match and lead to an outer journey, we have no true liberation at all. Most groups choose just one side or the other; very few choose both. That is what liberation theology is honest enough to point out.

+Adapted from *CAC Foundation Set: Gospel Call to Compassionate Action (Bias from the Bottom) and Contemplative Prayer* (CD, MP3)

ACTION AND CONTEMPLATION

Moses is the historical character at the heart of the Exodus event and the spirituality that grew from that experience (Exodus 3:1–15). This is the primal historical experience at the beginning of the Bible.

A murderer on the run, Moses has a burning bush experience out in the wild. It has nothing to do with formal religion. It is both a nature experience and one that follows upon an experience of failure and suffering (necessary disillusionment), which major religious experiences often are. The voice he hears from the burning bush tells him to confront the pharaoh and tell him to let his slaves go! *You do not think yourself into a new way of living as much as you live your way into a new way of thinking.* This is one of the core principles of the Center for Action and Contemplation.

So here you have a primary inner experience, which is described as a "bush that burns but is not destroyed"—and that inner fire experience immediately has *social, economic, and political implications!* That is what liberation theology is saying—contemplation and action are forever connected and must never be separated. Some people set out to act first, and their inner experience is given to them on the journey itself. It does not matter which side you start on, but eventually action and contemplation must meet and feed one another. When prayer is authentic it will always lead to actions of mercy; when actions of mercy are attempted at any depth, they will always drive you to prayer.

+Adapted from *CAC Foundation Set: Gospel Call to Compassionate Action (Bias from the Bottom) and Contemplative Prayer* (CD, MP3)

PROPHETIC KNOWING

Very early in the Judeo-Christian tradition there is a split between the Exodus tradition, which I believe is the mainline and original tradition of full liberation, and the tradition that develops in Leviticus and Numbers, which is called the priestly tradition. If you read these two books, for the most part they have none of the drama of Exodus, but they reflect what happens when the priestly mentality takes over and tries to organize and control and perpetuate the initial experience—always around *their* services, I might add.

About eight centuries before Christ, we finally meet the spiritual geniuses—the Jewish prophets—who tried desperately to link two traditions: inner God experience and outer work for justice and truth. That linkage is forever needed and yet forever resented and avoided to this day. We continue to have *halfhearted* religious divisions in the form of right or left, liberal or conservative, establishment or disestablishment, contemplative or activist. They really do need one another, but in most of history the priestly tradition has been in control and defined religion. The divisions of Leviticus and Numbers usually trump any real exoduses from slavery to freedom. We always and forever need the prophets, who are invariably pushed off to the side.

+Adapted from *CAC Foundation Set: Gospel Call to Compassionate Action (Bias from the Bottom) and Contemplative Prayer* (CD, MP3)

BIBLE AS AN ALTERNATIVE HISTORY

The political terms *right* and *left* came from the *Estates General* in France. It's interesting that now we use them as our basic political categories. On the left sat the ordinary people, and on the right sat the nobility and the clergy! (What were the clergy doing over there?!) I think you see the pattern. The right normally protects continuity and the status quo. The left predictably looks for change and reform, and there is a certain need for both or we have chaos.

In history you will invariably have these two movements in some form, because we didn't have the phenomenon of the middle class until very recently. The vast majority of people in all of history has been poor, as in Jesus's time, and would have read history in terms of a need for change. The people who wrote the books and controlled the social institutions, however, have almost always been the comfortable people on the right. And much of history has been read and interpreted from the side of the winners, or the right, except for the unique revelation called the Bible, which is an alternative history from the side of the enslaved, the dominated, the oppressed, and the poor, leading up to the totally scapegoated Jesus himself.

+Adapted from *CAC Foundation Set: Gospel Call to Compassionate Action (Bias from the Bottom) and Contemplative Prayer* (CD, MP3)

IDEOLOGY CAN NEVER BE HUMBLE

When you truly know, the giveaway is that you know that you do *not* know! Truly holy people are always humble. If you are not humble, you have not experienced the Holy One. If you don't see humility and patience in religion, you know it's not on the right course.

The prophets are always calling Israel to such humility. They represent the self-critical and honest part of religion. *Without the prophetic element, religion is always self-serving and idolatrous.* True prophets please nobody, neither left nor right, which are mere ideologies (having the answers before you know what the real questions are).

According to Jesus, the whole world will hate you if you follow him (Matthew 10:22).

When you are truly prophetic, both the left and the right will invariably mistrust and attack you. A great disappointment in our time is that organized religion itself has become more ideological than transformative. It has taken on the arguments and, even worse, the very form of argumentation of conservative and liberal politics, and it has lost its own unique Gospel agenda. The medium must also be the message.

+Adapted from *CAC Foundation Set: Gospel Call to Compassionate Action (Bias from the Bottom) and Contemplative Prayer* (CD, MP3)

BIAS FROM THE BOTTOM

We see in the Gospels that it's the lame, the poor, the blind, the prostitutes, the drunkards, the tax collectors, the sinners, the outsiders, and the foreigners who tend to follow Jesus. It is those on the inside and the top who crucify him (elders, chief priests, teachers of the Law, scribes, and Roman occupiers). Shouldn't that tell us something really important about perspective? Every viewpoint is a view from a point, and we need to critique our own perspective if we are to see and follow the full truth.

We fail to appreciate liberation theology because of seventeen hundred years of interpreting the Scriptures from the perspective of the empowered clergy class, rather than from the perspective of the marginalized, who first received the message with such excitement. Once Christianity became the established religion of the Roman Empire (after 313), we largely stopped reading the Bible from the side of the poor and the oppressed. We read it from the side of the political establishment and, I am sorry to say, from the priesthood side, which was often eager to keep us codependent on their ministrations, instead of from the side of people hungry for justice and truth. No wonder Jesus said, "I did not come for the healthy but for the sick" (Mark 2:17). This priority has the power to constantly detach religion from its common marriage to power, money, and self-importance.

+Adapted from *CAC Foundation Set: Gospel Call to Compassionate Action (Bias from the Bottom) and Contemplative Prayer* (CD, MP3)

TIME TO GROW UP

It seems to me that it is a minority that ever gets the true and full Gospel—in any denomination. Most of us just keep worshiping Jesus and arguing over the right way to do it. The amazing thing is that Jesus never once says, "Worship me!" whereas he frequently says, "Follow me" (see, for example, Matthew 4:19).

Christianity is a *lifestyle*—a way of being in the world that is simple, nonviolent, shared, and loving. However, we made it into an established religion (and all that goes with that) and avoided the lifestyle change itself. One could be warlike, greedy, racist, selfish, and vain throughout most of Christian history, and still believe that Jesus is one's personal Lord and Savior or continue to receive the sacraments in good standing. The world has no time for such silliness anymore. The suffering on earth is too great.

+Adapted from *CAC Foundation Set: Gospel Call to Compassionate Action (Bias from the Bottom) and Contemplative Prayer* (CD, MP3)

PROPHETS AND PRIESTS

Historically, mysticism was often seen as the opposite of prophecy. There was the *prophetic* strain, which was working for social justice, making a difference, solving problems, fixing the world, and bringing about the Kingdom of God. Then there were these other mystified people who locked themselves in hermitages and monasteries and didn't care much about the suffering of the world. This would be the *priestly* strain of theology. Now we know that was a radical misunderstanding from both sides.

When we read the prophets, we see that without exception they talk about an intimate and loving relationship with Yahweh that led to radical social critique. Jeremiah talks about a love that "seduces him and that lets him be seduced" (Jeremiah 20:7). The normal language of the prophets Amos and Hosea is an intimate language of divine encounter that always overspills into social concerns. They blast a common understanding of Judaism and Temple worship, which puts them in direct conflict with the priestly class. It seemed to lead to the murdering of the prophets according to Jesus (Matthew 23:31–35).

In the Jewish Scriptures, the priests are invariably competing with the prophets and the prophets are critiquing the priests—and this tells me it must be a necessary and creative tension. Maybe both sides get refined because of it. Today, however, we have mostly priestly concerns or as Jeremiah put it, "the sanctuary, the sanctuary, the sanctuary" (Jeremiah 7:4), and little concern for immigrants, health care for the poor, earth care, or even minimal peacemaking. The patterns never seem to change since the priests control the home front and the prophets invariably work at the edges.

+Adapted from *Following the Mystics through the Narrow Gate....*
Seeing God in All Things (CD, DVD, MP3)

EXPERIENTIAL KNOWING

Mysticism is when God's presence becomes experiential and undoubted for a person. You can see a kind of courage and self-confidence in the mystics. That puts them in an extraordinary category. Most of us believe things because our churches tell us to believe them and we don't want to be disobedient members of the church, so we say "I believe," as we do in the Nicene or Apostles' Creed.

Mystics don't say, "I believe." They say, "I know." A true mystic will ironically speak with that self-confidence but at the same time with a kind of humility. So when you see that combination of calm self-confidence, certitude, and humility all at the same time, you have the basis for mysticism in general. The only things we know at any deep and real level are the things we have personally experienced. Creedal belief, however, *holds onto us* until we have that experience! This is an important distinction, and it is why we need creeds as well. Each generation and person cannot start at zero.

MYSTICISM OF THE STREETS

Up to the year 1100 most of the mystics were identified with the early desert fathers and mothers of Egypt, Syria, and Palestine, thus more in the
East than in the West. Later, mysticism was localized in the monasteries
and hermitages of the Augustinians and Benedictines, where it became
academic in its explanation to others. This might be exemplified by such
places as the monastery of St. Victor in Paris. Although we already had it
among bishops and others—as in Cappadocia in eastern Turkey with Basil,
his brother Gregory of Nyssa, his sister Abbess Makrina, and their friend
Gregory Nazianzen. What family gatherings they must have had! Paul's
Trinitarian theology was still very alive in Asia Minor, where it was first
taught.

St. Francis brought mysticism from the monasteries and academia to the
streets. He said, "Don't speak to me of Benedict and Augustine. God has
shown me a different way." So we Franciscans were never called monks.
We are friars. A friar is one who mixes with the ordinary people and in the
city. Our emphasis was not on academia or a daily monastic schedule but
on ordinary life itself. "Preach the Gospel at all times, and when necessary
use words" is the summary statement attributed to Francis.

This was the beginning of an *alternative orthodoxy* that continues to
this day. I can only mention Waldensians, Mennonites, Quakers, Amish,
Catholic Workers, and many lay groups and individuals who do not even
know they are living an alternative orthodoxy by emphasizing daily life
practice instead of theory or "correct" liturgy.

MYTH VERSUS PARABLE

Our "myth" is the symbol system out of which we think and operate. It is largely unconscious and prerational, which is probably why the word *myth* (ineffable or unspeakable) is used, even if commonly misunderstood. Everyone has a myth, even those who fear the word. We have to have our myth because it creates a sometimes livable world and it provides the frame of reference necessary for sanity—or insanity, if our myth is destructive. A myth creates a habitable and meaningful world for us.

In contrast, a parable confronts our world and subverts it. It does not create but *re-creates* our destructive and illusory myths. It has a hard job, and so it usually does not call for discussion, debate, or questioning. A parable is not God-as-information. Rather it is God-as-invitation-and-challenge. A parable calls us to insight and decision. A parable doesn't lead us to more and more mental analysis; it's either a flashing insight or it's nothing. It calls us more to decision and a change of perspective.

Jesus is never afraid to put things in a challenging, parabolic way. He seems to even prefer this method (Matthew 13:3, 34). Jesus is not afraid of using a word or idea that's likely to be misunderstood (I wish I had that courage!). He puts his truth out there; dealing with it is the listener's problem (which is actually to respect the listener's spiritual intelligence). Jesus is saying, in effect, "Struggle with what I'm saying!" In general, Jesus doesn't spend a great deal of time qualifying his point and making sure everybody understands it clearly.

As Rainer Maria Rilke might later describe it, "Be patient toward all that is unsolved in your heart and try to love the questions themselves. Do not now seek the answers, which cannot be given you because you would not be able to live them. And the point is to live everything. Live the questions now" (Rilke, *Letters to a Young Poet*, 1934).

+Adapted from *The Good News According to Luke: Spiritual Reflections*, pp. 120, 162

KNOWING THROUGH RELATIONSHIP

The Gospel cannot happen in your head alone.

The Gospel is about relationship. Unless there is someplace on this earth where it's happening between you and another person, I don't believe you have any criterion to judge whether it's happening at all. Unless you're in right relationship with at least one other person on this earth, unless there is someplace you can give and receive love, I don't think you have any reason to think you are giving or receiving divine love either.

Is there at least one place in your life where you are giving and receiving love? If it happens in one place, it can happen everywhere. If you are truly capable of loving one person, you're capable of loving more than one, and eventually even your enemy, and finally *all*. Love is one piece. Thus, we rightly speak of being "in love" and Paul speaks of being "in Christ." Love is all or nothing. You either express love or you don't. The Scholastic philosopher Josef Pieper said it very well: "The proper habitat for truth is human relationship." How we relate to anyone is how we relate to everything else, too.

+Adapted from *The Good News According to Luke: Spiritual Reflections*, p. 138

TRUE PERSONHOOD IS RECEIVED PERSONHOOD

All of Jesus's rules of ministry, his tips for the road, are very specific and interpersonal (see Matthew 10:1–42). They put people in touch with other people, which becomes his very school of conversion (no hint of monasteries, universities, or seminaries yet!). We are essentially social beings, *just as the Trinity is both one self and yet three selves at the same time.* Person-to-person is the way the essential message is communicated: Person-in-love-with-person, person-healing-person, person-forgiving-person, person-touching-person, person-crying-with-person, person-surrendering to-person—all become the opening of the floodgates of both soul and Spirit, the waterwheel of Trinitarian grace.

When you see life being created between people and within people too, you see God. Restraint *and* passion are the paradoxical experience of the holy. Holding the self and then giving the self away are equally important, but it takes time to learn how to do that properly. You grow into your ability to love another in a way that totally gives yourself and entrusts yourself to them, and yet honors their boundaries and yours too. In my opinion, Jesus does both very well. He teaches us how to hold ourselves, lose ourselves, and paradoxically find ourselves in the process. He surely learned this as part of his own Trinitarian life. He is the Son who receives the Father totally, holds this identity proudly, and yet hands this mystery on to all of us as Holy Spirit! *God is a verb called* relate *more than a noun called* monarch.

+Adapted from *The Good News According to Luke: Spiritual Reflections*,
pp. 141, 110

HOW DO WE LOVE GOD?

We have put our emphasis on trying to love God, which is probably a good way to start—although we do not have a clue how to do that. What I consistently find in the mystics is an overwhelming experience of how God has loved *them*. God is always the initiator, God is the doer, God is the one who seduces us. All we can do is respond in kind and, exactly as Meister Eckhart said, "The love by which we love God is the very same love with which God has first loved us."

The mystics' overwhelming experiences are full body blows of the Divine loving them, God radically accepting them. And they spend the rest of their lives trying to verbalize those experiences, invariably finding ways to give that love back through forms of service, compassion, and nonstop worship. But none of this is to earn God's love; it's always and only to return God's love. Love is repaid by love alone.

+Adapted from *Following the Mystics through the Narrow Gate....*
Seeing God in All Things (CD, DVD, MP3)

A BALANCING ACT BETWEEN INNER
AND OUTER AUTHORITY

In finding your True Self, you will have found *an absolute reference point that is both utterly within you and utterly beyond you at the very same time.* This grounds the soul in big and reliable Truth. "My deepest *me* is God!" St. Catherine of Genoa shouted as she ran through the streets of town, just as Colossians had already shouted to both Jews and pagans, "The mystery is Christ within you—your hope of Glory!" (1:27).

The healthy inner authority of the True Self can now be balanced by a more objective outer authority of Scripture and mature Tradition. In other words, your experience is not just *your* experience. That's what tells you that you are not crazy. That God is both utterly beyond me and yet totally within me at the same time is the exquisite balance that most religion seldom achieves, in my opinion. Now the law is written both on tablets of stone (Exodus 31:18) and within your heart too (Deuteronomy 29:12–14), and the old covenant has rightly morphed into the new (Jeremiah 31:31–34).

+Excerpted from *Immortal Diamond: The Search for Our True Self*, p. 5

INTIMACY AS A WAY OF KNOWING

Intimacy could be described as our capacity for closeness and tenderness toward things. It is often revealed in moments of risky self-disclosure. Intimacy lets itself out and lets the other in. It makes all love possible, and yet it also reveals your utter incapacity to love back as the other deserves. Intimacy therefore encompasses a loneliness, but a sweet loneliness. In intimate moments, *you have been touched by something you cannot yet endure or carry, but you still love the touch and the invitation to carry.* You are always larger after any intimate encounter; in fact, it might well be the only way to enlarge spiritually. It is always grace.

+Excerpted from *Immortal Diamond: The Search for Our True Self,* pp. 159–160

VATICAN II FOUND THE TRILATERAL BALANCE

Fullness in a person cannot permit love because there are no openings, no handles, no give-and-take, and no deep hunger. It is like trying to attach two inflated balloons to one another. Human vulnerability gives the soul an immense head start on its travels—maybe the only start for any true spiritual journey. Thus the Risen Christ starts us off by revealing *the human wounds of God*, God's total solidarity with human suffering. He starts with self-disclosure from the divine side, which ideally leads to self-disclosure from our side.

The Bible first opened up for me in my 1960s seminary training with the Second Vatican Council. The Council said that divine revelation was not God disclosing ideas about God or religion, but actually God disclosing himself and first of all through the natural world (*Dei Verbum*, 2–3). Quickly Scripture, and religion itself, became not mere doctrines or moralisms for me, but lovemaking—an actual mutual exchange of being and intimacy. In the inspired documents of Vatican II, I found my best teacher in putting together Scripture, Tradition, and Experience in a quite reasonable (rational) way.

+Adapted from *Immortal Diamond: The Search for Our True Self*, p. 167

LOVE AS THE SECRET AND BEST WAY
OF KNOWING

The mystics, and those like Moses (Exodus 33:12–23), Jesus (John 5:19–20), and John the Divine (1 John 1:1–3) who personally claim to know God, are always aware that they have been let in on a big and wondrous love secret. Anyone not privy to an inner dialogue, that is, some kind of I-Thou relationship, would call such people presumptuous, emotional, foolish, or even arrogant.

How could they presume to claim an actual union with the divine? But this is without doubt "God's secret, in which all the jewels of wisdom and knowledge are hidden" (Colossians 2:3). The insiders know that "anyone who loves is born of God and knows God. Anyone who fails to love can never know God, because God is love" (1 John 4:7–8). Such an amazing, but seldom-quoted line lets you in on the big secret and also makes it universal and available to all.

+Excerpted from *Immortal Diamond: The Search for Our True Self*, pp. 167–168

CONTEMPLATION AS AN ALTERNATIVE MIND

The ability to stand back and calmly observe our inner dramas, without rushing to judgment, is foundational for spiritual seeing. It is the primary form of "dying to the self" that Jesus lived personally and the Buddha taught experientially. The growing consensus is that, whatever you call it, *such calm, egoless seeing is invariably characteristic of people at the highest levels of doing and loving in all cultures and religions.* They are the ones we call sages or wise women or holy men. They see as the mystics see. Many of us call it "the contemplative mind," Paul calls it "the mind of Christ" (1 Corinthians 2:10–16), but have no doubt that it is an alternative consciousness to our ordinary, calculating mind.

Do not let the word *mystic* scare you. It simply means *one who has moved from mere belief systems or belonging systems to actual inner experience.* All spiritual traditions agree that such a movement is possible, desirable, and available to everyone. In fact, Jesus seems to say that this is the whole point! (See, for example, John 10:19–38.)

+Adapted from *The Naked Now: Learning to See as the Mystics See*, pp. 30, 32–33. Also, *Everything Belongs: The Gift of Contemplative Prayer* develops the difference between the contemplative mind and the calculative mind.

THE TRUE SEMINARY

Why is it that Mother Teresa could stand up before crowds of thousands and repeat simple New Testament phrases and seemingly pious clichés, and still blow people away?!

She didn't say anything new: "Jesus loves you," she assured us. "We're all sons and daughters of God, and we have to love Jesus's poor." Yet people walked out renewed, transformed, and converted.

She wasn't a priest or minister. She wasn't well educated. Her authority came from her lifestyle, her solidarity with human suffering, and, thus, her pure goodness.

Loving servanthood and foundational surrender are the true basis for teaching authority in the Church, much more than title, vestment, role, or office. Such lives have the living authority of Jesus himself and need no special ordination or public validation. Jesus says to Simon Peter that he, and we ourselves, must first "be sifted like wheat," and only then are we in a position "*to recover* and in turn strengthen others" (see Luke 22:31–32). Such undergoing is the seminary that finally matters and that changes others' lives. It was Jesus's essential and first recovery program.

+Adapted from *Radical Grace: Daily Meditations*, pp. 384–385. For more on this theme, please consider *The Art of Letting Go: Living the Wisdom of St. Francis* with Fr. Richard Rohr (CD)

KNOWING FROM THE EDGE OF THE INSIDE

John the Baptist is the prophet who rejects the status quo without apology, eats the harsh food of that choice, and wears alternative clothing (why else do they take so much time describing it?) outside his own system of religion and culture—when his mom and dad were of the priestly class (Luke 1:5–6). He even changes the venue for transformation from Temple to river, which was clearly a judgment on the Temple system (John 1:19), and, thus, he was not trusted or liked by the authorities (Matthew 21:26–27).

Like the native peoples in New Mexico, he goes on his vision quest into the desert where he faces his aloneness, boredom, and naked self. He returns with a message, with clarity and a sureness of heart that reveals a totally surrendered man (but with an excess of asceticism and moralism, which Jesus corrects and redirects, see Matthew 11:11b and Luke 5:33). Nevertheless, John listens long and self-forgetfully; then he speaks, acts, and accepts those consequences, and is thus still pointed to as one than whom "no greater has ever been seen" (Matthew 11:11a).

You see, *transformed people transform people*, and John's new offbeat ritual down by the riverside (outside of the Temple where his father served) has become for us the very symbol of Christian transformation and orthodoxy. Really quite amazing when you think about it—and Jesus totally went along with it himself! Paul does the same thing with the early Christian status quo (Acts 15:1–12; Galatians 2:11–13), and probably has had more influence on Christian history than the twelve apostles put together. We must think about such things in a serious way now, if we are to faithfully imitate John the Baptist, Jesus, and Paul.

+Adapted from *Radical Grace: Daily Meditations*, pp. 24–25. For more on this theme, please consider *The Art of Letting Go: Living the Wisdom of St. Francis* with Fr. Richard Rohr (CD)

EXPERIENCE NEEDS DISCERNMENT
OF THAT EXPERIENCE

In her *Dialogues*, St. Catherine of Siena pictures the spiritual life as a large tree:

The trunk of the tree is *love*.

The core of the tree, that middle part that must be alive for the rest of the tree to be alive, is *patience*.

The roots of the tree are *self-knowledge*.

The many branches, reaching out into the air, are *discernment*.

In other words, says Catherine, *love* does not happen without *patience*, *self-knowledge*, and *discernment*.

Today we have little encouragement toward honest self-knowledge or training in spiritual discernment from our churches. We prefer the seeming clarity of black-and-white laws. By nature, most of us are not very patient. All of which means that love is not going to be very common. We need St. Catherine's tree again.

+Adapted from *Radical Grace: Daily Meditations*, pp. 184–185. For more on this theme, please consider *The Art of Letting Go: Living the Wisdom of St. Francis* with Fr. Richard Rohr (CD)

A NEW STRUCTURE FOR KNOWING
(EMERGING CHRISTIANITY)

The Jewish prophets had one foot in Israel and one foot outside and beyond. So must you have one foot in your historical faith community and one foot in the larger world; one foot rooted in a good tradition of accountability and another in your own world of service, volunteerism, occupation, subgroup, or what I call "lifestyle Christianity" and some call "Emerging Church," which desires to move beyond mere belief and worship systems to actual lifestyle choices and new accountability systems for giving your life away.

How else can we imitate the surrender of Jesus, who did exactly the same in relation to his own Jewish religion? He never left it, and yet in some ways he always left it when it did not heal or help real people. He formed his own little parachurch within yet alongside the Jewish priestly system, which became, rightly or wrongly, its own separate religion and which we now call Christianity.

As the twelfth step of Alcoholics Anonymous recognizes, we do not really appropriate things ourselves until we actively hand them on to others. We have to find the Love, and then give the Love away, and it is amazing how the two events do not always happen within the same group. I think they are both training grounds, one for the other. The first is our spring and our well (home base); the other is the channel away from home base that keeps our well from becoming brackish and stagnant.

+For more on this theme, please consider *The Art of Letting Go: Living the Wisdom of St. Francis* with Fr. Richard Rohr (CD)

BIAS TOWARD ACTION

The works that the Father has given me to complete, the very works that I am doing, testify on my behalf that the Father has sent me.

—John 5:36

The Scriptures very clearly teach what we call today a bias toward action. They are not just belief systems or dogmas and doctrines, as we have often made it. The Word of God is telling us very clearly that if you do not do it, you, in fact, do not believe it and have not heard it (James 1:19–27, as well as much of the rest of this primitive letter, which likely precedes the later theological emphasis in Paul's letters).

The only way that we become convinced of our own sense of power, dignity, and the power of God is by actually participating in it—by crossing a line, a line that has a certain degree of nonsensicalness and unprovability to it—and that's why we call it faith. In crossing that line, and acting in a new way, then and only then, can we really believe what we say we believe in the first place. Lifestyle issues, like nonconsumer living, nonviolent actions, community building, service, and volunteerism, ask much more of us than mere belief systems ever do.

+Adapted from *Preparing for Christmas with Richard Rohr*, pp. 48–49

A THREE-STEP USE OF SCRIPTURE

When the Scriptures are used maturely, they proceed in this order:

They *confront* us with a bigger picture than we are used to: God's kingdom, which has the potential to deconstruct our false and smaller kingdoms.

They then have the power to *convert* us to an alternative world view by proclamation, grace, and the sheer attraction of the good, the true, and the beautiful (not by shame, guilt, or fear which are low-level motivations, but which operate more quickly and so churches often resort to them).

They then *console* us and bring deep healing as they reconstruct us in a new place with a new mind and heart. If you seek consolation as the first meaning of a biblical text, you never get very far, because the small self or ego is still directing the mind and heart. As many have said before me, the truth will set you free, but first it must make you miserable.

+Adapted from *Preparing for Christmas with Richard Rohr*, pp. 64–65

EXPERIENCE TRUMPING ANY SCRIPTURE
OR TRADITION

Kingdom people are history makers. They break through the small kingdoms of this world to an alternative and much larger world, God's full creation. People who are still living in the false self are history stoppers. They use God and religion to protect their own status and the status quo of the world that sustains them. They are often fearful people, the nice, proper folks of every age who think like everybody else thinks and have no power to break through, or as Jesus's opening words state, "to change" (Mark 1:15; Matthew 4:17) and move beyond their small agenda. Courage is certainly the foundational virtue. Without it, faith, love, and hope do not happen. It takes immense courage to trust your own experience, and to be willing to pay the price if you are wrong. And you just might be!

Why do we piously admire kingdom people like Mary and Joseph and then not imitate their faith journeys, their courage, their non-reassurance by any religious system?

These were two uneducated laypeople who totally trusted their inner experience of God (angels and dreams) and who followed these to Bethlehem and beyond. Mary and Joseph walked in the courage and blind faith that their own experience was true—with no one to reassure them they were right. Their only safety net was God's love and mercy, a safety net they must have tried out many times or they would never have been able to fall into it so gracefully.

+Adapted from *Preparing for Christmas with Richard Rohr*, pp. 66–68

WE KNOW THROUGH THE CONCRETE
MORE THAN BY UNIVERSAL THEORIES

God's revelations are always pointed, concrete, and specific. They are not a Platonic world of ideas and theories about which you can be right or wrong or observe from a distance. Divine Revelation is not something you measure or critique. It is not an ideology but a Presence you intuit and meet! It is more Someone than something.

All of this is called the "mystery of incarnation"—*enfleshment* or *embodiment,* if you prefer—and for Christians it reaches its fullness in the incarnation of God in one ordinary-looking man named Jesus. God materialized in human form, so we could fall in love with a real person, which is the only way we fall in love at all. Walter Brueggemann called this clear Biblical pattern "the scandal of the particular." We first get the truth in one specific ordinary place and moment (like the one man Jesus), and then we universalize from that to the universal truth (the cosmic Christ). Our Franciscan philosopher John Duns Scotus called this the principle of "thisness" (*haecceity* or *haecceitas* in Latin). We can only know in focused moments what is always and everywhere true.

+Adapted from *Things Hidden: Scripture as Spirituality*, p. 17

.

FOUNDATION

If God is Trinity and Jesus is the face of God, then it is a benevolent universe. God is not someone to be afraid of but is the Ground of Being and is on our side.

INTRODUCTION

Your image of God creates you—or defeats you. There is an absolute connection between how you see God and how you see yourself and the whole universe. The word *God* is first of all a stand-in for *everything*—reality, truth, and the very shape of your universe. This is why theology is important, and why good theology and spirituality can make so much difference in how you live your daily life in this world. Theology is not just theoretical, but ends up being quite practical—practically upbuilding or practically defeating.

After years of giving and receiving spiritual direction, it has become obvious to me and to many of my colleagues that most people's operative, de facto image of God is initially a subtle combination of their mom and their dad, or other early authority figures. Without an interior journey of prayer or experience, much of religion is largely childhood conditioning, which God surely understands and works with. But this is what atheists and many former believers rightly react against because such religion is so childish and often fear-based, even if their arguments are blowing down a straw man.

The goal, of course, is to grow toward an adult religion that includes both reason and faith and inner experience you can trust. A mature God creates mature people. A big God creates big people.

If your mom was punitive, your God is usually punitive too, and you actually spend much of your life submitting to that punitive God or angrily reacting against it. If your dad (or your minister or early religion teachers) were cold and withdrawn, you will assume that God is cold and withdrawn—all Scriptures, Jesus, and mystics to the contrary. If all authority in your life came through males, you probably prefer a male image of God, even if your heart says otherwise. As we were taught in Scholastic philosophy, "Everything is received according to the manner of the receiver." This is one of those things hidden in plain sight, but it still remains well hidden to most Christians.

Frankly, if your early authority figures were merciful and forgiving, you have a great big emotional head start in understanding the Gospel and who God might really be. This is why denominational affiliations in the end mean very little. Yes, good theology and preaching will help, but I have met evangelicals with very limited theology who are bright and alive. They invariably had a bright and alive upbringing, and their hearts tends to be generous.

I also meet Catholics and Anglicans with a more expansive theology who nevertheless are dour and dominating. They invariably had an early world view that was all about counting, measuring, making inner lists, and doling out rewards and punishments. The expansive and open world of grace is actually a scandal to them. They are upset because God is so "generous" (see Matthew 20:16). Such people find it sincerely hard to live in the frame of reference that Jesus calls "the Reign of God." They are much more secure in a meritocracy of quid pro quo and resent anyone getting anything they have not worked for and deserved.

This is all mirrored in our political world views, of course. Good theology makes for good politics and positive social relationships. Bad theology makes for stingy politics, xenophobia, and highly controlled relationships. No wonder that both Freud and Jung believed that low-level religion creates mostly "anal retentive" people, to use a rather unkind but truly descriptive phrase.

For me as a Christian, the mostly undeveloped image of God as Trinity is the way out and the way through all limited concepts of God. Jesus comes to invite us into that flow—which flows only in one entirely positive direction.

GOD IS NOT SANTA CLAUS

If we want to go to the mature, mystical, and non-dual levels of spirituality, we must first deal with the often faulty, inadequate, and even toxic images of God that most people are dealing with before they have authentic God experience. Both God as Trinity and Jesus as the image of the invisible God reveal a God quite different—and much better—than the Santa Claus god who is "making a list, checking it twice, who's going to find out who's naughty or nice" or an "I will torture you if you do not love me" god (worse than your worst enemy, I would think). We must be honest and admit that this is the god that most people are still praying to. Such images are an unworkable basis for any real spirituality.

Trinity reveals that God is the Divine Flow under, around, and through all things—much more a verb than a noun, relationship itself rather than an old man sitting on a throne. Jesus tells us that God is like a loving parent who runs toward us while we are "still a long ways off" (Luke 15:20), then clasps and kisses us. Until this is personally experienced, most of Christianity does not work. This theme moves us quickly into practice-based religion (orthopraxy) over mere words and ideas (orthodoxy).

GOD IS ALWAYS THE INITIATOR
(All else is a manufactured god!)

When Jesus came up from the water, the heavens were opened to him,
and he saw the Spirit of God descending like a dove and alighting upon
him. And suddenly a voice came from heaven, saying,
"This is my beloved Son, in whom I am well pleased."
—Matthew 3:16–17

It has been said many times that after transformation you seldom have the feeling you have found anything. It feels much more like Someone has found you! You find yourself being grabbed, being held, and being loved by Someone. At first, you do not even know what is going on. All you know is that it is a most wondrous *undergoing*, but an undergoing nevertheless. You do not do much yourself but, like Mary, you know something "has been done unto you" (Luke 1:38).

Finally, you allow yourself to stand before one true mirror for your identity—you surrender to the naked now of true prayer and full presence. You become a Thou before the great I AM. Henceforward, as Teresa of Avila said, "You find God in yourself and yourself in God."

+Adapted from *The Naked Now: Learning to See as the Mystics See*, p. 19

BOTH ABYSS AND GROUND

The creation story (Genesis 1:26) states, "Let us make humans in *our* image." From the very beginning we know that we are being brought into a larger and shared life. The secret is somehow planted within us, and slowly reveals itself—if we are attentive to this "reverence humming within us."

Our DNA is divine, and the divine indwelling is never earned by any behavior or any ritual, but only *recognized* and *realized* (see Romans 11:6; Ephesians 2:8–10) and fallen in love with. When you are ready, you will be both underwhelmed and overwhelmed at the boundless mystery of your own humanity. You will know you are standing under the same waterfall of mercy as everybody else and receiving an undeserved *radical* grace, which gets to the root of your own soul.

Without that underlying experience of God as both *abyss* and *ground*, it is almost impossible to live in the now, in the fullness of who I am, warts and all, and almost impossible to experience the Presence that, paradoxically, always fills the abyss and shakes the ground. *Abyss* lets you know that you will never know fully, and God must always remain a "mystery" (Judges 13:18). This keeps you humble and searching. *Ground* gives you something solid to stand on and move out from. The Jewish Scriptures frequently call their God a "rock" experience (see Deuteronomy 32:18, 31 and Psalm 18:46, for example).

This keeps you confident and hopeful.

+Adapted from *The Naked Now: Learning to See as the Mystics See,* p. 22

GOD IS EVERYWHERE
(Answer to Question 16, "Where is God?"
in the old *Baltimore Catechism*)

You cannot *not* live in the presence of God. You are totally surrounded by God all the time and everywhere. You have no choice in the matter, except to bring it to consciousness. St. Patrick said it well in the prayer attributed to him:

> God beneath you,
>
> God in front of you,
>
> God behind you,
>
> God above you,
>
> God within you.

You cannot earn this God by any practice whatsoever. You cannot prove yourself worthy of this God. Knowing God's presence is simply a matter of awareness, of fully allowing and enjoying the present moment. There are moments when it happens naturally, normally *when we are out of the way*. Then life makes sense. Once I can see the Mystery here, and trust the Mystery even in this little piece of clay that I am, in this moment of time that I am—then I can also see it in you, and eventually in all things.

That would be full enlightenment, "when God is all in all" (1 Corinthians 15:28). There's no question and answer here as in the *Baltimore Catechism*; there is no problem-solving going on here. It is simply pure and unbounded awareness on our part. Any attempt by any religion to say God is here and not there is pure heresy. God is in all things precisely in God's ever newness and God's ever-possibility.

+Adapted from *Everything Belongs: The Gift of Contemplative Prayer*, pp. 56–57

WHO IS DOING THE PRAYING?

Prayer is not about changing God, but being willing to let God change us, or as Step 11 in the *Big Book* of Alcoholics Anonymous says: "Praying only for the knowledge of his will." Jesus goes so far as to say that true prayer is *always* answered (Matthew 7:7–11).

Now we all know that this is not factually true—unless he is talking about prayer in the sense that I will try to describe it. *If you are able to switch minds to the mind of Christ, your prayer has already been answered! The new mind knows, understands, accepts, and sees correctly, widely, and wisely. Its prayers are always answered because they are, in fact, the prayers of God, as well.*

True prayer is always about getting the "who" right. Who is doing the praying, you or God-in-you, little old you or the Eternal Christ Consciousness? Basically prayer is an exercise in *divine participation*—you opting in and God always being there!

+Adapted from *Breathing under Water: Spirituality and the Twelve Steps*,
pp. 96–97

GOD AS A SYNERGY

Contemplation (the prayer beyond words and ideas) is a way to describe what Jesus did in the desert. It is not learning as much as it is unlearning. It is not explaining as much as containing and receiving everything and holding onto nothing. It is refusing to judge too quickly and refining your own thoughts and feelings by calm observation and awareness over time—in light of the Big Picture.

You cannot understand anything well once you have approved or disapproved of it. There is too much of *you* invested there. Contemplation is loosening our attachment to ourselves so that Reality can get at us, especially the Absolute Reality that we call God.

Contemplation is the most radical form of self-abandonment I can imagine. It is most difficult if there is not a profound trust that there is Someone to whom I can be abandoned! Such self-forgetfulness paradoxically leads one to a firm and somewhat fearless sense of responsibility. Now I can risk responsibility precisely because I know the buck does *not* stop here. There is a cocreation going on, a life giving *synergism* that is found somewhere between surrender and personal responsibility—God fully "cooperating with those who love God" (Romans 8:28), and we slowly learning to second the motion.

+Adapted from *Near Occasions of Grace*, pp. 18–19

EXPANSIVE QUESTIONS,
NOT CONSTRICTIVE ANSWERS

Your image of God, your de facto, operative image of God, lives in a symbiotic relationship with your soul and creates what you become. Loving and forgiving people have always encountered a loving and forgiving God. Cynical people are cynical about the very possibility of any coherent or loving Center to the universe. So why wouldn't they become cynical themselves? Of course they do.

When you encounter a truly sacred text, the first questions are not "Did this literally happen just as it states? How can I be saved? What is the right thing for me to do? What is the dogmatic pronouncement here? Does my church agree with this? Who is right and who is wrong here?" These are largely ego questions, I am afraid. They are questions that try to secure your position, not questions that help you go on a spiritual path of faith and trust. They constrict you, whereas the purpose of the Sacred is to expand you. I know these are the first questions that come to our minds because that is where we usually live—inside our mental ego. They are the questions we were trained to ask, because everybody else asks them, unfortunately!

Having read sacred text, I would invite you to ponder these questions:

1. What is God doing here?
2. What does this say about who God is?
3. What does this say about how I can then relate to such a God?

+Adapted from the webcast *A Teaching on Wondrous Encounters*
(CD, DVD, MP3)

GOD IS NEVER LESS LOVING THAN THE MOST
LOVING PERSON YOU KNOW

What is God doing in the Scripture reading? With that question in mind, I want to give you an operative principle, which, I believe, had it been used in the last five hundred years, would have ensured a much more exciting and positive Christian history. If you are meditating on a Bible text, Hebrew or Christian, *and if you see God operating at a lesser level than the best person you know, then that text is not authentic revelation.* "God is love" (1 John 4:16), and no person you meet could possibly be more loving than the Source of love itself. It is as simple as that. You now have a foundational *hermeneutic* (interpretive key) for interpreting all of Scripture wisely. Literalism is the lowest and most narrow hermeneutic for understanding conversation in general and sacred texts in particular.

Haven't you read texts and not known what to think? See, for example, where Yahweh presumably tells the Israelites to kill every Canaanite in sight—men, women and children—and then imposes a ban on every pagan town, telling the Israelites to enter, burn, and destroy everything in sight (as in Joshua 6—7). *Do you really think that is God talking? I don't think so.* They have created God in their own image instead of letting God re-create them in his image.

"Well," you say, "it is in the Bible, and that makes it true and right." That is why we have to use a whole different lens for interpreting any authoritative text. How we deal with sacred texts is how we deal with reality in general. And how we deal with reality in general is how we deal with sacred texts. And both reality and all sacred texts are also fragmented and imperfect (1 Corinthians 13:12). It takes a certain level of human and spiritual maturity to interpret a Scripture. Vengeful and petty people find vengeful and hateful texts (and they are there, but some find them even when they are not there)! Loving and peaceful people will hold out until a text resounds deep within them (and there are plenty there!). In short, *only love can handle big truth.*

+Adapted from the webcast *A Teaching on Wondrous Encounters*
(CD, DVD, MP3)

NOT WHAT WE EXPECTED OR EVEN WANTED

"Rejoice heart and soul, daughter of Zion! Shout with gladness, daughter
of Jerusalem! See now, your king comes to you; he is victorious, he is triumphant, humble and riding on a donkey, on a colt, the foal of a donkey."
— Zechariah 9:9

Luke builds on this Old Testament image as he has Jesus entering the Holy
City on Palm Sunday. Jesus is taking charge of his possession—namely, his
people—and Luke has him coming in, according to the prophecy, as a very
different kind of king. He is a not an enthroned monarch, or even a mounted
warrior, but his triumph and victory come by doing power in a whole new
way. He seems to have created this well-staged drama with chosen props
and stage setting so his message could not be ignored (Luke 19:28–33). He
inaugurated a new kind of leadership, not one based in dominative power
but one based in humble service. The capital city hardly notices this kind
of power, as we probably wouldn't have either. It is political power that fascinates us, not men on donkeys. Any philosophy of religion assumes that
God should be omnipotent, omnipresent, and omniscient. If Jesus is the
image of God, he is turning that entire assumption on its head. God is not
who we think God is.

+Adapted from *The Good News According to Luke*, p. 180

GOD AS SERVANT?

There is no real story of the Last Supper in the Gospel of John as found in the Synoptic Gospels of Matthew, Mark, and Luke. There is no passing of the bread or passing of the cup. Instead we come upon the story of Jesus on his knees washing the apostles' feet (John 13:1–20). This is really quite amazing, and it is even more amazing that this foot-washing was never made into a sacrament! It is much more explicit and clear in the Scriptures than many other actions we made into sacraments. In fact, Jesus even appears to mandate it (John 3:14–15)!

Perhaps John realized that, seventy years after the Synoptic Gospels had been read, he wanted to give a theology of the Eucharist that revealed *the meaning behind* the breaking of the bread. He made it into an active ritual of servanthood and solidarity, instead of the priest-centered cult that it has largely become.

Peter symbolizes all of us as he protests, "You will never wash my feet!" (John 13:8). But Jesus answers, "If I do not wash you, you can have nothing in common with me." That is strong! Many of us find it hard to receive undeserved love from another. For some reason it is very humiliating to the ego. We want to think we have earned any love that we get by our worthiness or attractiveness. So Jesus has to insist on being the servant lover. Thank God Peter surrenders, but it probably takes him the rest of his life to understand what has happened.

+Adapted from *Radical Grace: Daily Meditations*, p. 143

POWER THAT FEELS LIKE POWERLESSNESS

The supreme irony of the whole crucifixion scene is this: he who was everything had everything taken away from him. He who was seemingly perfect (Hebrews 1:3; 5:9) was totally misjudged as sin itself (Romans 8:3–4). How can we be that mistaken? The crucified Jesus forever reveals to us how wrong both religious and political authorities can be, and how utterly wrong we all can be—about who is in the right and who is sinful (John 16:8). The crowd, who represents all of us, chooses Barabbas, a common thief, over Jesus. That is how much we can misperceive, misjudge, and be mistaken.

Jesus hung in total solidarity with the pain of the world and the far too many lives on this planet that have been "nasty, lonely, brutish, and short." After the cross, we know that God is not watching human pain, nor apparently always stopping human pain, as much as God is found *hanging with us* alongside all human pain. Jesus's ministry of healing and death, of solidarity with the crucified of history, forever tells us that *God is found wherever the pain is.* This leaves God on both sides of every war, in sympathy with both the pain of the perpetrator and the pain of the victim, with the excluded, the tortured, the abandoned, and the oppressed since the beginning of time. I wonder if we even like that. There are no games of moral superiority left for us now. Yet this is exactly the kind of Lover and the universal Love that humanity needs.

This is exactly how Jesus "redeemed the world by the blood of the cross." It was not some kind of heavenly transaction, or paying a price to an offended God, as much as *a cosmic communion with all that humanity has ever loved and ever suffered.* If Jesus was paying any price, it was to the hard and resistant defenses around our hearts and bodies. God has loved us from all eternity.

CHRIST IS THE STAND-IN FOR EVERYBODY

Christ has been raised from the dead,
the first fruits of all who fall asleep.
—1 Corinthians 15:20

St. Paul seldom leaves the message at the level of "believe this fact about Jesus." He always moves it to "This is what it says about you!" or "This is what it says about history!" Until we are pulled into the equation, we find it hard to invest ourselves in a distant religious belief.

Paul normally speaks of "Christ"—which includes *all of creation*—for he never knew Jesus in the flesh but only as the eternal Body of Christ. Christ Crucified is all of the hidden, private, tragic pain of history made public and given over to God. Christ Resurrected is all suffering received, loved, and transformed by an all-caring God. How else could we have any kind of cosmic hope? How else would we not die of sadness for what humanity has done to itself and what we have done to one another?

The cross is the standing statement of what we do to one another and to ourselves. The resurrection is the standing statement of what God does to us in return.

SOME EFFECTS OF MYSTICAL (EXPERIENTIAL)
ENCOUNTERS

After the first effects of enlargement, connection, or union, and some degree of emancipation, mystical experiences lead to a kind of foundational *optimism*. You would usually call it "hope." You wonder where it comes from, especially in the middle of all the terrible things that are happening in the world. Hope is not logical, but a "participation in the very life of God" (just like faith and love, which were called "theological virtues" as opposed to virtues acquired by practice, temperament, or willpower). That doesn't mean we should not practice being hopeful, but it is still not a matter of pure willpower. Faith, hope, and love are always somehow a gift—a cooperation with Someone Else, a participation in Something larger than ourselves.

The next descriptor I'd like to add is a sense of safety and security. If you can't feel safe with a person, deep love cannot really happen. *If, in the presence of God, you don't feel safe and even protected, then I don't think it is God—it is something else.* It's a god that is not God. It's probably what Meister Eckhart is referring to when he says, "I pray God to rid me of God." He means that the God we all begin with is necessarily a partial God, an imitation God, a word for God, a try-on God. But as you go deeper into the journey, I promise you, you will always be more naturally hopeful (even when you don't *feel* it!), and you will usually sense a deep safety and security (even when your mental ego momentarily presents scenarios of doom).

+Adapted from *Following the Mystics through the Narrow Gate....
Seeing God in All Things* (CD, DVD, MP3)

GOD DOES NOT LOVE YOU BECAUSE YOU ARE GOOD, YOU ARE GOOD BECAUSE GOD LOVES YOU

The great thing about God's love is that it's not determined by the object. *God does not love us because we are good. God loves us because God is good.* It takes our whole lives for that to sink in, along with lots of trials and testing of divine love, because that's not how human love operates.

Human love is largely determined by the attractiveness of the object. When someone is nice, good, not high maintenance, attractive physically, important, or has a nice personality, we find it much easier to give ourselves to them or to "like" them. That's just the way we humans operate. We naturally live in what I call the meritocracy of quid pro quo. We must be taught by God and grace how to live in an *economy of grace*. Divine love is a love that operates in a quite unqualified way, without making distinctions between persons and seemingly without such a thing as personal preference. Anyone who receives divine love feels like God's favorite in that minute! We don't even have the capacity to imagine such a notion until we have received it! Divine love is *received by surrender instead of any performance principle whatsoever.*

+Adapted from *Following the Mystics through the Narrow Gate....
Seeing God in All Things* (CD, DVD, MP3)

REVERSE ENGINES!

Each of the four Gospels leads up to Jesus finally standing alone, without anyone really comprehending what he's talking about when he pounds them with successive metaphors about the Reign of God. Jesus must finally realize that he has to do it visually and personally in his body. He's got to stop talking about it. He's got to let it happen. Maybe you've had the experience that it's not until someone dies that we ask bigger questions and reframe our universe.

That's what we mean when we say Jesus *had* to die for us. It's not that he had to literally pay God some price, which makes God appear rather petty and powerless. Is God that unfree to love and forgive? Does not God organically and naturally love what he created? It can't be true. John Duns Scotus (1266–1308), a Franciscan philosopher and theologian, taught that good theology will always *keep God free for humanity and humanity free for God*. Love can only happen in the realm of freedom, and ever-expanding freedom at that. We pulled God into our way of loving and forgiving, which is always mercenary and tit-for-tat. It was the best any of us could do until we sat stunned before the cross.

Quite simply, until someone dies, we don't ask bigger questions. We don't understand in a new way. We don't break through. The only price that Jesus was paying was to the human soul, so that we could break through to a new kind of God. Most of religious history believed that humanity had to spill blood (human sacrifice or animal sacrifice) to get to God, but after Jesus some were able to comprehend that actually God was spilling blood to get to us. That reversed the engines of history forever, but the human mind still resists that reversal. It is too good to be true.

+Adapted from *The Four Gospels* (CD, MP3)

GOD SEEMS TO CARE ABOUT HUMAN SUFFERING

Mark's is primarily a Gospel of action. Of the four Gospels, his includes the least verbal teaching. Jesus is constantly on the move from place to place preaching and healing, preaching and healing, but it is mostly action and narrative. Jesus is the invasion of God's Big Picture into our small worlds, and he does this much more than he talks about it. We have to look at Jesus's actions and how his physical healings consistently rearranged faulty relationships—with our own self-image, with others, with society as a whole, and with a God who was henceforth seen as on our side.

There is not much profit in just thinking, "Wow, Jesus worked another miracle!" But there is much profit in noting the changed status, self-image, courage, and relationship to family or community that the cure invariably entails. This is the real transformative message. I am not denying that Jesus could and undoubtedly did perform physical healing. It still happens, and I have seen it, but the healings and exorcisms in Mark's Gospel are primarily to make statements about power, abuse, relationships, class, addiction, money, exclusion, the state of women and the poor, and the connections between soul and body—the exact same issues we face today.

Further, Jesus doesn't heal as a reward for good behavior (usually there is no mention of any pre-requisites whatsoever, and often it is others who have the faith, not the one cured). Neither is there any primary concern about a later life in heaven in Mark's Gospel. We projected that onto the text. All of the healing stories are *present-tense concerns for human suffering in this world*. They tell us that God cares deeply about the tragic human condition *now*. How could we miss this? In general, you should see all rewards and punishments as inherent and current (Sin is its own punishment, and virtue is its own reward now!) And surely what God does today,

God will do forever! What is true now is true forever. That is our promise of any life and our warning against any eternal death.

+Adapted from *The Four Gospels* (CD, MP3)

GOD HAS NO GRANDCHILDREN, ONLY CHILDREN

Jesus practically begs for some trust from his disciples, even after they've witnessed his miracles and heard his profound teaching. He eventually puts this question to them: "Who do you say that I am?" *Don't give me your theologies. Who is the Jesus you know? That's the only Jesus that can really touch you and liberate you.* Finally, Peter responds: "You are the Christ!" (Mark 8:29). "And Jesus gave him strict orders not to tell anyone" (8:30). Why? Because each one of us has to walk the same journey of death and doubt for ourselves—and come out the other side enlarged by love.

No one can do this homework for you. Every generation has to be converted anew, and the Gospel has to always be preached in new contexts and cultures in ways that are good news to that time and people. Yes, institutions and denominations are necessary and somehow inevitable, but when they imagine that they can prepackage the message in eternal formulas and half-believed (half-experienced?) doctrines and Scriptures, they often become their own worst enemy. Too many people join a club instead of going on a journey toward God, love, or truth.

+Adapted from *The Four Gospels* (CD, MP3)

GOD AND GENDER

Most people, not all, first experienced unconditional love not through the image of a man, but through the image of their mother. She therefore became the basis for many people's real and operative God. I am convinced that many people sour on religion because the God they are presented with is actually less loving than their mother or father was.

For much of the human race, the mother has been the one who parts the veil for us, and opens us up to any inner life of emotions or soul. She gives us that experience of grounding, intimacy, tenderness, and safety that most of us hope for from God. However, many people also operate from a toxic and negative image of God. For those people, little that is wonderful is going to happen as long as that is true. Early growth in spirituality is often about healing that inner image, whether male-based or female-based.

Most of us know that God is beyond gender. When we look at the book of Genesis, we see that the first thing God is looking for is quite simply "images" by which to communicate who-God-is (Genesis 1:26–27). God is not looking for servants, for slaves, or for people who are going to pass loyalty tests. God is just looking for images—images and likenesses of the Inner Mystery. Whoever God is, is profoundly and essentially what it means to be both male *and* female in perfect balance. We have to find and to trust images that present both a healthy feminine face for God and a healthy masculine face for God. Both are true and both are necessary for a vital and loving relationship with God. Up to now, we have largely relied upon the presented masculine images of God (which closed many people down) while, in fact, our inner life is much more drawn to a loving feminine energy. That is much of our religious problem today, and I do not believe that is an exaggeration.

+Adapted from *On Transformation: Collected Talks, Volume 1: The Maternal Face of God* (CD)

THE FEMININE FACE OF GOD

All this women's stuff is not only important; it is half of conversion, half of salvation, half of wholeness, half of God's work of art. I believe this mystery is reflected in the woman of the twelfth chapter of the Apocalypse: "Pregnant, and in labor, crying aloud in the pangs of childbirth...and finally escaping into the desert until her time" (Revelation 12:1–6).

Could this be the time? The world is tired of Pentagons and pyramids, prelates and princes, empires and corporations that only abort God's child. This women's stuff is very important, and it has always been important, more than this white male priest ever imagined or desired! My God was too small and too male in the first half of my life. It kept me from the deeper mystical path.

Much that many feminists have said is very prophetic and necessary for the Church and the world. It is time for the woman to come out of her desert refuge and for the men to welcome her, as we see in the churches today. This is still quite difficult if you have been an "alpha male" all of your life. No surprise that Jesus came "meek and humble of heart" to undo the male addiction to power and performance (Matthew 11:29). Mary is the standing archetype of how the gift of God is received. One almost wonders if the Roman and Orthodox churches do not worship Mary to avoid actually following her on her oh-so-natural and simple path.

+Adapted from Radical Grace: Daily Meditations, p. 279.

A BROWN MADONNA

In one generation after 1531, under the mother symbol of the Lady of Guadalupe, almost all of the native peoples of Mexico accepted Christianity. Such a quick and massive conversion had never been recorded. A new kind of Christianity unfolded in the New World precisely at the time it was fighting and dividing in the Old World. I believe that Christ takes on the face and features of each people God loves. In this case God knew that the face and features had to be feminine and compassionate, after centuries of a tyrannical sun-god and a new Catholic-Spanish machismo. The Lady of Guadalupe is clearly an archetype of the eternal feminine—the heart, hope, and strength of all new life revealed in a marvelous brown and pregnant woman—to people who could not read. Her image is the real operative flag of Mexico!

She believed in a little one, Juan Diego, who could not believe in himself. She spoke sweetly to him in his native Nahuatl language, and not the Spanish language of the new oppressors. She encouraged him beyond his shame, and made him special and beloved in a love he could understand. She empowered him to face again and again the distant father (bishop), and finally revealed the inner and transcendent woman on his own chest. The disbelieving bishop finally kneels at the young Indian's feet. No logic is offered, no theological subtleties—only December roses given and received. The symbolism is not attractive to any *conquistador* mentality, but only to a feminine soul.

Maybe it is only the Eternal Feminine who will be able to heal the wars, the oppression, the mistrust, and the status symbols that divide the children of God. (We have only begun to see women at international peace talks in very recent years. Could that be why they seldom succeeded in the past?)

+Adapted from *Radical Grace: Daily Meditations*, pp. 325, 216

THE FLIGHT FROM THE FEMININE

One of the most influential books I read when I was a young man was Karl Stern's classic *The Flight from Woman*, which made much sense to me on many levels and formed my early appreciation of an alternative consciousness to the one that was forming Western militarism and capitalism. Thank God, the twentieth century will be known for the emergence of the feminine mind into mainstream consciousness. Before this time that has not been the case, and it is still not true in much of Africa, Asia, and the Middle East. Christianity must take much of the credit here, and liberals would be honest to admit this. But in general, the feminine and women have been demeaned or dismissed as inferior, even in Christianity, which should have known better.

There were occasional Christians who took Paul seriously when he said that "in Christ there is neither male nor female" (Galatians 3:28). For example, Lady Julian of Norwich (1342–1416), my favorite mystic, calls Jesus "our Mother." She says, "Jesus is our true mother in whom we are endlessly carried and out of whom we will never come."

For many Christians, Mary became the archetypal image of the maternal face of God. It was the only way they could break through, especially if they never had a good man in their lives. Many Catholics, especially in macho cultures, actually loved Mary much more than Jesus, or God "the Father," or the neuter Holy Spirit. It was perhaps bad theology, but it was needed and brilliant psychology.

+Adapted from *On Transformation: Collected Talks, Volume 1:*
The Maternal Face of God (CD)

JESUS AND "THE CHRIST" ARE NOT EXACTLY THE SAME

Jesus is the microcosm; Christ is the macrocosm. There is a movement from Jesus to the Christ that you and I have to imitate and walk, as well. A lot of us have so fallen in love with the historical Jesus that we worship him as such and stop right there. We never really follow the same full journey that he made, which is the death and resurrection journey—Jesus died and Christ rose.

Unless we make the same movement that Jesus did—from his one single life to his risen and transformed state (John 12:24)—we probably don't really understand, experientially, what we mean by the Christ—*and how we are part of that deal!* This is why he said, "Follow me." The Jesus you and I participate in and are graced by and redeemed by is the *risen* Jesus who *has become the Christ* (see Acts 2:36), which is an inclusive statement about all of us and all of creation too. Stay with this startling truth in the days ahead, and it will rearrange your mind and heart, and change the way you read the entire New Testament. Paul understood this to an amazing degree, which is why he almost always talks about Christ and hardly ever directly quotes Jesus. It is rather shocking once you realize it.

+Adapted from *The Cosmic Christ* (CD, MP3)

SAME PATTERN ON TWO LEVELS

As many mystics and saints throughout history have said, God created because God needed something to love beyond the internal love of the Trinity. And then, to take this one step further, God created humans so that one species could love God back *freely.* Robots cannot love. Trees cannot love consciously, at least in the way we understand consciousness. Now set this parallel to your relationship with your own children. Your fondest desire, maybe at an unconscious level, if you consciously conceived a child, was to bring forth a love object. "I want to love this child in every way I can, and even hope that this child will love me in return. And the way I love them, paradoxically, becomes their empowerment to love me back." Now apply this pattern to God and us.

I think this is why the reproductive process is given to us in this unique and special way, precisely so that we can experience the reciprocal character of love. God is creating an object of love that God can totally give himself to, so that eventually we will be capable of freely loving God back in the same way. Humans are like two-way mirrors, both receiving and reflecting. Humans are like tuning forks that pick up a tone and hand it on as resonance.

+Adapted from *The Cosmic Christ* (CD, MP3)

HOLY SPIRIT

We are always waiting for the Holy Spirit—somehow forgetting that the Spirit was given to us from the very beginning. In fact, she was "hovering over the chaos" in the very first lines of Genesis 1:2, soon turning the "formless void" into a Garden of Eden.

We are threatened by anything we cannot control, that part of God "which blows where it will" (John 3:8) and which our theologies and churches can never perfectly predict nor inhibit (see Acts 10:44–48). The Holy Spirit has rightly been called the forgotten or denied Person of the Blessed Trinity. We cannot sense the Spirit, just as we cannot see air, silence, or the space between everything. We look for God out there and the Spirit is always in here and in between everything. Now even science is revealing to us that the energy of the universe is not in the particles or planets—but in the relational space between them! And we are having a hard time measuring it, controlling it, predicting it, or inhibiting it. It sounds an awful lot like Spirit.

GOD AS FLOW

The day of Pentecost frees the apostles to believe in a God who is actively involved in their lives and no longer a mere intellectual concept. The Holy Spirit has become wind, fire, joy, excitement, universal shareability, and not just another boring Sabbath obligation or more commandments to obey. Notice how all the metaphors of Spirit presence are dynamic, alive, moving, and universally available.

The Spirit will always be totally unmerited grace. She always takes the initiative, because Spirit is omnipresent, and thus there *first*! In the first Pentecost account the Holy Spirit is experienced as intimacy, enlightenment, joy, and fire, and as the power to love beyond boundaries and ethnicities, which became a universal language (Acts 2:1–13). She is presented as surprising, elusive, and free, and yet totally *given*. The Spirit comes from no place we can control, least of all by our good behavior or even our bad behavior. All we can do is surrender, enjoy, and share. Spirit-filled lives become like a pass-through savings account—which gains lots of interest for you and others when it is consciously enjoyed.

+Adapted from *Radical Grace: Daily Meditations*, p. 193

ORTHOPRAXY OVER ORTHODOXY

A Christian, or any holy person, is someone who is animated by *the Holy Spirit*, a person in whom *the Spirit* of Christ can work. That doesn't have to mean that you consciously know what you are doing or that you even have to know or that you even belong to the right Jesus group. As Paul said to the Athenians, "The God whom I proclaim is in fact the one you already worship without knowing it" (Acts 17:23).

In Matthew 25, the dead say, "When have we seen you hungry? When have we seen you thirsty?" And the Christ says in return, "Because you did it for these little ones, you did it for me." In each case, they did not know, at least consciously, that they were doing it for God or Jesus or even love. They just did it, and presumably from a pure heart, without any obvious religious affiliation or impure motive.

It never depends upon whether we say the right words or practice the right ritual, but whether we live the right reality. It is rather clear to me now that the Spirit gets most of her work done by stealth and disguise, not even caring who gets the credit, and not just by those who say, "Lord, Lord!" (Matthew 7:21). Jesus seems to be making this exact point in his story of the two sons (Matthew 21:28–32). The one who actually *acts*, even if he says the wrong words, "does the Father's will" and not the one who just says the right words.

+Adapted from *Simplicity: The Freedom of Letting Go,* p. 157

A TRINITARIAN PRAYER

In the name of the Holy Formless One,

In the name of the Son, who took Form,

In the name of the Spirit between these Two,

All things are made one.

God for us, we call You Father

God alongside us, we call You Jesus,

God within us, we call You Holy Spirit.

But these are only names.

You are the Eternal Mystery that enables and holds and enlivens all things

—even us and even me.

Every name falls short of Your goodness and Your greatness.

We can only see who You are in *what is*.

In the beginning, now, and always.

Amen.

+A prayer accompanying *The Divine Dance* on God as Trinity

WITH THREE YOU GET JOY

Our Franciscan St. Bonaventure (1221–1274), who wrote a lot about the Trinity, was deeply influenced by a lesser-known figure, Richard of St. Victor, who died in 1173. Richard said, "For God to be good, God can be one. For God to be loving, God has to be two because love is always a relationship." But his real breakthrough was saying, "For God to be supreme joy and happiness, God has to be three." Lovers do not know full happiness until they both delight in the same thing, like new parents with the ecstasy of their first child.

When I was first becoming known, people wanted to get close to me and be my friends or have special relationships with me. I asked myself how I would choose between all these friends and I realized that the people I really found joy in were not people who loved me so much as *people who loved what I loved*. That helped me understand what I think Richard of St. Victor was trying to teach. The Holy Spirit *is* the shared love of the Father and the Son, and shared love is always happiness and joy. The Holy Spirit is whatever the Father and the Son are in love with; the Holy Spirit *is* that excitement and joy—about everything that has been created!

+Adapted from *The Shape of God: Deepening the Mystery of the Trinity*
(CD, DVD, MP3)

A MYSTERY OF PARTICIPATION

In our attempts to explain the Trinitarian Mystery in the past, we over-emphasized the individual qualities of the Father, Son, and Holy Spirit, but not so much the relationships between them. It is in the relationships themselves that all the power is! This is where all the meaning is! We can name them all with masculine words (as we have done up to now), we can name them with feminine or neuter words if you wish, but in both cases you can miss the precise way that they relate to one another—and thus miss the major point.

The Mystery of God as Trinity invites us into a dynamism, a flow, a relationship, a waterwheel of love, or a "fountain fullness of love" as Bonaventure put it. The idea of Trinity says that God is a verb much more than a noun, an energy and action more than a concept. God as Trinity invites us *into* a shared experience, where we are invited as participants. Some of our Christian, Sufi, and Jewish mystics trusted that all of creation was being taken back into this flow of eternal life, almost as if we are a Fourth Person of the Eternal Flow of God or, as Jesus clearly put it, "I will return to take you with me, so that where I am you also may be" (John 14:3). Only a Trinitarian theology makes heaven make sense. Otherwise, we simply have rewards and punishments administered by a monarch on a throne.

+Adapted from *The Shape of God: Deepening the Mystery of the Trinity*
(CD, DVD, MP3)

INTERBEING

Paul says, "God's weakness is stronger than human strength" (1 Corinthians 1:25). That awesome line gives us a key into the Mystery of Trinity. I would describe human strength as self-sufficiency or autonomy. God's weakness I would describe as *Interbeing* or shared intimacy.

Human strength admires holding on. Human weakness is about letting go into the Other, handing over the self to another and receiving your self from another. Human strength admires personal independence. But God's Mystery is total mutual dependence and interdependence. We like control more than surrender. God loves vulnerability. We admire needing no one. The Trinity is total intercommunion with all things and all being. We are practiced at hiding and protecting ourselves. God seems to be in some kind of total disclosure for the sake of creating and loving the other.

Our strength, we think, is in asserting and protecting our boundaries. God is into dissolving boundaries between Father, Son, and Holy Spirit, yet finding them anew in that very outpouring! The space created by outpouring is automatically filled up by infilling. Take the rest of your life to try to unpack such a total turnaround of Reality.

+Adapted from *The Shape of God: Deepening the Mystery of the Trinity*
(CD, DVD, MP3)

THE PARADIGM FOR ALL OF REALITY

A threefold God totally lets go of any boundaries for the sake of the Other and then receives them back from Another. It is a nonstop waterwheel of Love. Each accepts that He is fully accepted by the Other, and then passes on that total acceptance. Thus indeed, "God is Love"! It's the same spiritual journey for all of us, for it takes most of our life to accept that we are accepted—and to accept everyone else as a result.

Most can't do this easily because internally there is so much self-accusation (self-flagellation in many cases) and self-preservation at work. Most are so convinced that they are not the body of Christ, that they are unworthy, that they are not in radical union with God, and so they live in an economy of scarcity and self-protection. The Gospel announces a world view of abundance, and the Church is supposed to use every means to convince us of this inherent safety and dignity, which is why it is called "Good News."

The Good News is that the question of union has already been resolved once and for all. We cannot create our union with God from our side. It is objectively already given to us by the Holy Spirit who dwells within us (see Romans 8:9, for one example). Once we know we are that grounded, founded, and home free, we can then stop protecting ourselves and pour ourselves out (2 Timothy 4:6) just as Father does to Son, Son to Spirit, and Spirit to Father in a fountain fullness of generosity and abundance.

+Adapted from *The Shape of God: Deepening the Mystery of the Trinity*
(CD, DVD, MP3)

GOD AS SHARED FOOD

When we start making the Eucharistic meal something to define member-ship instead of to proclaim grace and gift, we always get in trouble; that's been the temptation of every denomination that has the Eucharist. Too often we use the Eucharist to separate who's in from who's out, who's wor-thy from who's unworthy, instead of to declare that all of us are radically unworthy, and that worthiness is not even the issue. If worthiness is the issue, who can stand before God? Are those who receive actually saying they are worthy? I hope not. It is an ego statement to begin with. In fact, we Catholics even say, "Lord, I am not worthy" right before we come to the altar. I guess we don't really mean that, and it is just a pious bluff.

The issue is not worthiness; the issue is trust and surrender. It all comes down to "confidence and love," as Thérèse of Lisieux said. I think that explains the joyous character with which many celebrate the Eucharist. We are pulled into immense love and joy for such constant and unearned grace. It doesn't get any better than this! All we can do at the Eucharist is kneel in love and then stand in confidence. (St. Augustine said that the proper posture for prayer was standing proud and erect, because we no longer have to grovel before God or fear God, if God is like Jesus.)

+Adapted from *Eucharist as Touchstone* (CD, MP3)

SPACIOUS SILENCE ALLOWS A SPACIOUS GOD

This is one good thing that silence and waiting has taught me: *our lives are always useable by God. We need not always be effective, but only transparent and vulnerable.* Then we are instruments, no matter what we do. Silence is the ability to trust that God is acting, teaching, and using me—even before I perform or after my seeming failures. Silence is the necessary space around things that allows them to develop and flourish without my pushing.

God takes it from there, and there is not much point in comparing who is better, right, higher, lower, or supposedly saved. We are all partial images slowly coming into focus, as long as we allow and filter the Light and Love of God, which longs to shine through us—*as us*!

+Adapted from *Contemplation in Action,* p. 134

THE GOD YOU MEET IN PRAYER

The True Sacred, which is what you are seeking in prayer and silence, always reveals that:

God is One, timeless, and inclusive of all.

God is above any national or group ownership or personal manipulation.

God is available as a free gift and not through sacrificing things.

God needs no victims and creates no victims. Jesus ends religion as sacrifice "once and for all" by revealing the tragic effects of scapegoating through what happened to him on the cross (Hebrews 7:27; 10:10).

Jesus personifies this type of God and speaks defiantly in defense of such a God. Nowhere is he more succinct than when he quotes the prophet Hosea, "Go and learn the meaning of the words: '*Mercy is what pleases me, not sacrifices*'" (Matthew 9:13).

+Adapted from *Jesus' Plan for a New World: The Sermon on the Mount*, p. 5

HOW DOES ONE REALLY LOVE GOD?

Ordinary Christianity has emphasized that *we* should love God. This makes sense, but do we really know how to do that? What I find in the mystics is an overwhelming experience of how God has loved *us!* That's what comes through all of their writings, and I do mean *all*—that God is forever the aggressive lover, God is the protagonist, God is the one who seduces me out of my unworthiness. It's all about *God's* initiative! Then the mystics try desperately to pay back, to offer their lives back to the world, to the poor and rejected, and, thus, back to God. Love is repaid by love alone.

Mystics are not trying to *earn* God's love by doing good things or going to church services. That question is already and profoundly resolved. The mystic's overwhelming experience is this full body blow of divine embrace, a *radical acceptance by God* even in a state of fragmentation and poverty. That's what makes it amazing and grace (see Romans 11:6).

+Adapted from *Following the Mystics through the Narrow Gate....*
Seeing God in All Things (CD, DVD, MP3)

TRUE SELF AND GODSELF

Evelyn Underhill defines mysticism as "an overwhelming consciousness of God and an overwhelming consciousness of one's own soul *at the same time*." In my experience, that is exactly what I see happening. There's this wonderful sense of my own value, my own significance, my own validation from above and beyond me. "I was once blind, but now I see." I once was nobody and now I'm everybody—and this change in self-image is simultaneous with a discovery of a true and all-accepting image of God. No wonder so many people cry, laugh, or sing in tongues, when this happens. Their proper boundaries are blown away.

Mystical experience is the best possible cure for low self-esteem. You know you were chosen by the One who does the choosing! You know you are intimately loved by the One who creates all the loving! When the "Unmoved Mover" says you are good, you would do well to accept his or her version of reality and let go of your petty carping and complaining about yourself.

+Adapted from *Following the Mystics through the Narrow Gate....*
Seeing God in All Things (CD, DVD, MP3)

GOD DOES NOT LOVE US *IF* WE CHANGE, GOD LOVES US SO *THAT* WE CAN CHANGE

Those who pray learn to favor and prefer God's judgment over that of human beings. God always outdoes us in generosity and in receptivity. God is always more loving than the person who has loved you the most! All you can bring is today's latest product, whatever it is, for a new dose of love. It will always be immature on some level. It will always be inadequate, but that is not the point. It is not the perfection of the gift, but the willingness to lovingly offer the gift that pleases all parents and surely, then, the Super Parent that some of us call God.

God does not lead the soul by shaming it, just as a good parent would not shame his or her child. It doesn't work anyway. We all have done it at times, and if we were raised in a punitive way ourselves, we still tend to think that is the way to motivate people—by shaming them or making them feel guilty. I've done it enough and I've received it enough to know that it eventually backfires. It never works. We close down and stop trusting after that, and we use all kinds of defense mechanisms to avoid further vulnerability. So God's way actually works—to love us at even deeper levels than we can know or love ourselves. It is really quite wonderful, and one wonders why anyone would want to miss out on this.

+Adapted from *Following the Mystics through the Narrow Gate…. Seeing God in All Things* (CD, DVD, MP3)

EVERY PRAYER IS ALREADY
A PREVIOUS RESPONSE

We are told that St. Francis used to spend whole nights praying the same prayer: "Who are you, O God? And who am I?" Evelyn Underhill claims it's almost the perfect prayer. The abyss of your own soul and the abyss of the nature of God have opened up, and you are falling into both of them simultaneously. Now you are in a new realm of Mystery and grace, where everything good happens!

Notice how the prayer of Francis is not stating anything, is not sure of anything, but just asking open-ended questions. It is the humble, seeking, endless horizon prayer of the mystic that is offered out of complete trust. You know that such a prayer will be answered, because there has already been a previous answering, a previous epiphany, a previous moment where the ground opened up and you knew you were in touch with infinite mystery and you knew you were yourself infinite mystery. You only ask such grace-filled questions (or any question, for that matter) when they have already begun to be answered.

+Adapted from *Following the Mystics through the Narrow Gate....*
Seeing God in All Things (CD, DVD, MP3)

LIGHT AND DARKNESS
DO NOT ELIMINATE ONE ANOTHER

German Jesuit Karl Rahner said something like this (his German is hard to translate): "The infinite mystery that you are to yourself and the infinite mystery that God is in God's self proceed forward together as one." In simple English, as you uncover God's loving truth, you uncover your own, and as you uncover your own truth, you fall deeper into God's mercy and love. I've certainly seen this in my own little journey. When I come to a breakthrough in my own shadow work, my own sinfulness, my own self-knowledge, or in wonder at my own soul, it invariably feeds and invites the other side, and I want to go deeper with God.

In the same way, when my heart opens up inside the safety and spaciousness of God, it always invites me into deeper and daring honesty, deeper self-surrender, deeper shadow work with my own illusions and my own pretensions. The two will always feed one another, and that's why people who go deeper with God invariably have a very honest evaluation of themselves. They are never proud people. They can't be, because the closer you get to the Light, the more you see your own darkness. And the closer you get to your own ordinariness (which sometimes includes darkness), the more you know you need the Light.

+Adapted from *Following the Mystics through the Narrow Gate....*
Seeing God in All Things (CD, DVD, MP3)

A GOSPEL OF PURE GRACE

Luke's Gospel is the most broad-minded and the most forgiving of all four Gospels. Every chance he gets, Luke has Jesus forgiving people, right up to the thief on the cross and the prayer for his persecutors. Luke is quite ready to see God as generous, gratuitous, and merciful. Mercy and inclusivity—Jesus's ministry to outcasts, to gentiles, to the poor—are emphasized a great deal in Luke. In this approach, Luke's sacred text is also called the gospel of women. Far more than any other evangelist, Luke brings women into Jesus's life and shows Jesus's unique way of relating to women. He wants to make Jesus available to the forgotten and diminished, and women usually were.

Luke's Gospel has also been called the gospel of absolute renunciation. For Luke, becoming a disciple means letting go of everything—not just money or other external idols, but inner idols and ego concerns as well. Luke advocates radically new social patterns of relationship. His is an upside-down gospel: "The first will be last and the last will be first" (Luke 13:30). Luke uses every story he can to show that what impresses people does not impress God; that people who think they are at the top are often, in God's eyes, at the bottom; and that people who think they are at the bottom are, in God's eyes, often at the top.

+Adapted from *The Good News According to Luke: Spiritual Reflections*, pp. 38, 40

DO NOT BE AFRAID

One could sum up the Bible as an interplay of fear and faith. In general, people are obsessed and overpowered by fears; we all fear whatever we cannot control. God is one of our primary fears because God is totally beyond us. The Good News, the Gospel, according to Luke, is that God has breached that fear and become one of us in Jesus. God says, in effect, "It's okay. You don't have to live in chattering fear of me." God's response to Mary's quaver at the angel's appearance is, "Do not be afraid" (Luke 1:30) and, in fact, I am told it is the most common one-liner in the whole Bible.

In Luke's infancy narrative, Mary is presented as prototypical and archetypal, because God comes into her life and announces the Divine Presence within her. Through the same Spirit, God comes into our lives and announces the Divine Presence within us. This annunciation event is a paradigm of every mystical experience. God offers the Godself to us even before we invite God to do so. There is no indication of previous holiness or heroics in Mary's life. All we can do is be present and open. When Mary manifests this presence and openness, she becomes the Christ-bearer to the world. It is the same for us.

+Adapted from *The Good News According to Luke: Spiritual Reflections*, p. 66

JESUS LIVED IN DARKNESS AND FAITH, JUST AS WE DO

Luke tells us that Jesus walked the journey of faith just as you and I do, and thus has him pray. Jesus needed strength and resorted to prayer—during his temptation in the desert, before choosing the apostles, during his debates with his adversaries, in the garden, and on the cross. We like to imagine that Jesus did not flinch, doubt, or ever question God's love. The much greater message is that in his humanity he *did* flinch, have doubts, and ask questions—and still remained faithful. He is indeed our "pioneer and perfecter" in the ways of faith, who "disregards the shamefulness of it all" (see Hebrews 12:2).

You see Jesus's faith tested in the temptation scenes in Luke 4:1–13. The basic question put before him three times is this: "Is God to be trusted?" That is the great question the human race is asking at the most basic level. We hear Jesus ever more resoundingly answer, "Yes, God is on your side. Yes, God is more *for you* than you are for yourself."

+Adapted from *The Good News According to Luke: Spiritual Reflections*, p. 92

RIVER OF LOVE

I believe that faith might be precisely an ability to trust the river, to trust the Flow and the Lover. It is a process that we don't have to change, coerce, or improve, and is revealed in the notion of God as a Trinitarian relationship that flows unguarded! We only need to allow the Flow to flow—and through us. That takes immense confidence in God's goodness, especially when we're hurting. Usually, I can feel myself get panicky. I want to make things right, quickly. I lose my ability to be present, and I go up into my head and start obsessing. I am by nature goal-oriented, as many of us are, trying to push or even create the river—the river that is already flowing through me, with me, and in me (John 7:39).

The people who know God well—the mystics, the hermits, the prayerful people, those who risk everything to find God—always meet a lover, not a dictator. God is never found to be an abusive father or a manipulative mother, but a lover who is more than we dared hope for.

+Adapted from *Everything Belongs: The Gift of Contemplative Prayer*, pp. 142–143, 131

APPROACH/AVOIDANCE

In his book *The Idea of the Holy,* Rudolph Otto says that when someone has an experience of the Holy, they find themselves caught up in two opposite things at the same time: the *mysterium tremendum* and the *mysterium fascinosum,* or the scary mystery and the alluring mystery. We both draw back and are pulled forward into a very new space.

In the *mysterium tremendum,* God is ultimately far, ultimately beyond—too much, too much, too much (Isaiah 6:3). It inspired fear and drawing back. Many people never get beyond this first half of the journey. If that is the only half of holiness you experience, you experience God as dread, as the one who has all the power, and in whose presence you are utterly powerless. Religion at this initial stage tends to become overwhelmed by a sense of sinfulness and separateness. The defining of sin and sin management becomes the very nature of religion, and clergy move in to do the job.

Simultaneously, with the experience of the Holy as beyond and too much is another sense of fascination, allurement, and seduction, a *being pulled into something very good and inviting and wonderful* or the *mysterium fascinosum.* It's a paradoxical experience. Otto says if you don't have both, you don't have the true or full experience of the Holy. I would agree, based on my experience.

+Adapted from *Following the Mystics through the Narrow Gate....*
Seeing God in All Things (CD, DVD, MP3)

A WHOLE NEW GOD

Mysticism begins when the totally transcendent image of God starts to recede, and there's a deepening sense of God as imminent, present, here, now, safe, and even within me. In Augustine's words, "God is more intimate to me than I am to myself" or "more me than I am myself." St. Catherine of Genoa shouted in the streets, "My deepest me is God!"

So you must overcome this gap to spiritually know things and then, ironically, you'll know that Someone Else is doing the knowing through you. God is no longer out there. At this point, it's not like one has a new relationship with God; it's like one has a whole new God! "God himself is my counselor, and at night my innermost being instructs me," says the Psalmist (16:7). God is operating with you, in you, and even *as* you.

The mystics are those who are let in on this secret mystery of God's love affair with the soul, each knowing God loves *my* soul in particular; God loves *me* uniquely. All true love gives us this sense of being special, chosen, and like nobody else. That is why we are so joyful in the presence of our lover, who mirrors us with a divine mirror.

+Adapted from *Following the Mystics through the Narrow Gate....*
Seeing God in All Things (CD, DVD, MP3)

LANGUAGE OF THOSE WHO KNOW

Any true experience of the Holy gives one the experience of being secretly chosen, invited, and loved. Surely that is why bride and bridegroom, invitations, and wedding banquets are Jesus's most common metaphors for eternal life.

The mystics of all religions talk of being seduced and ravished and of deep inner acceptance, total forgiveness, mutual nakedness, immense and endless gratitude, endless yearning, and always a desire and possibility of more. This is religion at its best and highest and truest. The mystics know themselves to be completely safe and completely accepted at ever-deeper levels of trust, exposure, and embrace. It is a spiral that goes ever deeper and closer. This is very different from fear of hell or punishment, which characterize so much common religion. This keeps us on the far edge of the only dance there is.

+Adapted from an unpublished talk given in Tucson, Arizona

PRAYER JUST HAPPENS,
AND SOMETIMES YOU ARE THERE!

Mary's understanding and full acceptance of her nothingness, is also saying something about all of us. Our worthiness is also and always given. It is not attained. It is God in you searching for God. It is God in you that believes and hopes and cares and loves. And there is nothing that you can take credit for. It is something you just thank God for!

The same is true of prayer and all spiritual initiatives. Eventually you realize that you don't just say a prayer by yourself. Rather, you recognize that prayer is happening, and you just happen to be the channel and instrument. When your mind, your heart, and your body are all present, which is always a gift, that full presence is prayer. At that moment God is able to use you because you are out of the way, and God is leading the way.

+Adapted from an unpublished talk given in Tucson, Arizona

MARY'S HYMN

The ego-liberated attitude of Mary is the language of allowing, receiving, surrendering, trusting. Luke sums this all up in Mary's beautiful song, the Magnificat. It was once considered against the law to recite this prayer at public demonstrations in Argentina. (You have to give them credit for seeing the immense political implications of this seemingly sweet and pretty prayer.)

THE CANTICLE OF MARY

And Mary said:
 "My soul glorifies the Lord
and my spirit rejoices in God my Savior,
for Yahweh has been mindful
of the humble state of his servant.
From now on all generations will call me blessed,
for the Mighty One has done great things for me—
And holy is God's name.
Yahweh's mercy extends to those who reverence him,
from generation to generation.
God has performed mighty deeds with his outstretched arm;
Yahweh has scattered those who are proud in their inmost thoughts.
God has brought down the mighty from their thrones
and has lifted up the little ones.
Yahweh has filled the hungry with good things
but has sent the rich away empty.

God has helped his servant Israel,

remembering to be merciful, even as he said to our ancestors,

to Abraham and his descendants forever."

+Luke 1:46–55

GOD IS ALWAYS CREATING SOMETHING OUT OF NOTHING

We have in Mary's story what some call the second creation story in the Bible. Again it is a creation that is ex nihilo, or out of nothing (Genesis 1:2). Mary is the one quite willing to be the nothing. Ironically this is what makes her—and us—something!

God does not need worthiness ahead of time; God creates worthiness by the choice itself. It seems God will not come into the world unreceived or uninvited. God is gentle and does not come into your world unless you actually want God to.

Presence is a reciprocal or mutual encounter. One can give it, but it has to be received or there is no presence. For many, Mary is indeed the model of how "real presence" effectively happens. It is not just through a priests' transubstantiation of bread, but by the transformation of the persons who eat that bread. She was the first "priest" who first transformed matter into Christ, and she could do that because she fully allowed her own transformation.

+Adapted from *Things Hidden: Scripture as Spirituality*, pp. 178–179

FRAME

There is only one Reality. Any distinction between natural and supernatural, sacred and profane is a bogus one.

INTRODUCTION

The clarification here is fundamental and central. A historian of religion once said (I cannot remember where I read it) that *all religion begins by the making of a false distinction between the holy and the seemingly unholy.* Soon a clerical caste, moral distinctions, purity codes, and temple systems emerge to keep these two worlds defined and apart and to keep us separate from the unholy. This makes the ego feel safe and superior, so it usually works if you stay at the early level (of religion), where not much self-knowledge has yet been acquired. This becomes the very "business" of religion, and you can understand business here on several true levels: It keeps us busy, it keeps the customers coming back, and it is often a very subtle process of "buying and selling" of God. It does give us clergy a good job, and most of us run to the occasion—because the crowds like it for some reason, and we get to feel important as protectors of the sacred (scriptures, rituals, and moralities). No one has told them any differently for the most part—except Jesus.

Try, for example, his absolutely upside-down story of the Pharisee and the tax collector (Luke 18:9–14)—although there are many others too. The "Pharisee," by definition, is fully orthodox and seemingly law-abiding inside the Jewish Law of Holiness, which is largely about *separation from unholy things* (see Leviticus 17–27). He "prided himself on being virtuous and despised everyone else," the text states. He prays secretly, proudly, and rather unkindly "to himself." Because he is trapped inside himself, there is no real contact with the Mystery beyond himself.

This Pharisee is compared to the tax collector or "publican" who was an officially defined sinner, dealing in unholy and unjust taxes for the Roman occupiers and in daily commerce with the Gentiles, but his prayer at least is honest and humble. Without denying his objective unholy status, Jesus says, "This man went home at rights with God, the other did not" (Luke 18:14). Once you get this pattern in Jesus, you will see that it is everywhere and constant in his ministry. He refuses and rejects his own religion's distinction between objectively holy and unholy things and *moves morality to the interior level of motivation and intention* (what Jeremiah described as the "circumcised heart" instead of the circumcised physical member). This is basically what gets Jesus in trouble with the religious authorities (see Mark 7:5). He refuses most "purity codes" and "debt codes" that keep people codependent on the public ministrations of paid clergy and says, "You clean the outside of the dish, and leave the inside full of extortion and intemperance" (Matthew 23:25). Much of Matthew 23 and Mark 7 make this same point in a dozen different ways.

There are only unholy hearts and minds for Jesus, but not inherently holy or unholy places, actions, or people. Let's now let the meditations speak for themselves.

IDOLATRY IS THE ONLY SIN

Almost all religion begins with a specific encounter with something that feels holy or transcendent: a place, an emotion, an image, music, a liturgy, an idea that suddenly gives you access to God's Bigger World. The natural and universal response is to "idolize" and idealize that event. It becomes sacred for you, and it surely is. The only mistake is that too many then conclude that this is *the* way, the best way, the superior way, the "only" way for everybody—that I myself just happen to have discovered. Then, they must both protect their idol and spread this exclusive way to others. (They normally have no concrete evidence whatsoever that other people have not also encountered the holy.)

The false leap of logic is that other places, images, liturgies, scriptures, or ideas can *not* give you access. "We forbid them to give you access, it is impossible!" we seem to say. Thus, much religion wastes far too much time trying to separate itself from—and create purity codes against—what is perceived as secular, bad, heretical, dangerous, "other," or wrong. Jesus had no patience with such immature and exclusionary religion, yet it is common to this day. Idolatry has been called the only constant and real sin of the entire Old Testament, and idolatry is *whenever we make something god that is not God*, or whenever we make the means into an end. Any attempt to create our own golden calf is usually first-half-of-life religion, and eventually false religion.

THE PRIMAL SACRED

Two thousand years ago was the *human* incarnation of God in Jesus, but before that there was the first and original incarnation through light, water, land, sun, moon, stars, plants, trees, fruit, birds, serpents, cattle, fish, and "every kind of wild beast" according to our own creation story (Genesis 1:3–25). This was the Cosmic Christ through which God has "let us know the mystery of his purpose, the hidden plan he so kindly made from the beginning in Christ" (Ephesians 1:9). Christ is not Jesus's last name, but the title for his life's purpose.

All of creation, it seems, has been obedient to its destiny, "each mortal thing does one thing and the same/...myself it speaks and spells, / crying *"What I do is me, for that I came"'* (Gerard Manley Hopkins, "As Kingfishers Catch Fire"). Wouldn't it be our last and greatest humiliation, if we one day realized that all other creatures have obeyed their inner destiny with a kind of humility and with trustful surrender? All, except us? We rebel against and resist who we are.

We sometimes called it "natural law" (that things had an inherent goodness and unfolding to them). Genesis called it image and likeness (1:26). Peter finally understands when he says "God has made it clear to me that I must not call anyone profane or unclean" (Acts 10:28), and Paul says it in one succinct phrase "Ever since God created the world, his everlasting power and deity—however invisible—have been there for the mind to see in the things that God has made" (Romans 1:20). The sacred is established from the beginning and it is universal. We live in a sacred and enchanted universe.

+Adapted from *Radical Grace*, Vol. 23, No 2, p. 3

RECONCILING PARADOXES

You already know. The Spirit is with you, and the Spirit is in you.

— John 14:17

Jesus seemed to caution his contemporaries to humility and patience before the subtle mystery of who he was: "You do not know where I came from and where I am going" (John 8:14). He seemed to know that this mystery of being both divine and human would take a very long time to absorb, understand, accept, or reconcile. It is the ultimate paradox, and every Christian and every human being struggles with it anew, both in themselves and in him, and every day.

We could not hold the mystery together in Jesus, despite being assured that he is "the one single New Man" (Ephesians 2:15), the archetypal person who reconciles and recapitulates everything inside himself (Colossians 1:15-20). The sad result is that we could not see, honor, and reconcile the mystery inside ourselves or in one another. We could not let Jesus save us, you might say. It is the third eye, or spiritual eye, that allows us to say Yes both to the infinite mystery of Jesus and to the infinite mystery that we are to ourselves. They are finally the same mystery and the same surrender.

+Adapted from *The Naked Now: Learning to See as the Mystics See*, pp. 69–70

A COSMIC CHRIST

The human spiritual longing expressed by "Come, Lord Jesus" is a longing for universal order and meaning. In the centuries of fighting over the humanity and the divinity of Christ, the Western Church has gradually lost touch with the larger and more universal message: "The image of the unseen God, the firstborn of all creation, for in him were created all things in heaven and on earth…and he holds all things in unity…because God wanted all perfection to be found in him and all things to be reconciled through him and for him" (Colossians 1:15–20).

This is not a problem-solving Christ, not a denominational or cultural Christ, not a Christ domesticated by the churches. This Christ names in his life and person what *matters*, what *lasts*, and finally what *is*. He holds it all together in significance, reveals the redemptive pattern that we call the life and death of things, and holds the meaning and value of our lives *outside of ourselves!*

Remember: *Your life is not about you. You are about life!*

+Adapted from *Radical Grace: Daily Meditations*, pp. 387–388

ORIGINAL PARTICIPATION

Before 800 B.C., the thinking on the whole planet, no matter the continent, was invariably tribal, cosmic, mythic, and ritualistic (according to German philosopher Karl Jaspers). Owen Barfield calls it "original participation." Simply by watching the sky, birds, and trees, the seasons, darkness and light, people knew they belonged. Though we call these people uncivilized people, many conjecture that they might have had healthier psyches than we do because *they lived in an inherently enchanted universe where everything belonged, including themselves.* And they knew that simply by listening and by observing and living! (Almost too simple.) The cycles of darkness and light, of growth and death, of fertility and fecundity—which were everywhere all the time, were their primary and natural teachers.

Why do we call them uncivilized people? The very word *pagan* is a dismissive word meaning "those who live in the country." We thought by moving into so-called civilization, into cities, we were better and smarter, and maybe we were in some ways. But they perhaps were in other ways! Native peoples learned of the divine, the sacred, God, through the natural world. They already saw the Great Spirit in everything, as Pope John Paul II said to the natives gathered in Phoenix, Arizona, some years ago. Religion was much more about healing and harmonizing than sin management. Salvation wasn't a reward for good moral behavior you got after you died, but as the very root word (*salus*) reveals, it was a healing and harmonizing *now*. It had the power to make the world a much more livable place than we have made it.

+Adapted from *Soul Centering through Nature: Becoming a True Human Adult* (CD, DVD, MP3)

A BIT OF HISTORY

Most of the world religions, in their foundational forms, emerged between 800 and 200 B.C. when humans began conceptualizing and thinking abstractly; yet religion was still deeply connected to myth, story, and the pre-rational. You see this amazing combination in the Greeks with their mathematics and philosophy, while still having all their mythic gods too (probably why they stood out among all the cultures of the world!).

Richard Tarnas, in his brilliant book *The Passion of the Western Mind: Understanding the Ideas that Have Shaped Our World View*, says that all of philosophical history is a pendulum swing between the romantic and the rational and only now and then do they come together in good balance. Whenever you have the balancing of the romantic and the rational, the natural and the culturally created, the energetic and the self-critical, you have an explosion of genius. Humans have both capacities, and both must be honored.

With the scientific and industrial revolutions came the birth of *individualism—and individual self-consciousness*. It was a mixed blessing—responsibility, ethics, and personal subjective experience emerged but alongside a new privatized self-absorption, ego defensiveness, and mental overanalyzing. Healthy and mature religion must again combine the best of both worlds: the mythic and nonrational to intuitively open us up to the Whole—along with the critical rational to keep us honest and humble about what we can know and what we don't know.

+Adapted from *Soul Centering through Nature: Becoming a True Human Adult*
(CD, DVD, MP3)

SPIRITUAL GLOBALIZATION

Everything has been moving apart into greater individuation for more than two thousand years now (for good and for ill) until this globe we live on started filling up, and we started meeting one another on the other side—other religions, cultures, ethnicities, and world views. This globalization made us aware that God loves not only Catholics from Kansas (like me), but Hindus, Jews, Muslims, and Buddhists as well. We are finding we have only one thing in common. What's literally grounding all of this is that all of us are standing on the same ground and earth! She feeds us all.

What we have in common is that we are all breathing the same air, relying upon the same Brother Sun and walking on this same Mother Earth. That is the common collective. That gives us the power to read reality with foundational truth, beyond any ideology. We are first and foremost and universally members of the one earth community (Ephesians 4:4–6 surely intuited this). But we are able to do this now, as in no other period of history. It's forced upon us now because we know that if we keep following this artificial separation and over-individuation, my rights over the common good, the whole thing is over in a century or so.

I wonder about these Christians who are waiting for the second coming of Christ, some of them seemingly hoping we'll actually destroy this planet so he can come earlier. I sincerely hope Christ is going to have something left to return to—both "a new heaven and a new earth" (Revelation 21:1).

+Adapted from *Soul Centering through Nature: Becoming a True Human Adult* (CD, DVD, MP3)

THE SACRED GENERATES THINGS FROM WITHIN

When I first joined the Franciscan order in 1961, my novice master told me we could not cut down a tree without permission of the provincial (the major religious superior). It seemed a bit extreme, but then I realized that a little bit of Francis of Assisi had lasted eight hundred years! We still had his awareness that wilderness is not just "wilderness." Nature is not just here for our consumption and profit. The natural is of itself also the supernatural. Both natural elements and animals are not just objects for our plunder. Francis granted true dignity and subjectivity to nature by calling it Brother Sun, Sister Fire, Brother Wind, and Sister Water. No wonder he is the patron saint of ecology and care for creation.

Once you grant subjectivity to the natural world, everything changes. It's no longer an object and you're the separated and superior subject, but you share subjectivity with it. You address it with a title of respect, and allow it to speak back to you! For so long creation has been a mere commodity at best, a useless or profitable wilderness, depending on who owned it. With the contemplative mind, questions of creation are different than those of consumption and capitalism, and they move us to appreciate creation for its own sake, not because of what it does for me or how much money it can make me. For those with spiritual eyes, the world itself has to be somehow the very "Body of God." What else could it be for one who believes in creationism? As Paul puts it, "From the beginning until now, the entire creation has been groaning in one great act of giving birth" (Romans 8:22), so it is not only an evolutionary body but an eternally pregnant body besides. God's creation is so perfect that it continues to create itself from within. The Franciscans were not wrong in not cutting down ordinary trees without a very good reason.

+Adapted from *Soul Centering through Nature: Becoming a True Human Adult*
(CD, DVD, MP3)

EVOLUTION

God has let us in on "the mystery of his purpose, the hidden plan" (Ephesians 1:9). And it sure is hidden, hidden so well that few saw the plan God so kindly made "from the very beginning in Christ." "Christ" is the name for God's plan to *materialize his formless Spirit*. This is very clear in Colossians 1:15–20, Ephesians 1:3–14, and John 1:1–5, but you cannot see what you were never told to pay attention to. The divine, it seems, wants to manifest itself in visible form. This mystery is going to keep being recapitulated at every level of creation as it evolves, as it emerges, and then the real second coming of Christ is the recognition that it's been the Christ all along!

Picture the boxed Russian dolls, each one enclosing a smaller one. The first doll and the last doll are the Christ mystery, "the Alpha and the Omega" of history as it states in Revelation. In the end, God will bring together everything under the title of Christ, "everything in heaven and everything on the earth" (Colossians 1:16). This is not an individualistic or anthropocentric notion of salvation. It's happening to the whole of creation, exactly as Paul says in Romans 8:18–39, which is his masterpiece of theology, in my opinion. The very fact that Christians have wasted time and energy fighting the notion of evolution shows that we didn't understand the Cosmic Christ at all. Our Christ and our Jesus have both been too small.

Christians should have been the first to appreciate evolution and to recognize what God is doing—that God creates things that continue to create themselves from the inner divine Spirit. Christ is "the image of the invisible God, the firstborn of all creation" (Colossians 1:15), the first little Russian doll in the mind of God. For "in him is recapitulated all things in heaven and on earth" (Colossians 1:20). The Eternal Christ is the microcosm of the macrocosm or what Shakespeare would call "the play within the play." His role is to forever hold together matter and spirit, divine and human, and to say they always have been one, but you just don't know it yet. So God is going to hold them together in front of your face—until you do.

+Adapted from *Soul Centering through Nature: Becoming a True Human Adult*
(CD, DVD, MP3)

DEGREES OF CONSCIOUSNESS

When did the incarnation begin? It began 14.5 billion years ago, and we're the first generation that's ever known that, that was able to give a number to it—that this materialization of the Formless One into form began 14.5 billion years ago. What was God doing 5 billion years ago? What was God doing 10 billion years ago? Was he really waiting for the pope to appear and declare his infallibility? Was she waiting for the Bible to become the *King James Version*—both of which happened only in the last nanosecond of history? We've got to recognize the immense cosmos inside which we are living. For many, it has become a new name and shape for theology. Like no other generation, we are the first one free to begin to recognize the unfathomable character of the universe. And it is still expanding!

As humans, we do have the advantage of consciousness, but that doesn't mean that everything else doesn't also share in some rudimentary form of consciousness. Maybe it's a quantitative difference, but not a qualitative difference, so Paul calls it the "first fruits of the Spirit" (Romans 8:23) in this whole "groaning" of creation. That does not mean there are not other fruits, and that the other groanings don't matter to God. Maybe we are the ones who can know it consciously first, and give it a name. The little sheep and the little dog, the insect and the fish are also creatures of God, and carry his "fingerprint," as St. Bonaventure would say. We hope the animals know it in a natural, cellular way. They seem to carry that calm dignity as they each do their thing so patiently and humbly. But we are also able to know it for and with the natural world—and therefore grant things their inherent dignity and sacrality. This is a wonderful role, and we can do it much better.

+Adapted from *Soul Centering through Nature: Becoming a True Human Adult*
(CD, DVD, MP3)

PLATO OR JESUS?

I sincerely hate to say it, but I fear that Platonic philosophy has had more influence in Christian history than Jesus. The Jesus and Christ event says that matter and spirit, divine and human are not enemies, but are two sides of the same coin. They, in fact, reveal one another. For Plato, the body and the soul are mortal enemies and largely incompatible. Our poor sexual theology and our history of lackluster care for the earth and its resources, our disrespect for animals and all growing things shows that Christians have not seen matter and spirit as natural friends. For much of our history, Catholic, Orthodox, and Protestant theology has created Platonists much more than Incarnationalists or Christians.

Matter and spirit have never been separate. That's really the ultimate Christian heresy, and what Jesus came to undo. At its best, religion did try to put matter and spirit together ("sacramentalism"), but you can't put together what is already together. You are taking yourself too seriously. *That is God's job, and all we can do is come along later and second the motion.* That's what Christians should mean when they say Jesus has become "both Lord and Christ" (Acts 2:36); Jesus is the epiphany in personal form of what has always been true. Yet this really is a switch for most of us raised in organized Christianity. We overplayed the Jesus card and largely ignored the Christ card. Most Christians just believe in Jesus. They have never moved to the level of cosmic mystery that Paul could say was revealed both in the bread he called the Body of Christ (1 Corinthians 11:23ff) and the people that he also called the Body of Christ (1 Corinthians 12:12ff).

Some do not like Paul for other reasons, but he did express Incarnational Christianity with a very specific implication and corollary. He was the true

Christian philosopher, but the dualistic Western mind preferred Plato instead.

+Adapted from *Soul Centering through Nature: Becoming a True Human Adult*
(CD, DVD, MP3)

THE EARLY SACRED

The first half of life is invariably about creating identity, finding some boundary markers (traditions, trustworthy authorities, and structures), making some money, getting an education, marrying, and raising children—which we then must defend for the rest of our lives. Most of us are so invested in these first answers by the age of forty that we can't imagine anything more—not realizing that we think, "It's still all about me!"

Christians in the first half of life become obsessed with dying a happy death and going to heaven. Even religion becomes a rather privatized "evacuation plan for the next world" (as Brian McLaren calls it), and the clergy seldom recognize that much of religion is trapped at the individualistic and egocentric level. No actual love of neighbor, outsider, the poor, or even God was really necessary. This is garden variety first-half-of-life religion, and it has passed for the real thing for much of the Christian era.

+Adapted from *Loving the Two Halves of Life: The Further Journey* (CD, DVD)

THE LATER SACRED

To live in the first half of life is largely a matter of survival. All it takes is what some call the "reptilian brain." Like any good reptile, it is largely concerned with reproduction, food, and survival. All that is important at this stage is my private, moral superiority that was supposed to make me pleasing to God for some reason. First-half-of-life morality is largely concerned with various "purity codes." As one monk said to me, you could be "pure as an angel while still proud as a devil." I am afraid that is as far as first-half-of-life values can get you.

Identity, security, and boundary questions are basically concerns of the ego. That does not make them bad, but they are just a starting point. The soul has different concerns. Our politicians continually assure us that they will keep us safe. This is usually enough to get them elected, because most people are not yet asking higher questions in the hierarchy of needs—questions about things such as education, affordable housing, earth care, justice, the arts, immigration, penal reform, and the morality of war itself.

+Adapted from *Loving the Two Halves of Life: The Further Journey*
(CD, DVD, MP3)

CENTER AND CIRCUMFERENCE

How do we find what is supposedly already there? How do we awaken our deepest and most profound selves? By praying and meditating? By more silence, solitude, and sacraments? Yes to all, but the most important way is to *live and fully accept our reality*. This solution sounds so simple and innocuous that most of us fabricate all kinds of religious trappings to avoid taking up our own inglorious, mundane, and ever-present cross.

Living and accepting our own reality will not feel very spiritual. It will feel like we are on the edges rather than dealing with the essence. Thus, most run toward more esoteric and dramatic postures instead of *bearing the mystery of God's suffering and joy inside themselves*. But the edges of our lives—fully experienced, suffered, and enjoyed—lead us back to the center and the essence.

We do not find our own center; it finds us. Our own minds will not be able to figure it out. Our journeys around and through our realities, or "circumferences," lead us to the *core reality*, where we meet both our truest selves and our truest God. We do not really know what it means to be human unless we know God. And, in turn, we do not really know God except through our broken and rejoicing humanity.

+Adapted from *Everything Belongs: The Gift of Contemplative Prayer*, pp. 17–19

PATRIOTISM AS THE FALSE SACRED

"Jesus is Lord" (Romans 10:9) was proclaimed by the early Church as its most concise creedal statement. No one ever told me this was a political and subversive statement, but then I learned a bit of Bible history. To say "Jesus is Lord!" was testing and provoking the Roman pledge of allegiance that all Roman citizens had to proclaim when they raised their hands to the imperial insignia and shouted, "Caesar is Lord!" Early Christians were quite aware that their "citizenship" was in a new universal kingdom, announced by Jesus (Philippians 3:20), and that the kingdoms of this world were not their primary loyalty systems. How did we manage to lose that? And what price have we paid for it?

Jesus showed no undue loyalty either to his Jewish religion nor to his Roman-occupied Jewish country; instead, he radically critiqued both of them, and in that he revealed and warned against the idolatrous relationships most people have with *their* country and *their* religion. It has allowed us to justify violence in almost every form and to ignore much of the central teaching of Jesus.

+Adapted from *Spiral of Violence: The World, the Flesh, and the Devil* (CD, MP3)

A BIG SURPRISE

I bless you, Father, Lord of heaven and earth, for hiding these things from the learned and the clever, and revealing them to the little ones.
—Luke 10:21

We grow spiritually much more by doing it wrong than by doing it right. That might just be the central message of how spiritual growth happens; yet nothing in us wants to believe it, and those who deem themselves morally successful are often the last to learn it.

If there is such a thing as human perfection, it seems to emerge precisely from how we handle the imperfection that is everywhere, especially our own. What a clever place for God to hide holiness, so that only the humble and earnest will find it! A "perfect" person ends up being one who can consciously forgive and include imperfection (like God does), rather than one who thinks he or she is totally above and beyond any imperfection.

It becomes sort of obvious once you say it out loud. In fact, I would say that *the demand for the perfect is often the greatest enemy of the good.* Perfection is a mathematical or divine concept; goodness is a beautiful human concept. We see this illusionary perfectionism in ideologues and zealots on both the left and the right of church and state. They refuse to get their hands dirty, think *compromise* or *subtlety* are dirty words, and end up creating much more dirt for the rest of us, while they remain totally clean and quite comfortable in their cleanliness.

+Adapted from *Falling Upward: A Spirituality for the Two Halves of Life,*
pp. xxii–xxiii

TEMPLE RELIGION

Jesus enters the Temple and drives out the salesmen who "were selling and buying there" (Matthew 21:12), trying to sell worthiness, purity, and access to God (Luke 19:45–46), just as the Catholic Church did later with indulgences and stipends of various sorts. This is the great temptation of all religion. Jesus symbolically dismantles this system by not allowing it to operate in its present form and by releasing the animals that were sold for sacrifice (John 2:15–16). The temple of religion (read church or mosque too) is henceforth to become personal, relational, embodied in him and other people, and not a physical building (John 2:21).

The precise message of the Raised Up Christ is that God is available everywhere, as his body moved beyond any limits of space and time. For some reason we like to keep God elsewhere or "just here," where we can control God by our theologies, tabernacles, and services. We often tell God whom he can love or not love. Poor God must conform to our moral systems and judgments.

This public demonstration against and inside the sacred space of the Temple is surely the historical action that finally gets Jesus killed. The trouble with declaring one space sacred is that we then imagine other spaces are not! Here he takes on the major detours of false religion, which are any attempt to buy God by exclusionary purity and debt codes, and by emphasizing sacrifices (which the clergy just happen to control) over basic mercy and compassion (Matthew 9:13).

Jesus really did come to liberate God for humanity and humanity for God.

RESURRECTION AS THE REVELATION OF WHAT WAS ALWAYS TRUE

In the Risen Christ, God reveals the final state of all reality. God forbids us to accept as-it-is in favor of what-God's-love-can-make-it. To believe in resurrection means to cross limits and transcend boundaries. Because of the promise of the resurrection of Jesus we realistically can believe that tomorrow can be better than today. We are not bound by any past. There is a future that is created by God, and much bigger than our own efforts.

We should not just believe in some kind of survival or immortality or just "life after death"—but *resurrection*, an utterly new creation, a transformation into Love that is promised as something that can happen in this world and is God's final chapter for all of history. That is why a true Christian has to be an optimist. In fact, if you are not an optimist, you haven't got it yet.

+Adapted from *Radical Grace: Daily Meditations*, p. 150

START WITH A STONE

Abraham Maslow points out in his hierarchy of needs that one cannot meet higher needs at any level of depth if the lesser needs are not first tended to. One cannot do an end-run to levels of communion and compassion, for example, when one's basic security and survival needs have not been met. As Jesus might put it, when you are "worried about many things" (Luke 10:41), you cannot have faith. When you cannot enjoy the lilies of the field or the sparrows in the sky, don't waste time thinking you can enjoy God or respect people at any depth. So, start at the bottom if you can, and try to love a rock! If you can do that, it only gets bigger, wider, higher, deeper, and better.

History tells of too many people who have tried to be spiritual before they have learned how to be human! It is a major problem. Maybe this is why Jesus came to model humanity for us—much more than divinity. Once we get the simplest human parts down (stop slamming doors and start loving rocks), God will most assuredly take it all from there. Get the ordinary human thing down, and you will have all the spirituality you can handle.

+Adapted from *Contemplation in Action*, pp. 83–84

FINAL REUNION

I remember once seeing a painting, in a European museum, of the ascension. It was huge, and at the very top, right beneath the frame, were the bare feet of Jesus as he ascended into heaven. It felt almost comical. Most of the painting was of the apostles looking up in various poses of fear, confusion, disbelief, and awe. It struck me that the ascension was the final stage of Jesus's human life, and every human life—when the material world is reunited to its spiritual Source. At least that is what the artist seemed to be saying, with the various poses of the apostles illustrating our various stances toward eternal life and divine union.

The ascension is about the final reunion of what appeared to be separated for awhile: earth and heaven, human and divine, matter and Spirit, feet and freedom. They are again one in the end, and it was important, the artist seemed to say, that we see ordinary human feet going into heaven! If the Christ is the archetype of the full human journey, now we know how it all resolves itself in the end. "So that where I am, you also will be" (John 14:3).

GOD'S HOMING DEVICE

The love of God has been poured into our hearts by the Holy Spirit,
which has been given us.
— Romans 5:5

To span the infinite gap between the Divine and the human, God's agenda is to plant a little bit of God, the Holy Spirit, right inside of us! (Jeremiah 31:31–34; John 14:16ff).

This is the very meaning of the new covenant, and the replacing of our "heart of stone with a heart of flesh," as Ezekiel promised (36:25–26). Isn't that wonderful? It is God doing the loving, in and through us, back to God, toward our neighbor and enemy alike, and even toward the sad and broken parts of ourselves. "You will know him because her Spirit is with you, he is within you" (John 14:17).

+Adapted from *Things Hidden: Scripture as Spirituality*, p. 97

THE IN-BETWEEN OF THINGS

One reason so many theologians are interested in the Trinity now is that we're finding both physics (especially quantum physics) and cosmology are at a level of development where the sciences in general, our understanding of the atom and our understanding of galaxies, is affirming and confirming our use of the old Trinitarian language—but with a whole new level of appreciation. *Reality is radically relational, and all the power is in the relationships themselves! Not in the particles or the planets, but in the space in between the particles and planets. It sounds a lot like what we called the Holy Spirit.*

No good Christians would have denied the Trinitarian Mystery, but until our generation none were prepared to see that the shape of God is the shape of the whole universe!

Great science, which we once considered an enemy of religion, is now helping us see that we're standing in the middle of awesome Mystery, and the only response before that Mystery is immense humility. Astrophysicists are much more comfortable with darkness, emptiness, non-explainability (dark matter, black holes), and living with hypotheses than most Christians I know. Who could have imagined this?

+Adapted from *The Shape of God: Deepening the Mystery of the Trinity* (CD, DVD, MP3)

EUCHARIST AS FOCUSED TRUTH

I believe that the primary healing of human loneliness and meaninglessness is contact with reality itself, natural reality, and especially in its concrete forms (instead of just ideas and concepts). But, as T.S. Eliot said in
the *Four Quartets*, "Mankind cannot bear very much reality." What human
existence often prefers is highly contrived and costumed ways of avoiding
the real, the concrete, the physical. We fabricate artificial realities instead,
even religion itself. So Jesus brought all of our fancy thinking down to
earth, to one concrete place of ordinary incarnation—one loaf of bread
and this cup of wine! "Eat it here, and then see it everywhere," he seems
to be saying. Get it in one shocking moment—and universalize. If you can
comprehend the sacred in one moment, know it is in all moments too. As
St. Augustine essentially said in an Easter sermon, *"You are what you eat."*

If it's too idealized and pretty, if it's somewhere floating around up in the
air, it's probably not the Gospel. Jesus gave us a marvelous touchstone for
orthodoxy in the Eucharist. The first incarnation in creation personifies in
the body of Jesus and is spread out in space and time as a Eucharistic meal
in ordinary food. Note how John almost embarrassingly keeps insisting on
the fleshly physicality of it all (John 6:53–66), and even admits that "many
left him and stopped going with him" (John 6:66).

It is still an embarrassment intellectually and theologically, so we high
churches surround the scandal with all kinds of pretty gold, flowers,
candles, and lovely ministers in brocade and lace. The nonliturgical
churches, who purportedly love Scripture, just avoid the whole thing alto-
gether. I am not sure that either of these groups are ready for the hard

contact with reality that Jesus offers in full incarnation and in his passion, death, and resurrection.

+Adapted from *Eucharist as Touchstone* (CD, MP3)

SIGNS OF CONTRADICTION (LUKE 2:34)

The hiding place of God and also the revelation place of God is the material world.

You don't have to put spirit and matter together; they have been together ever since the Big Bang, 13.77 billion years ago. You have to recognize this momentous truth as *already and always so*. But big truth can only be understood on small and specific stages. The Eucharist offers microcosmic moments of what is cosmically true. It will surely take a lifetime of kneeling and surrendering, trusting and letting go, believing and saying, "How could this be true?" Even Gandhi said, "If I really believed what you believe, I wouldn't get up from my knees."

The only trouble is that many fervent Christians kneel before the Eucharistic Body of Christ but not the Human Body of Christ that Paul describes (1 Corinthians 12:12–26). In most of the first millennium, the people of the Church were called the *Corpus Verum* (the true Body), and the Eucharist was the *Corpus Mysticum* (the mystical Body), which was exactly reversed in the second millennium. I find that very telling and even disappointing.

Remember, it is much easier for priests and congregations to transform bread than to actually transform people, and further, *the bread is for the sake of the people* and not an end in itself, as both St. Augustine and even present canon law clearly teach.

+Adapted from *Eucharist as Touchstone* (CD, MP3)

PERENNIAL PHILOSOPHY

The perennial tradition was defined by Aldous Huxley in his book *The Perennial Philosophy*. He felt that this teaching was ageless and universal, which would make sense if the Holy Spirit is guiding all of history or, humanly speaking, if there is such a thing as the collective unconscious.

The perennial philosophy recognizes again and again in different religions and in different ways and with different vocabulary that (1) there is a Divine Reality substantial to the world of things, (2) there is an inner compatibility and coherence between humans and God, and (3) the goal of human existence is quite simply union with that Reality. Jesus, of course, says the same thing (Mark 12:30) and, in fact, equates love of others, love of self, and love of God throughout his teaching. Only some form of unitive or non-dual consciousness is capable of understanding such teaching and such a philosophy. The dualistic mind just takes sides and stands isolated on one of them. Either God is great (too much religion), or humans and creation are great in and of themselves and by themselves (which cannot be logically sustained), but the real synthesis is that *both* are great. This is the basis for all sustainable sacredness in the universe, and the practical goal of religion.

THE UNIVOCITY OF BEING

The perennial tradition is not just a metaphysical principle, but it's also a psychological principle that allows us to find in ourselves something similar to and capable of actual union with Divine Reality. "It is not because you do not know the truth that I am writing to you, but rather because you know it already," John says in his first letter (1 John 2:21). John Duns Scotus (1266–1308) called this "the univocity of all being." In other words, we could speak of all being with one voice and one consistent meaning, and *like can know like*. This provides a philosophical basis for mysticism and divine union, and is the pride of the Franciscan Order. Maybe it is why we have so many saints and mystics!

The assumption is that you have no way to understand another thing, even minimally, unless there is a little bit of it already in you. Your neurons are able to mirror what they see because they already hold the same image within on some level.

If something is completely foreign to you, you're normally bored by it or do not even notice it. There has to be a little bit of something in you to recognize, or to be attracted to, or to be drawn to another thing. We certainly cannot deeply experience, much less desire union with, something that is totally foreign or alien to us. So God planted a little bit of God inside of us—and all things. It seduces us into even more universal love and life. Some might call it the Holy Spirit, some might call it the soul, some might simply speak of inner resonance. The practical point is that *pure being* can move in both directions up and down from God to rocks, with humans as the free and conscious connector in between.

LIFE AND DEATH ARE NOT TWO

Let us look at the phenomenon that some have called "falling upward." The very activity we discern in the planets and evolution seems to be that through loss, crisis, stress, limitation—use whatever word you want—we move into deeper states of consciousness and freedom. I think even physicists today would say that actual loss is not real. Nothing totally dies. There is only transformation.

The common metaphor is that the liquid world is moving to solid to vapor and eventually back again. Just wait a while. It looks like a death, a loss in each case, but, in fact, it is a becoming. Now we recognize that spiritual teachers were saying this all along. In Christianity it was called "the paschal mystery"—a phrase used by St. Augustine to teach the paradox that dying must precede resurrection. Jesus, for Christians, became the Icon and living image of that mystery. Christians believe that his crucified body in fact transmuted—transformed into the Risen Christ and he is a stand-in, a corporate personality for all of creation. He holds the two sides of life together in one hopeful place.

+Adapted from *The Art of Letting Go: Living the Wisdom of St. Francis* (CD)

MAJOR MISPLACEMENT OF ATTENTION

The Christian tradition became so concerned with making Jesus into *its* God and making sure everybody believed that Jesus was God that it often ignored his very practical and clear teachings. (Has Christianity been known for loving its enemies or even building bridges of understanding between peoples?) Instead, we made the important issues abstract theological questions about the nature of God, which ask almost nothing of us except argument. Much of our Church life has been on that level, and no one ever really wins, and so it goes on for centuries. Churches divide and separate largely over nonessential Gospel issues. "Who can pour the water, when, and what do they say?"

What the Buddha made clear to his people is that the crucial questions are first of all psychological and personal, and here and now. I think Jesus was also first talking about the human situation and describing the issues of human liberation right here and now. Clearly the Kingdom of God, as Jesus describes it, is first of all here and now and is the very thing we ask for in our official "Our Father" prayer—"thy kingdom come" here!

Despite it all, we turned Jesus's message into a contest of reward or punishment (that would, we hope, come later) instead of a transformational experience that was verifiable here and now by the fruits of the Holy Spirit (Galatians 5:22–23). Probably more than anything else, this *huge misplacement of attention, anesthetized and weakened the actual transformative power of Christianity*. It all got moved into later and frankly only for a few. For both Jesus and for the Buddha rewards and punishments are first of all *inherent to the action and in this world*. Goodness is its own reward and evil is its own punishment, and then we must all leave the future to the mercy and love of God, instead of thinking we are the umpires and judges of who goes where, when, and how. What a cosmic waste of time and energy and attention.

+Adapted from *Jesus and Buddha: Paths to Awakening* (CD, DVD, MP3)

IS IT ABOUT HOLDING OUT OR LETTING GO?

The important and fundamental question we must ask is this: "When is the real life?" "Now!" the modern materialist would say—the good life, the real life, is *now* and then it ends. Many reincarnationalists and most pious Christians and mainline religious people believe that the real life is *later*, after this life. This falsehood has wrongly framed the Christian religion more than anything else despite the fact that Jesus clearly said the kingdom of God is first of all now, and therefore also later—and even forever: As now, so then. *This* becomes the promise of *that*. Here is the assurance and guarantee of *there*. That is the important sequence.

Once Jesus's great and good news became a reward-punishment system that only kicked into place in the next world instead of a transformational system in this world, Christianity, in effect, moved away from a religion of letting go and trusting and became instead a religion of holding on, hunkering down, and self-protecting. Religion's very purpose, for many people, was to protect the status quo of empire, power, war, money, and the private ego. In many ways, we have not been a force for liberation, peace-making, or change in the world. One thing for sure is that healthy religion is always telling *us* to change our lives instead of giving us ammunition to try to change others. Authentic Christianity is a religion of constantly letting go of the false self so the True Self in God can stand free and revealed—now.

+Adapted from *The Art of Letting Go: Living the Wisdom of St. Francis* (CD, MP3)

HOW YOU DO THIS MOMENT
IS PROBABLY WHO YOU ARE

Isn't it strange that a religion that began with a call to change or let go has become a religion so impervious and resistant to change? Many Catholics think that what it means to be a Christian is to be in love with the thirteenth century (or the sixteenth century, if you are Protestant), thinking that "this is when Christians were really Christians and God was really God." There is no evidence that this is true but it allows us to create religion as nostalgia instead of religion as actual transformation. Some Catholics hanker for a "true Latin Mass" not realizing that Jesus never spoke Latin— the language of his oppressors! Anything to avoid living right now where God is fully present!

What healthy religion is saying is that the real life is both now and later. You have to taste the Real first of all now. The constant pattern, however, is that most Christians either move both backwards (religion as nostalgia) or into the distant future (religion as a carrot on the stick) and consistently avoid where everything really happens and matters—the present moment. Catholics once beautifully called this "the sacrament of the present moment." The full now is always a taste of something really real. It therefore entices us to imagine the eternal and live in an eternal now. We are just practicing for heaven. How we do anything is, finally, how we do everything.

+Adapted from *The Art of Letting Go: Living the Wisdom of St. Francis* (CD, MP3)

AN ALTERNATIVE KINGDOM TO ANY OTHER

Authentic God experience gives you another place to stand, another identity, a *spacious and gracious place*, which invites you to stand outside of the dominant consciousness that surrounds you and that everybody accepts as reality.

Authentic God experience liberates you from the usual domination systems, liberates you from needing everything to be perfect or right, and liberates you to be who you really are—ordinary and poor—just like everybody else.

Until you can be at home in the alternative Kingdom of God, you will almost always be completely conformed to the superficial systems of this world, while calling it freedom and independence. Some do it by conforming to styles and fashions of their particular groupthink, while others do it by various conformities to the political correctness of either left or right. Some even do it by conforming to the rebellious group, but that is not freedom either.

Gospel freedom allows you to act *from deep within*, where the Holy Spirit dwells, and *not for or against* any outside group whatsoever (unless they happen to be responding to the same deep Spirit!).

+Adapted from *Spiral of Violence* (CD, DVD)

WHICH LOYALTY SYSTEM?

If we try to make the Church into the Kingdom of God, we create a false idol that will disappoint us. If we try to make the world itself into the Kingdom, we will always be resentful when it does not come through. If we make a later heaven into the Kingdom, we miss most of its transformative message for now. We are not waiting for the coming of an ideal Church or any perfect world here and now, or even for the next world. The Kingdom is more than all of these. It is always here and not here. It is always now and not yet. No institution can encompass it. That is rather clear in the texts where Jesus describes the kingdom.

All false religion proceeds in a certain sense from one illusion. When people say piously, "Thy kingdom come" out of one side of their mouth, they need also to say, "My kingdom go!" out of the other side. The Kingdom of God supersedes and far surpasses all kingdoms of self and society or personal reward.

+Adapted from *Preparing for Christmas with Richard Rohr*, p. 13

INCARNATIONALISM

Pure, unspoiled religion, in the eyes of God our Father is this: to come to
the help of orphans and widows when they need it, and keeping free from
the enticements of the system.

—James 1:27

Whenever the human and the divine coexist at the same time in the same
person we have Christianity. I don't know that it finally matters what
Scriptures you read, liturgies you attend, or moral positions you hold about
this or that—as much as how you live trustfully inside of God's one world?"
This creates honest people, people who don't waste time proving they're
right, superior, or saved. They just try to live and love the daily mystery
that they are in the loving presence of God. "God comes to you disguised
as your life," as Paula D'Arcy loves to say. Imagine that!

There are basically four world views: (1) Reality is just matter, (2) Reality
is just spirit, (3) Through religion and morality we can work to put matter
and spirit together (the most common religious position), and (4) The
material world has always been the place where Spirit is revealed. You
cannot put them together. They already are—as in Jesus. Only the fourth
position, incarnationalism, deserves to be called authentic Christianity. It
has little to do with the right rituals, only the right reality.

+Adapted from *Great Themes of Paul: Life as Participation* (CD)

THE FINAL AND BIG PICTURE

Jesus announced, lived, and inaugurated for history a new social order based on grace and not on merit. He called it the "Reign" or "Kingdom of God." It is without doubt his most common message and metaphor, so it must be very important. Maybe we should just call his Kingdom "the final and big picture." Many of us would put it this way: "In the end it all comes down to..." There we believe that all will be found and revealed inside of the love and mercy of God—for everyone without exception—and for all of creation. All of our little divisions and dramas will be revealed to be just that. All smaller kingdoms and criteria will pass away and mean very little. To live with that final consciousness today is to live in the Reign of God.

This now and not-yet Reign of God is the foundation for both our personal hope and our cosmic optimism, but it is also the source of our deepest alienation from the world as it is, which is all based on largely meaningless merit badges, and various forms of win or lose (at which almost all lose!).

I must warn you that living in this Big Picture of God will leave you in many ways as a "stranger and pilgrim" on this earth (Hebrews 11:13). It is not a popular position, because you can no longer easily fit into ordinary superficial conversations and anti–any group jokes. Nevertheless, our task is to learn how to live lovingly in both worlds until they become one world—at least in us. True Kingdom people bridge worlds and do not again create separate or superior little kingdoms. This is a common mistake.

+Adapted from *Jesus' Plan for a New World: The Sermon on the Mount*, pp. 3–4

A SALVATION OF HISTORY MORE THAN
PRIVATE INDIVIDUALS

The Reign of God has much more to do with *right relationship* than with being privately right. It has much more to do with *being connected* than with being personally correct. Can you feel the total difference between these two? The one encourages an impossible notion of individual salvation and creates individualists; the other introduces cosmic salvation and creates humans, citizens, caretakers, neighbors, and saints.

The Reign of God is not about a world without pain or mystery but simply a world where we can be in real contact with all things, where we can be inherently connected and in communion with what the poet Mary Oliver calls "the daily presentations." Then the whole world is our temple and our church. Then we can realistically hope for both "a new heaven and a new earth" (Revelation 21:1), as the Bible finally promises.

Jesus was a consummate Jew and he was quite aware from his own Scriptures that God was saving history itself, and all of us in its sweep—and all of us in spite of ourselves, just as he always loved Israel in spite of its constant infidelities. Salvation for the Jews was a social and historical notion, not this much later regression into "How can I personally go to heaven?" This gross individualism pretty much destroyed the historical influence and sweep of the Judeo-Christian religions. Individuals sought to be privately correct instead of learning how to stay connected with everything else. This has really done us in.

+Adapted from *Jesus' Plan for a New World: The Sermon on the Mount*, p. 11

POWER VERSUS LOVE

There are always two worlds. The world as it operates is largely about power; the world as it should be, or the Reign of God, is always about love. Conversion is almost entirely about moving from one world to the next, and yet having to live in both worlds at the same time. As you allow yourself to loosen your grip on the ego or bad forms of power, you will gradually see the inadequacy and weakness of mere domination and control. God will then teach you how to tighten your grip around the second world, which is the ever-purer motivation of love.

Any exercise of power apart from love leads to brutality and evil; but any claim to love that does not lead to using power for others is mere sentimentality and emotion. I must admit, it is rare to find people who hold both together in perfect balance—who have found their power and use it for others or people who have found love and use it for good purposes. I think the Reign of God includes both love and power in a lovely dance.

I think that is what Jesus means when he tells us to be "cunning as serpents but gentle as doves" (Matthew 10:16). It is a beautiful combination of both authority and vulnerability.

+Adapted from *Jesus' Plan for a New World: The Sermon on the Mount*, p. 41

INSTITUTIONS AND "DEEP CHURCH"

Jesus says that the Reign of God "is close at hand" (Mark 1:15; Matthew 4:17). So we should not project it onto a later or other world. The Kingdom of God breaks into this world whenever people act as God would act.

It is sad to say, but institutions as institutions can seldom operate at a Kingdom level, except in vision, philosophy, and mission statements, in corporate decisions they make now and then, and writings that stand over time. They can also raise up, educate, protect, and promote enlightened individuals, as many churches and organizations often do. There has to be a container to carry the message from age to age, or we all have to start at zero, so I am not so naïve as to think we do not need institutions.

When Big Truth can happen in terms of structures, organizations, or groups, then you have a momentary taste of the true Kingdom descending to earth. This seldom happens with more than "two or three" rightly gathered (Matthew 18:20). It is the critical mass, or leaven and salt, who can and will change the world and reform institutions. *This is Jesus's basic and first image of church.* Nowhere is there found an institutional image of church as such. Deep church is invariably something shared between a small group of believers, which is probably why Jesus speaks of "two or three gathered in my name" (Matthew 18:20).

+Adapted from *Jesus' Plan for a New World: The Sermon on the Mount*, p. 110

INCARNATION

In most pictures of people waiting for the Holy Spirit they are looking upward, they have their hands out or raised—the assumption being that the Spirit is "up there." In the Great Basilica in Assisi there's a little bronze statue of St. Francis honoring the Holy Spirit. His posture and perspective are completely different from the usual. He's got his hands folded looking into the earth. This is a very good artistic image of what we called our Franciscan "alternative orthodoxy." We started looking down for the Holy Spirit instead of up, which was continued in saints like Vincent de Paul, Thérèse of Lisieux, and Dorothy Day. The full mystery of incarnation ("enfleshment") takes a long time to sink into humanity's heart.

If Divinity became flesh in Jesus, if God entered the world as a human being, then it was this world that became the hiding and the revealing place of God. It was henceforth the physical, the animal, the elements, sexuality, embodiment, it was the material universe—whatever your place of connection has been—that are the hiding places and the revealing places of God. That changes everything, and it was supposed to change everything.

INCARNATION MAKES EVOLUTION INEVITABLE

St. Bonaventure, who lived shortly after St. Francis (1181–1226), and John Duns Scotus a little later yet, both observed as intellectuals what St. Francis was seeing and doing intuitively. They saw that he, exactly like Jesus, found the transcendent not "out there" but "in here"—the transcendent was largely revealed at the depth and "inner" of things. Years ago, a dear friend and theologian, Walter Wink, made the strong case that this was what we actually mean when we say, "Angels." Angels are *the transcendent within things*. Everything, therefore, has its angel or messenger! They make all things fly, as it were, and all things are messengers of deeper messages.

What's happening is inherent, and all things blossom from within and at their depths. Grace is not something you invite into the world as if it's not already there. This is why a Christian should never have the least trouble with evolution. People only have trouble with it because they believe grace is extrinsic to the universe. Too many evangelical Protestants and conservative Catholics did not learn from Franciscanism. For them, God is doing everything from outside and God's love is not organic to creation. It is from the depths and from the inside that life is generated, as all DNA, every seed, nuclear fusion, and all things born make very clear.

NOT JUST BY ANALOGY!

What John Duns Scotus taught me was the Univocity of Being. *Univocity*, in Latin, means "one voice." He said that when you speak of God, when you speak of angels, when you speak of humans, when you speak of animals, when you speak of trees, when you speak of fish, when you speak of the earth, you are using the word *being* univocally, or *with one voice* and meaning. They all participate in the same being in varying ways. And being is one, just as God is One.

Now that might seem like an abstract philosophical position, but I hope you can see how it creates an inclusive universe where everything is sacred, where you can't divide the world into the sacred and profane anymore. Most of the Catholic tradition, including Thomas Aquinas, believed, at best, in "the Analogy of Being." In other words, God was pure Being, and all the rest of creation participated in that Being by analogy—or metaphorically speaking. For us, that created too big a divide, and then it was it too hard to overcome in practice. This has surely proven to be true for too many Christians, producing Pelagianism (not Pelagius's fault!), Jansenism, immense fear of God, and false searching for private perfection to please this too-distant God.

We don't have exclusionary Christianity in early Franciscanism. It's one world. "In all creatures you may see and honor God. If you do not do this the whole world will rise against you," says Francis. He's paralleling Jesus's own phrase that "the very stones will cry out" (Luke 19:40) if you do not let the disciples recognize and honor the Christ Mystery, who at that moment is seated on a donkey (Luke 19:35), an event that Jesus has gone to great effort to orchestrate (Luke 19:28–36). Jesus was a master of incarnational message.

FRANCISCANISM

The two adjectives most applied to God by Franciscan mysticism were the *goodness* of God and the *humility* of God. Hardly any of us would say God is humble, but Francis did. He and Clare fell in love with the humility of God; because if God emptied himself and hid himself inside the material world, then God, who was revealed in Jesus, was surely a very humble God. This is a total surprise to history, and so much a scandal that most Christians still resist it consciously or unconsciously.

Francis fell in love more with the humanity of Jesus than with his divinity. It was Jesus's humanity that Francis wanted to draw close to, and that he fell in love with. He just wanted to be the most humble man around, which was his "imitation of God" (Ephesians 5:1). Only in that humble state could he find God, because that's where God had gone; Francis wanted to go where Jesus went and where God was hiding.

Art historians say that even Christian art changed after Francis. Beginning with Giotto, we have a new interest in things ordinary, human, animal, mundane, and nature-based. Not just glowing divine icons, but now light shining through the ordinary world.

So you see the basis for a different kind of holiness. It's not God from above. It's now God from within—incarnationalism instead of transcendentalism.

SURFACE VERSUS DEPTH

If we just stay on the fearful or superficial side of the religious spectrum, religion is invariably defined by exclusionary purity codes that always separate things into the sacred and profane. God is still distant, punitive, and scary. Then our religious job becomes putting ourselves only on the side of "sacred" things (as if we could) and to stay apart from worldly or material things, even though Jesus shows no such preference himself.

After the beginnings of mystical experience (which is just prayer experience), one finds that what makes something secular or profane is precisely to live on the surface of it. It's not that the sacred is here and the profane is over there. *Everything is profane if you live on the surface of it, and everything is sacred if you go into the depths of it—even your sin.*

To go inside your own mistakenness is to find God. To stay on the surface of very good things—like the Bible, sacraments, priesthood, or church—is to often do very unkind and evil things, while calling them good. This important distinction is perfectly illustrated by Jesus's parable of the publican and the Pharisee (Luke 18:9–14).

So the division for the Christian is not between secular and sacred things, but between superficial things and things at their depth. The depths always reveal grace, while staying on the surface allows one to largely miss the point (the major danger of fundamentalism, by the way). Karl Rahner, the German Jesuit and one of my heroes of Vatican II, loved to call this "the mysticism of ordinary life."

+Adapted from *Following the Mystics through the Narrow Gate....*
Seeing God in All Things (CD, DVD, MP3)

LIMINAL SPACE

What some call "liminal space" or threshold space (in Latin, *limen* means a threshold, a starting line in a race, or a beginning place) is a very good phrase for those special times, events, and places that open us up to the sacred. It seems we need special (sacred) days to open us up to all days being special and sacred; we need special and sacred times to universalize to all time. (It is only some forms of late-blooming Protestantism that never recognized this need.) Even ancient initiation rites were both intensely sacred time and space to send the initiate into a newly discovered sacred universe.

What became All Saints Day and All Souls Day (November 1–2) were already called "thin times" by the ancient Celts, as also were February 1–2 (St. Bridget's Day and Candlemas Day when the candles were blessed and lit). The veil between this world and the next world was considered most "thin" and most easily traversed during these times. On these days, we were invited to be aware of deep time—that is, past, present, and future time gathered into one especially holy moment. On these pivotal days, we are reminded that our ancestors are still in us and work with us and through us; we call it the "communion of saints." The New Testament phrase for this was "when time came to a fullness," as when Jesus first announces the Reign of God (Mark 1:15) or when Mary comes to the moment of birth (Luke 2:6). We are in liminal space whenever past, present, and future time come together in a full moment of readiness. We are in liminal space whenever the division between "right here" and "over there" is obliterated in our consciousness.

THE COMMUNION OF SAINTS

Deep time, or the communion of saints professed in Christian creeds, means that *your goodness is not just your own, nor is your badness just your own.* We are intrinsically social animals. You carry the lived and the unlived (unhealed) lives of your parents, grandparents, and great-grandparents as far back as DNA and genomes can trace it—which is pretty far back. It does take a village to create a person. We are the very first generation to know that this is also literally and genetically true. Maybe the vast number of world religions which we dismissed as mere ancestor worshipers were not as naïve as we imagined. Maybe there is also healing and understanding when we honor the full cycle of life.

Living in the communion of saints means that we can take ourselves very seriously (we are part of a Great Whole) and not take ourselves too seriously at all (we are *just a part* of the Great Whole!) at the very same time. I hope this frees you *from* any unnecessary individual guilt—and more importantly frees you *to be* a full "partner in God's triumphant parade" through time and history (2 Corinthians 2:14). You are in on the deal and, yes, the really Big Deal. We are all a very small part of a very Big Thing!

THE FRANCISCAN RECOVERY OF THE GOSPEL

St. Bonaventure, building on the Incarnation of God in Jesus and Francis's love of all nature, saw the traces or footprints of God in everything. The whole world was also the "incarnation" of the God mystery, and indeed the very "Body of God" (see Romans 8:19–22). Jesus is the microcosm of the macrocosm, the hologram of the whole, the corporate personality for humanity, in other words, the stand-in for everything and everyone else (see Colossians 1:15–20).

"The journey of the soul into God," as Bonaventure put it, was to learn how to see the unity of all being, how to look for this partially hidden God, and how to honor those footprints everywhere once you could see them. It was a surrender to gratitude—and also to immense confidence that you were a part of something very good.

The result was a continuous life of appreciation and reverence, nonconsumption, and simple joy—while still living a very busy life in the world! These were the hallmarks of Franciscan spirituality.

+For more on this theme, please consider *The Art of Letting Go: Living the Wisdom of St. Francis* (CD)

NOT A COMPETITIVE RELIGION

Paul, a good Jew, quotes Deuteronomy, "The Word is near you, in your mouth and in your heart" (Romans 10:8), and begins with a challenge that we still need today, "Do not tell yourself that you have to bring Christ down!" (Romans 10:6). He knew that God had overcome the human-divine gap in the Christ Mystery once and for all. God is henceforth here, and not just there.

This is Christianity's only completely unique message. Full incarnation is what distinguishes us from all other religions. This is our only real trump card, and, for the most part, we have not yet played it. History, the planet—and other religions—have only suffered as a result. Incarnationalism does not put you in competition with any other religions but, in fact, allows you to see God *in all things*, including them! It mandates that you love and respect all others.

The mystery of the Incarnation is precisely *the repositioning of God in the human and material world and not just part of that world*. Common variety top-down religion often creates very passive, and even passive-dependent and passive-aggressive, Christians. Certainly that is very common in my own Roman Church. Bottom-up or incarnational religion, offers a God we can experience for ourselves and a God we can see—and must see—in everyone else. Any God on a throne does not achieve that purpose, but merely makes you fight other "thrones."

+Adapted from *Things Hidden: Scripture as Spirituality*, p. 121

CONSCIOUSNESS IS CONSCIOUSNESS
OF THE WHOLE

When God gives of God's self, one of two things happens: either flesh is inspirited or Spirit is enfleshed. This pattern is really very clear. I am somewhat amazed that more have not recognized this simple pattern: God's will is always *incarnation*. And against all of our godly expectations, it appears that for God, *matter really matters*. God, who is Spirit, chose to materialize! We call it the *Christ* Mystery.

This Creator of ours is patiently determined to put matter and spirit together, almost as if the one were not complete without the other. This Lord of life seems to desire a perfect but free unification of body and soul. So much so, in fact, that God appears to be willing to wait for the creatures to will and choose this unity for themselves—or it does not fully happen. Our Yes to incarnation really matters, just as Mary's did. Could this be the very meaning of consciousness? Certainly full consciousness of any event demands that we see its outer and its inner, its shape and also its meaning, its body and also its soul.

+Adapted from *Near Occasions of Grace*, p. 5

FEAST OF CHRISTMAS

Your all powerful Word, leapt down from heaven, from your royal throne.
—Wisdom 18:15

Do we have any idea what this sentence means, or what it might imply? Is it really true? If it is, then we are living in an entirely different universe than we imagine, or even can imagine. If the major division between Creator and creature can be overcome, then all others can be overcome too. To paraphrase Oswald Chambers, "this is a truth that dumbly struggles in us for utterance!" It is too much to be true and too good to be true. So we can only resort to metaphors, images, poets, music, and artists of every stripe.

I have long felt that Christmas is a feast that largely celebrates humanity's unconscious desire and goal. Its meaning is too much for the rational mind to process, so God graciously puts this Big Truth on a small stage so that we can wrap our minds and hearts around it over time. No philosopher would dare to predict the materialization of God, so we are just presented with a very human image of a poor woman and her husband with a newborn child. (I am told that the Madonna is by far the most painted image in Western civilization.)

Pope Benedict, who addressed 250 artists in the Sistine Chapel before Michelangelo's half-naked, and often grotesque, images, said quite brilliantly, "An essential function of genuine beauty is that it gives humanity a healthy shock!" And then he went on to quote Simone Weil who said that "Beauty is the experimental proof that incarnation is in fact possible."

If there is one moment of beauty, then beauty can indeed exist on this earth; if there is one true moment of Incarnation, then why not incarnation everywhere? The beauty of Christmas is enough *healthy shock* for a lifetime, and it leaves the shocked ones *dumbly struggling for utterance.* Once the Eternal Word has become human flesh it is very hard to put it back into words—only music, poetry, and art can begin to suffice.

+A Christmas meditation

NOT WHAT ANY OF US WOULD THINK

You Bethlehem, too small to be among the clans of Judah, from you shall come forth one who is to rule my people Israel.

— Matthew 2:6

We, like Bethlehem itself, are too tiny to imagine greatness within us, but God always hides inside of littleness and seeming insignificance, so only the humble and honest can find him. God appears at the edges, it seems. We do not have to see God if we do not want to. God trusts our desiring and lets us do all the discovering. The Mystery does not come from above, like the important capitals of Jerusalem, Rome, Paris, or Washington, D.C., but only little backwaters like Bethlehem, hardly worth noticing.

Those who can recognize God within their own puny and ordinary souls will be the same who will freely and daringly affirm the Divine Presence in other unexpected places. It is all one and the same pattern. See it once, here and now, and soon you can see it everywhere!

+Adapted from *Near Occasions of Grace*, p. 6

WHAT DOES IT MEAN TO BE HUMAN?

It is not about becoming spiritual beings nearly as much as about becoming human beings. The biblical revelation is clearly saying that we are already spiritual beings; we just don't know it yet. The Bible tries to let you in on the secret by revealing God in ordinary times and places. That's why so much of the text seems so mundane, practical, specific, and frankly, unspiritual! Maybe that is why Catholics never read it very much! It is not usually inspiring but filled with prostitution, adultery, murder, polygamy, gang rape, and frankly, just a lot of contradictions. Just like everything else. Just like life. Just like me.

We have created a sad kind of dualism between the spiritual and the so-called non-spiritual. We just couldn't see God's new unity or dare to believe it until God put them together in one human body called Jesus (see Ephesians 2:11–20). As many have said much better than I, we are not human beings trying desperately to become spiritual, we are already and essentially spiritual beings—and our problem has always been "What does it mean to be a human being?" I suspect that is why God had to model the answer in at least one human being called Jesus.

+Adapted from *Things Hidden: Scripture as Spirituality*, p. 17

RELIGIONLESS CHRISTIANITY

Listen carefully to the many examples, parables, and metaphors used by Jesus. You will notice that they are more nature-based, lifestyle-based, and relationship-based than grounded in any concepts of philosophy, academia, or churchiness. He says things like "Look at the lilies of the field" (Matthew 6:28), and "Observe the ravens" (Luke 12:24), he speaks of a woman looking for a coin, and a father running after his son. He does not talk about the candlesticks, priestly vestments, or what was later named "orthodoxy." In fact, he warns against such righteousness. Certainly in the three Synoptic Gospels there is no sense Jesus is walking around proclaiming eternal doctrines and dogmas. If so, he left an awful lot of room for misinterpretation, a contrary opinion, or even fuzzy thinking. Christian teachers must be honest here.

Jesus uses normal language that uneducated people can understand. Frankly, it is a bit disappointing. Jesus looks at things right in front of him, and talks about what's real and what's unreal, what lasts and what does not last at all. He often criticizes us for our *lack of common sense and lack of religious common sense*: "You know how to read the face of the sky, but you cannot see the signs of the times. This is an evil and unfaithful generation" (Matthew 16:3–4). The problem seems to be that we too quickly made Jesus into God before we just let him be our daily teacher, lover, and friend.

+Adapted from the webcast *What is the Emerging Church?* (CD, MP3)

ECUMENISM

Everything belongs and no one needs to be scapegoated or excluded.
Evil and illusion only need to be named and exposed truthfully,
and they die in exposure to the light.

INTRODUCTION

The issue here is first of all a psychological one, but one with immediate theological and social implications. It demands of us self-knowledge and the crucial need to recognize (1) when you are in denial about your own darkness, shadow, and capacity for illusion, (2) your capacity to project your own fears and darkness onto other people and groups, (3) your capacity to face and carry your own issues, and (4) the social, institutional, and political implications of not doing the above.

If some Christians think this is mere psychology, then they surely need to know that Jesus himself was a consummate analyst of human nature, really a brilliant psychologist, and named the very issues that today we have rediscovered and called "denial," "defense mechanisms," "projections," and "the shadow self," as well as the necessity of inner healing of hurts to avoid continuing the hurt in others. Much of Jesus's teaching is later reflected in Paul's instructions to his Christian communities.

Here are some of the outstanding examples:

"Why do you observe the splinter in your brother or sister's eye and never notice the log in your own.... Hypocrite! Take the log out of your own eye, first, and then you can perhaps see clearly enough to take the splinter out of your own eye." (Matthew 7:4–5)

"The lamp of the body is the eye. If your eye is sound, your whole body will be filled with light. But if your eye is diseased, your whole body will be filled with darkness." (Matthew 6:22–23)

"Do not give to dogs what is holy, and do not throw your pearls to swine. They will only trample you in turn, they will turn on you and tear you to pieces." (Matthew 7:6)

"A sound tree does not produce rotten fruit, and a rotten tree does not produce sound fruit.... A good person draws what is good from the goodness of her heart, and a bad person draws badness from the badness of his heart. A person's words flow out of what fills their heart." (Luke 6:43–45)

"We are not blind!" [they say] "Blind? If you were you would not be guilty, but [precisely] because you say 'We see!' your guilt remains." (John 9:40–41)

"Clean the inside of cup and dish first, and then the outside will be clean as well." (Matthew 23:26)

"Do not tell yourselves, 'We have Abraham for our Father' [We belong to the correct group!] I tell you God can raise up children of Abraham from these very stones!" (Luke 3:8)

"Physician, heal thyself!" (Luke 4:23)

"Everything exposed to the light becomes light." (Ephesians 5:13–14)

"If you pass judgment, you have no excuse. In judging others you condemn yourself, since you behave no differently from those you judge." (Romans 2:1)

"Put your sword back into its scabbard. All who live by the sword will die by the sword." (Matthew 26–52)

"Love your enemies, and do good to those who hate you.... Treat others as you would like them to treat you." (Luke 6:27, 30)

"The truth that I have now come to realize is that God has no favorites." (Acts 10:34)

"Everything will be subjected to [the Christ Mystery]...until God will finally be all in all." (1 Corinthians 15:28)

"There is only Christ: he is everything and he is in everything." (Colossians 3:11)

SOMETHING IS REEMERGING

We now know from cultural studies and historical experience that groups define themselves and even hold themselves together largely negatively—by who they are *not*, what they are *against*, and what they do *not* do. We need a problem or an enemy to gather our energies. We usually define ourselves through various purity codes to separate ourselves from the "impure" and the presumably unworthy. Simple worship (what we are *for*, or in *support* of, and what we *love*) is much harder to sustain. Thus most reformations and revolutions *need* someone else to be wrong much more than they need any discovery of a higher level of consciousness themselves. This is an absolutely core problem.

Thus, Jesus never affirmed opposition or contrariness, because he knew that it was merely a same-level or lower-level response to the problem (even when empowered by some new and good ideas). The new group was infected by the same hubris and oppositional energy, and would soon engender the same kind of reformation. Thus the endless progressive-conservative pendulum continues to swing and yet we do not move forward spiritually.

"Emerging Christianity" is trying *not* to make this mistake and hopes to be an inclusive notion of religion that is not against this or that. Evil and sin *do* need to be named and exposed (not directly fought!), however, and this is the prophetic role of religion. Without prophecy, religion cannot critique itself and ends up being largely self-serving. Jesus's starting point was never sin, but human suffering. This deeper and increasingly obvious teaching of Jesus is strongly reemerging in our time, this time from many different disciplines of wisdom and study.

EVIL DEPENDS UPON DISGUISE

We are all addicts. Human beings are addictive by nature. Addiction is a modern name and description for what the biblical tradition calls "sin" and the medieval Christians called "passions" or "attachments." They both recognized that serious measures, or practices, were needed to break us out of these illusions and entrapments; in fact, the New Testament calls them in some cases "exorcisms!" They knew they were dealing with nonrational evil, or so-called demons.

Substance addictions are merely the most visible form of addiction, but actually we are all addicted to our own habitual way of doing anything, our own defenses, and most especially our patterned way of thinking or how we process our reality. By definition, you can never see or handle what you are addicted to. It is always hidden and disguised as something else. As Jesus did with the demon at Gerasa, someone must say, "What is your name?" (Luke 8:30). You cannot heal what you do not first acknowledge.

+From *Breathing Under Water: Spirituality and the Twelve Steps*, pp. xxii–xxiii

YOU MUST NIP IT IN THE BUD

Remember, always remember, that the *heartfelt desire to do the will of God is, in fact, the truest will of God.* At that point, God has won, and the ego has lost, and your prayer has already been answered.

To sum up the importance of an alternative mind, this message says it all:

Watch your thoughts; they become words.

Watch your words; they become actions.

Watch your actions; they become habits.

Watch your habits; they become character.

Watch your character; it becomes your destiny.

+From *Breathing Under Water: Spirituality and the Twelve Steps*, p. 103

NON-DUAL THINKING IS NECESSARY

All-or-nothing reformations and all-or-nothing revolutions are not true reformations or revolutions. Most history, however, has not known this until now. When a new insight is reached, we must not dismiss the previous era or previous century or previous church as totally wrong. It is never true! We cannot try to reform things in that way anymore.

This is also true in terms of the psyche. When we grow and we pass over into the second half of life, we do not need to throw out the traditions, laws, boundaries, and earlier practices. That is mere rebellion, and it is why so many revolutions and reformations backfired and kept people in the first half of life. It is false reform, failed revolution, and non-transformation. *It is still dualistic thinking, which finally turns against its own group too.*

So do not waste time hating Mom and Dad, hating the Church, hating America, hating what has disappointed you. In fact, don't hate anything. You become so upset with the dark side of things that you never discover how to put the dark and the light together, which is the heart of wisdom and love and the trademark of a second-half-of-life person.

+Adapted from *Loving the Two Halves of Life: The Further Journey*
(CD, DVD, MP3)

EVERYTHING BELONGS

People who have learned to live from their center in God know which boundaries or edges are worth maintaining and which can be surrendered, although it is this very struggle that often constitutes their deepest dark nights. Both maintaining and surrendering boundaries ironically requires an "obedience" (Romans 16:26), because it requires listening to a Voice beyond your own.

I believe that we have no real access to *who we really are* except in God. Only when we rest in God can we find the safety, the spaciousness, and the scary freedom to be *who* we are, *all* that we are, *more* than we are, and *less* than we are. Only when we live and see through God can everything belong. All other systems exclude, expel, punish, and protect to find identity for their members in ideological perfection or some kind of purity. Apart from taking up so much useless time and energy, this effort keeps us from the one and only task of love and union.

+Adapted from *Everything Belongs: The Gift of Contemplative Prayer*, pp. 24–26

THE CELTIC KNOT

We are talking about a spiritual ecology. If you live in a fully connected world, you're saved every day just by playing your part. You are grabbed by God, and you belong to this universe, along with everything else.

At a retreat I gave on the Scottish island of Iona, which was the center point for the diffusion of Celtic Christianity, attendees remarked how often the Celtic knot was found on crosses, gravestones, in manuscripts, and on jewelry. It was apparently the Celts artistic way of saying that all is connected, everything belongs, and all is one in God. They knew about ecosystems long before we did, but in an even larger way. *All* was held together inside of the divine knot. T.S. Eliot ends his famous "Four Quartets" quoting Dame Julian, and saying the same: "And all shall be well and / All manner of thing shall be well / When the tongues of flame are in-folded / Into the crowned knot of fire."

+Adapted from *In the Footsteps of Francis* (CD, DVD)

LEARNING TO SEE

Jesus calls us to become like little children or, as the Zen master puts it, to have a "beginner's mind." Jesus says the only people who can recognize and be ready for what he's talking about are the ones who come with the mind and heart of a child. The older we get, the more we've been betrayed and hurt and disappointed, the more barriers we put up to beginner's mind. We must always be ready to see anew. But it's so hard to go back, to be vulnerable, to continue to say to your soul, "I don't know anything." (A man told me recently that was the mantra that has kept him a happy man).

Spirituality is always about how we see. It's not about earning or achieving some kind of merit. Once you see rightly, the rest follows and the road widens. You don't need to push the river, because you are already in it—and floating along! The Great Life is already living within us and we only gradually learn how to say Yes to this always-existent Life. This Life is so large and deep and spacious that it even includes its opposite, death.

+Adapted from *Everything Belongs: The Gift of Contemplative Prayer*, pp. 32–34

THE POWER OF NOW

The contemplative secret is to learn how to live in the now. Saints knew and taught this long before Eckhart Tolle retaught it in our time, but many Christians still called him "New Age." Jean Pierre de Caussade, S.J., already spoke of this as "the Sacrament of the Present Moment" in his classic book of spiritual direction in 1735. My book *Everything Belongs* came out in 1999, the same year as Tolle's immensely helpful book *The Power of Now*.

The now is not as empty as it might appear to be—or that we fear it may be. Try to realize that everything we really need is right here, right now. (Don't think at the lower dualistic level, or you can't get this). When we're doing life right, it means nothing more than it is right now, because God is always in this moment in an accepting and non-blaming way. When we are able to experience that, taste it, and enjoy it, we don't need to hold on to it, nor are we afraid to let go of it. The next moment will have its own taste and enjoyment.

Because our moments are not tasted—or full—or real—or in the Presence—we are never fulfilled and there is never enough. We then create artificial fullness and distractions and try to pass time our empty time with that. God is either in this now or God isn't in it at all. "This moment is as perfect as it can be" used to be a mantra we would repeat at the community of New Jerusalem in Cincinnati.

Perhaps this quote from Psalm 46:10 can be your entranceway into the now, if you slow down in this way:

Be still and know that I am God.

Be still and know that I am.

Be still and know.

Be still.

Be.

+Adapted from *Everything Belongs: The Gift of Contemplative Prayer*, pp. 60–62

EVIL IS ALSO CORPORATE EVIL

Up to now, we have almost entirely emphasized personal sin, with little notion of what John Paul II rightly called "structural sin" or "institutional evil." There has been little recognition of the deep connection between the structures that people uncritically accept and the personal evil things they also do.

The individual has usually gotten all the blame, while what Paul called the powers, the sovereignties, and the principalities (Romans 8:38; Colossians 2:15; Ephesians 3:10; 6:12) have gotten off scot-free for most of Christian history. These were his words for institutions and social systems. They have a life (and death!) of their own—that is usually above normal understanding and thus eludes any honest critique. In fact, we tend to worship them as mighty and strong, and therefore always good. "Too big to fail," we now say. We tend to demonize the individual prostitute, but not the industry of pornography at many levels. We tend to hate greedy people, but we idealize and try to be a part of the system that made them rich.

For example, people tend to support and even idealize almost all wars their country wages. In fact, few things are more romanticized than war, except by those who suffer from them. At the same time, we rail against violence in the streets, the violence of our young people, and the violence on the news every night. We are slowly learning that we cannot have it both ways. If violence is a way to solve international problems, then it is a way to solve problems at home, too. We can't say, "It's bad here, but it's good there."

We know how to name individual sin and evil, but we do not know how to name corporate sin and evil. We have ended up with a very *inconsistent* morality, which few take seriously anymore or even know how to follow. That is why we *need a consistent ethic of life.*

+Adapted from *Spiral of Violence: The World, the Flesh, and the Devil* (CD, MP3)

THE SIN OF EXCLUSION

Those at the edge of any system and those excluded from any system ironically and invariably hold the secret for the conversion and wholeness of that very group. They always hold the feared, rejected, and denied parts of the group's soul. You see, therefore, why the Church was meant to be that group that constantly went to the edges, to the least of the brothers and sisters, and even to the enemy. Jesus was not just a theological genius, but he was also a psychological and sociological genius. *When any church defines itself by exclusion of anybody, it is always wrong.* It is avoiding its only vocation, which is to be the Christ. The only groups that Jesus seriously critiques are those who include themselves and exclude others from the always-given grace of God.

Only as the People of God receive the stranger, the sinner, and the immigrant, those who don't play our game our way, do we discover not only the hidden, feared, and hated parts of our own souls, but the fullness of Jesus himself. We need them for our own conversion.

The Church is always converted when the outcasts are reinvited back into the temple. You see this in Jesus's common action of sending marginalized people that he has healed back into the village, back to their family, or back to the Temple to show themselves to the priests. It is not just for their reinclusion and acceptance, but actually for the group itself to be renewed.

+Adapted from *Radical Grace: Daily Meditations*, p. 28

HOW YOU KEEP GROWING

Until you can forgive and include all of the parts, every part belonging, every part forgiven, even the tragic parts now seen as necessary lessons, you cannot come home. The full gift of the final journey is discovering that we are already home. I hope you have seen it in at least some elders in your lifetime. They are at home in their own bodies, their own lives, and their own minds.

When you succeed at your *real* task, or what I like to call "the task within the task," then wherever God leads you, it doesn't really matter. Home is no longer a geographic place. It is a place where everything belongs, and everything can be held, and everything is another lesson and another gift.

Hell would be whenever life has come to a halt, where there is no rejoining, but all is exclusion, blaming, and denying. We no longer need to believe in hell as a doctrine or a geographic place. We see it in this world almost every day.

St. Gregory of Nyssa—one of the Eastern fathers of the Church, and one of my favorites—defined sin as "the refusal to keep growing." The saint and the true elder grow from everything, even and especially their failures.

+Adapted from *The Odyssey: The Further Journey* (CD/DVD)

A SEAMLESS GARMENT OF LIFE

Cardinal Bernardin, a true friend and confidant while I was in Cincinnati in the 1970s and early 1980s, was the first to publicly call for a consistent ethic of life. He made it clear that until the Church starts being honest and defending all life from beginning to end, it cannot truthfully call itself pro-life. Otherwise, the very moral principle falls apart. *All* policies that needlessly destroy life—abortion, war, capital punishment, euthanasia, poverty itself, and the selfish destruction of the earth and its creatures—are all anti-life and against the fifth commandment, "Thou shalt not kill." As you can see, we have a lot of time and a lot of moral maturing to go before we can match the clear, nonviolent teaching and example of Jesus himself (see Matthew 5:38–48). How can we expect the world to be nonviolent when the church itself has not taught it or practiced it in most of its history (except for some Quakers, Mennonites, and Amish)?

We not only need to be consistent between individual morality and social morality, but we need to be consistent between all of the various life issues. It is a "seamless garment," as Cardinal Bernardin brilliantly called it. Such a theology has teeth and real authority behind it and does not just pander to the cultural values of either the left or the right.

Like the Gospel itself, it challenges both sides and pleases nobody. He told me personally a couple of weeks after he gave his first lecture on this theme at Fordham University that he thought that phrase "seamless garment" (from John 19:23) would be the only thing he would ever be remembered for—and it came to his mind in a moment at the press conference afterward.

+Adapted from *Spiral of Violence: The World, the Flesh, and the Devil* (CD, MP3)

"NEW FUNDAMENTALS"
IS A CONTRADICTION IN TERMS

In recent years and elections, one might have thought that homosexuality and abortion were the new litmus tests of authentic Christianity. Where did this come from? They never were the criteria of proper membership for the first two thousand years, but they reflect very recent culture wars instead. And largely from people who think of themselves as traditionalists! (The fundamentals were already resolved in the early Apostles's Creed and Nicene Creed. Note that none of the core beliefs is about morality at all. The creeds are more mystical, cosmological, and about aligning our lives inside of a huge sacred story.) *When you lose the great mystical level of religion, you always become moralistic about this or that as a cheap substitute. It gives you a false sense of being on higher spiritual ground than others.*

Jesus is clearly much more concerned about issues of pride, injustice, hypocrisy, blindness, and what I have often called "The Three P's": power, prestige, and possessions, which are probably 95 percent of Jesus's written teaching. We conveniently ignore this 95 percent to concentrate on a morality that usually has to do with human embodiment. That's where people get righteous, judgmental, and upset for some reason. *The body seems to be where we carry our sense of shame and inferiority,* and early stage religion has never gotten much beyond these pelvic issues. As Jesus put it, "You ignore the weightier matters of the law—justice, mercy, and good faith…and instead you strain out gnats and swallow camels" (Matthew 23:23). We worry about what people are doing in bed much more than making sure everybody has a bed to begin with. There certainly is a need for a life-giving sexual morality and true pro-life morality, but one could sincerely question whether Christian nations and people have found it yet.

Christianity will regain its moral authority when it starts emphasizing social sin in equal measure with individual (body-based) sin and weave them both into a seamless garment of love and truth.

+Adapted from *Spiral of Violence: The World, the Flesh, and the Devil* (CD, MP3)

YES/AND. . .

The spiritual gift of discernment (1 Corinthians 12:10) is when seemingly good things can be recognized as sometimes bad things, and seemingly bad things can also be seen to bear some good fruit. Darn it! Discernment has largely been undeveloped among ordinary Christians, except among those good Jesuits! It invites people into what I call "Yes/And" thinking, rather than simplistic either/or thinking. This is the difference between merely having correct information and the true spiritual gift of wisdom (1 Corinthians 12:8). Both knowledge and wisdom are good, but wisdom is much better. It demands the maturity of discernment, which is what it takes to develop a truly *consistent ethic of life*. I admit the vast majority of people are not there yet.

Once we have learned to discern the real and disguised nature of both good and evil, we recognize that everything is broken and fallen, weak and poor—while still being the dwelling place of God—you and me, your country, your children, your marriage, and even your church and mosque and synagogue. That is not a put-down of anybody or anything, but actually creates the freedom to love imperfect things! As Jesus told the rich young man, "God alone is good!" (Mark 10:18).

In this, you may have been given the greatest recipe for happiness for the rest of your life. You cannot wait for things to be totally perfect to fall in love with them, or you will never love anything. Now, instead, you can love everything!

+Adapted from *Spiral of Violence: The World, the Flesh, and the Devil* (CD, MP3)

THE CRACK IN EVERYTHING

Leonard Cohen's song "Anthem" states in the refrain: "There is a crack in everything. That's how the light gets in." It sounds a lot like Paul's statement about carrying "the treasure in earthen vessels" (2 Corinthians 4:7). These are both much more poetic ways of naming what we unfortunately called "original sin"—a poor choice of words because the word *sin* implies fault and culpability, and that is precisely not the point! Original sin was trying to warn us that *the flaw at the heart of all reality* is nothing we did personally, but that there is simply a crack in everything, and so we should not be surprised when it shows itself in us or in everything else. This has the power to keep us patient, humble, and less judgmental. (One wonders if this does not also make the point that poetry and music are better ways to teach spiritual things than mental concepts).

The deep intuitions of most Church doctrines are invariably profound and correct, but they are still expressed in mechanical and literal language that everybody adores, stumbles over, denies, or fights. *Hold on for a while until you get to the real meaning, which is far more than the literal meaning!* That allows you to creatively both understand and critique things—without becoming oppositional, hateful, arrogant, and bitter. Some call this "appreciative inquiry" and it has an entirely different tone that does not invite or create the equal and opposite reaction of physics. *The opposite of contemplation is not action; it is reaction.* Much of the inconsistent ethic of life, in my opinion, is based on ideological reactions and groupthink, not humble discernment of how darkness hides and how the light gets in to almost everything. I hope I do not shock you, but it is really possible to have very ugly morality and sometimes rather beautiful immorality. Please think and pray about that.

+Adapted from *Spiral of Violence: The World, the Flesh, and the Devil* (CD, MP3)

HEAVEN AND HELL

Even Pope John Paul II said at a Vatican conference on June 28, 1999, that heaven and hell were primarily eternal states of consciousness more than geographical places of later reward and punishment. We seem to be our own worst enemies, and *we forget or deny things that are just too good to be true.* The ego clearly prefers an economy of merit, where we can divide the world into winners and losers, to any economy of grace, where merit or worthiness loses all meaning.

In the first case, at least a few of us good guys attain glory, although the vast majority of all of human history seems to be mere collateral damage to a God who is supposed to be merciful and compassionate. In the second case, God actually is merciful and compassionate as the world Scriptures and saints seem to agree upon. A notion of hell has to be theoretically maintained or humans have no freedom, and most religions have a similar concept, but it is interesting to me that the Roman Catholic Church has never declared a single person to be there, while it has declared tens of thousands to be in heaven!

+Adapted from *Falling Upward: A Spirituality for the Two Halves of Life*, p. 104

MEMORY

And Mary remembered all these things in her heart.
— Luke 2:19

Memory is the basis for both pain and rejoicing. We cannot have one without the other, it seems. Do not be too quick to heal all of those bad memories unless it means also feeling them deeply, which means to first learn what they have to teach you. God calls us to suffer (allow) the whole of reality, to remember the good along with the bad. Perhaps that is the course of the journey toward new sight and new hope. Memory creates a readiness for salvation, an emptiness to receive love and a fullness to enjoy it.

Strangely enough, it seems so much easier to remember the hurts, the failures, and the rejections. It is much more common to gather our life energy around a hurt than a joy, for some sad reason. Try to remember and give thanks for the good things even more than the bad, but learn from both of them. And most of all, as the prophet Baruch said, "Rejoice that you yourself are remembered by God" (5:5), which is the Big Memory that can hold and receive, heal and forgive, all of the smaller ones.

+Adapted from *Radical Grace: Daily Meditations*, p. 26

AN ETERNAL COVENANT WITH CREATION

The voluntary self-gift of Jesus on the cross was his free acceptance—and act of solidarity—with all of creation in its weakness and imperfection. He chose to become a divine brother to humanity, and by giving himself to God totally, he invites all of his brothers and sisters with him into that same relationship of belonging to everything. "Chosen in Christ from all eternity" is the way Ephesians 1:4 puts it.

The *raising up of Jesus* (which is the correct way to say it) is the confirmation of God's standing and universal relationship with what he created. The Jews brilliantly called it "a covenant" or "a testament" and it is one, consistent, and forever between God and humanity. Any new covenant or new testament is just when you finally get the first promise or covenant made to Israel—but now all the way through and now including everybody!

Jesus stands forever as our Promise, our Guarantee, and our Victory (1 Corinthians 1:30) of what God is doing everywhere and all the time. The only way you can absent yourself from this victory is to stand alone and apart. Inside communion you are forever safe and saved.

+Adapted from *Radical Grace: Daily Meditations*, p. 151

IMPLICATIONS OF MONOTHEISM

The Risen Christ is the eternal icon of the Divine Presence, which is beyond any boundaries or limits of space or time, or any attempts to limit God to here or there. We cannot achieve our divine sonship or our divine daughterhood. All we can do is awaken to it and start drawing upon a universal mystery. We live with an inherent dignity by reason of our very creation, a dignity that no human has given to us and no human can take from us. All things created bear the divine fingerprint, as St. Bonaventure put it.

Our inherent dignity has nothing to do with our race or religion or class. Hindus have it, and Buddhists have it, and so-called pagans in Africa have it. They are just as much children of God as we are. Objectively. Theologically. Eternally. Where else do you think they came from? Did some other god create them, except *the God*? Their divine DNA is identical to ours. We deny our supposed monotheism (there is one God) if we believe anything else. Far too many Jews, Christians, and Muslims have been anything but believers in one God who created all things.

+Adapted from *The Cosmic Christ* (CD, MP3)

CHRIST, CONSCIOUSNESS, AND LOVE
ARE PERHAPS THE SAME THING

You belong to Christ, and Christ belongs to God.
— 1 Corinthians 3:23

We are all the Body of Christ and even more so in our togetherness (1 Corinthians 12:12ff). Now that is quite scriptural, in many sacred texts, but perhaps it just seems too good to be true for most Christians: "There is only Christ, he is everything and he is in everything" (Colossians 3:11). The ego resists such inclusivity, because the ego is that part of you which wants to be special, separate, and superior instead. The ego ("flesh" for Paul) resists any change, vulnerability, or union with anything else.

The Risen Christ is our icon of God's universal presence, now unlimited by space or time. This is why the resurrection stories always show Jesus's body to be both here and there, passing through doors, visible and not visible, white light itself, everywhere and nowhere, as it were. He cannot be one object because he is *in* all objects (pan*en*theism).

Even to Mary Magdalene he says, "Do not cling to me" (John 20:17). Why? Because you can't! He is no longer bound by this one body. Christ is consciousness itself pervading all things—waiting and hoping for its inner Yes!

+Adapted from *The Cosmic Christ* (CD, MP3)

DEEP ECUMENISM

Christians believe in "Jesus Christ." Did anyone ever tell you those are two distinct faith affirmations? To believe in Jesus is to honor the one man who walked on this earth. To believe in "the Christ" is to include and honor all of creation, his whole Body. (Try Colossians 1:15–20 or Ephesians 1:3–14 if you think this is just my idea!) "Here comes everybody," was the way that James Joyce's *Finnegans Wake* described what a religion that calls itself "Catholic" should be.

Paul says in various places that Jesus is the "first of many brothers and sisters" and he is the first in "a great triumphal parade." The Christ is the symbolic beginning of the universal procession toward God, love, and life, and he is the end point too. Revelation says he is the "Alpha and the Omega, the Beginning and the End, the First and the Last" (22:13). This is a cosmological statement about the direction and meaning of history. It is not a statement about the Christian religion being superior or the only one true anything. Jesus died and Christ arose. Christ is the one truth pattern, and Jesus personified it in time, but many non-Christians actually live this truth pattern much, much better than many Christians. I know some of them.

+Adapted from *The Cosmic Christ* (CD, MP3)

THE WORLD, THE FLESH, AND THE DEVIL

Traditional Catholic moral teaching said there were three sources of evil—the world, the flesh and the devil. Dom Helder Camera, who was the holy and wise archbishop of Recife, Brazil, taught this in terms of a spiral of violence spiraling from the bottom up. The world (systemic evil) is the lie at the root of most cultures about power, prestige, and possessions; in the middle is the flesh (the personal evil and bad choices of individuals); and at the top is the devil (evil disguised as good power to enforce the first two), which are usually the unquestionable institutions like war, the laws of the market economy, most penal systems and many police forces, unjust legal systems and tax systems, etc. They are rightly called diabolical because starting with the snake in Genesis—high-level evil always disguises itself as good, charming, on your side, and even virtuous. Satan must present himself as too big or too needed to ever be wrong.

Up to now in human history most people's moral thinking has been overwhelmingly oriented around the personal evils of the flesh. There was not too much knowledge of the foundations of evil in cultural assumptions themselves, nor hardly any critique of major social institutions on a broad level until the 1960s! This is really quite amazing. The individual person got all the blame and punishment for evil, while the supportive world views and violent institutions were never called into account or punishment, as Jesus did when he critiqued the Temple system itself.

The biblical prophets of Judaism were the unique and inspired group who exposed all three sources of evil. It's why they have been largely ignored, as was Jesus, the greatest of the Jewish prophets. They didn't concentrate on the flesh, but largely on the world and what I just described as the devil, which very often passes as good and necessary evil. You see what we are up against and why evil continues to control so much of the human situation.

+Adapted from *Spiral of Violence: The World, the Flesh, and the Devil* (CD, MP3)

THE INVISIBLE SPIRAL OF VIOLENCE

If you cannot recognize evil on the level of what I call the world—then the flesh and the devil are inevitable consequences. They will soon be out of control, and everything is just trying to put out brush fires on already parched fields. The world or the system is the most hidden, the most disguised, and the most denied—but foundational—level of evil. It's the way cultures, groups, institutions, and nations organize themselves to survive.

It is not wrong to survive, but for some reason group egocentricity is never seen as evil when you have only concentrated on individual egocentricity (the flesh). That is how our attention has been diverted from the whole spiral of violence. The devil then stands for all of the ways we legitimate, enforce, and justify our group egocentricity (most wars; idolization of wealth, power, and show; tyrannical governments; and many penal systems), while not now calling it egocentricity, but necessity!

Once any social system exists, it has to maintain and assert itself at all costs. Things we do inside that system are no longer seen as evil because everyone is doing it. That's why North Koreans can march lockstep to a communist tyranny, and why American consumers can shop till they drop and make no moral connections whatsoever. You see now why most evil is hidden and denied, and why Jesus said, "Father forgive them, they don't know what they are doing" (Luke 23:34). We don't.

+Adapted from *Spiral of Violence: The World, the Flesh, and the Devil* (CD, MP3)

HIDDEN SOCIAL AGREEMENTS
REMAIN UNCRITIQUED

In Paul, it is clear that the second level of sin, the flesh, is individual sin, personal naughtiness, personal mistakes, and there is no denying that plenty of this evil exists in the world. When we point our finger at the second level of the spiral of violence, blaming individuals, punishing this person or that person, making people feel guilty because they are bad, we are mostly wasting our time unless we also critique the other two also. History will never change by such a one-shot-at-a-time approach. The underlying agreements are still in place. There is no point in telling a teenage girl she should not be vain or a young boy he should not be greedy when we all admire and agree upon these very things as a culture and when prelates and popes can be vain and greedy—but all for the welfare of the Church.

Up to now there has been little attention paid to the social systems that we uncritically accept—and the evil things they do. One of the great favors John Paul II did was to introduce into Catholic theology the terms "structural evil," "institutionalized sin," and "corporate evil." In that he was very prophetic, because that is the primary way that the biblical prophets spoke. Over 90 percent of their condemnations were of Israel itself, of wars, alliances, corrupt business practices, and a greedy priesthood in the Temple. They first named systemic evil, and then hoped the individual person could repent, and then the devil would have little chance of taking over because hidden evil had been exposed. Evil must be nipped in the bud, or it is always too late.

+Adapted from *Spiral of Violence: The World, the Flesh, and the Devil* (CD, MP3)

THE REAL DEVIL

When the first level of the spiral of violence, the world (group selfishness), is not exposed for what it is, and the second level, the flesh, operates out of control (murder, stealing, rape, lying, adultery, and greed), then a third level of fully justified and even idealized evil usually emerges. These are systems like oppressive governments, penal systems, legal systems, military systems, economic systems, and all the other systems we create to control disorder and violence. They ordinarily have a complete life of their own. These can, of course, be good, too. But when you worship them, when you let them have total power, when you refuse to critique these systems, they can wreak the greatest havoc in history—and they consistently have. Any system that says, "bow down and worship me" (Matthew 4:9) is *always* diabolical, whether it be church, state, the military, or the market.

The devil's secret is camouflage. The devil's job is to look very moral! It has to look like we are defending some great purpose or cause, like making the world safe for democracy or keeping the bad people off the streets. Then you can do many evils without any guilt, without any shame or self-doubt, but actually with a sense of high-minded virtue. Evil "must disguise itself as good," says St. Thomas Aquinas, and until Christians start understanding that, their capacity for "discernment of spirits" (1 Corinthians 12:10) remains very minimal. They are easily duped and always misled by such devils.

+Adapted from *Spiral of Violence: The World, the Flesh, and the Devil* (CD, MP3)

THE DEVIL, PART II

Be gone from me, Satan, you are to worship and serve God alone!
— Matthew 4:10

The third level of the spiral of violence, "the devil," will become absolutely necessary for survival once you have agreed to worship the foundational system. Such devils will not usually look like devils, except to those who are excluded because of them. (*The poor and marginalized see the devil first and most clearly. They have the power to reveal a culture's actual gods and their blindness!*) For most people, whatever system feeds and protects them, or panders to their superiority, is above criticism and, therefore, good. That is all they have and the highest they can think. They do not have their citizenship elsewhere, as Paul says (Philippians 3:20), or their heart is not yet interested in the Reign of God.

For most people, their only citizenship is here, and this is the citizenship they are defending. Not "all of God's people," but just "my people, which God most cares about." Whatever status quo benefits them is the full and final good. Pollsters know this is the way most people will vote. How foolish and how blind this is! Jesus showed no undue loyalty to his religion or to his country but radically critiqued both of them whenever they demanded to be worshiped. I challenge you to find one patriotic statement from Jesus. (The one that most people wrongly use about "giving to Caesar" [Mark 12:17] is actually a total dismissal of Caesar's rights in comparison to God's rights.)

+Adapted from *Spiral of Violence: The World, the Flesh, and the Devil* (CD, MP3)

THE WHOLE POINT

To more fully understand the concept of the Christ, we must be ready to receive a mystery that is just too good to be true. God is saving everything and everybody until, as Paul says, "Christ will be all in all" (1 Corinthians 15:28). Or, as St. Augustine put it, "In the end there will only be Christ, loving himself." Now this may sound like a shocking statement at first, but we are talking on a mystical and cosmological level about where history is going. Most of us did fairly well with the passion and death of the individual Jesus, but any comprehensive theology of what we mean by the Risen Christ has not really been developed. Some individuals seem to have gotten saved, but surely not the cosmos itself. Yet the precise genius of Jewish revelation is that it was a salvation of history itself, not just of persons. (Read the prophets and compare how often they speak to Israel as a whole corporate personality compared to a mere Jezebel or Azariah—probably ten to one!)

Christ is the code word for all of creation, all of humanity, what God has anointed (*Christened*) with love. The New Testament says that we are the first fruits or adopted sons and daughters of the one who first fully carried this awesome truth. Jesus is the symbolic firstborn Son (who fully accepts and believes what his Jewish Scriptures told him), and we all share in his same inheritance. That is the whole point! To use the language of the Pauline school in the Letter to the Ephesians: "Before the world began, we were chosen in Christ to live through love in his presence" (1:4–6).

Yes, Christ is a larger, older, and longer existence than Jesus of Nazareth. Yet Jesus's great act of love, courage, and surrender was precisely to let go of his Jesus so that Christ could arise and move forward, carrying all of us in his sweep. Pagans, Hindus, and Abraham and Sarah were objectively part of this one Eternal Christ Mystery. Forgive my seeming arrogance, but again—that is the whole point!

+Adapted from *The Cosmic Christ* (CD, MP3)

THE COSMIC CHRIST

In Paul's Letter to the Colossians, we have the premier texts of the evolving concepts of the *Cosmic Christ*: "He is the image of the invisible God, the firstborn of all creation" (Colossians 1:15). Did you get that? The firstborn of *all* creation! So what happened in him, and what it means to be born again, is to be born into this new experience. He was the firstborn and we are the second-born. "For in him all things were created, things in heaven and on earth" (Colossians 1:16). Here we have the Cosmic Christ. He is not just saving human beings, but all of creation is included—earth, birds, and animals, too.

Now we have a truly Cosmic Christ. Now we have a notion of salvation that includes everybody and everything that exists on this planet. Finally history coheres and "in him all things hold together" (Colossians 1:17).

+Adapted from *The Cosmic Christ* (CD, MP3)

THOMAS

The doors were closed where the disciples were gathered
for fear of the Jews.
— John 20:19

God has grown accustomed to our small and cowardly ways of waiting behind *closed doors* of fear and self-doubt. God knows that we settle for easy certitudes and common fears instead of Gospel freedom, for a very small god instead of a Big Mystery. Yet God seems surely determined to break through: "And Jesus came and stood in their midst, and said 'Peace!'" (John 20:26)

The Spirit eventually overcomes the obstacles that we present and surrounds us with enough peace so that we can, like the first doubting Thomas, touch and accept the "wounds in [Jesus's] hands and his side" (John 20:27)—which is really to accept his own woundedness—and the frailty of all created being. Until we know that the Christ is wounded too, we seem unable to accept that this might be the shape of all reality. His wound, of course, is his standing act of solidarity with all of suffering creation.

+Adapted from *Radical Grace: Daily Meditations*, pp. 192–193

LENIN AND FRANCIS

Shortly before he died, Lenin is supposed to have said that if the Russian Revolution were to take place over again, he would have asked for ten Francises of Assisi rather than more Bolsheviks. He eventually realized that something imposed by domination and violence from above only creates the same mirrored response from below. It is just a matter of time. He realized that the only communism that would ever be helpful to the world was the voluntary and joyous simplicity of a Francis of Assisi. (As a Franciscan, I am indeed a communist, as we share all things equally and from a common purse.) That element of the practice of the early Church (Acts 2:44) and of Jesus (John 13:29) was never expected of the rest of us. (One does wonder why some things become mandated from one mention by Jesus, and other things are totally forgotten.)

Voluntary simplicity was normally not lived by the clergy—certainly not the higher clergy—and therefore why would we, or how could we, ask it of the rest of the Church? Jesus was training the leaders first, because you can only ask of others what you yourselves have done. He was initiating them as spiritual elders, much more than ordaining them as priests (which is an Old Testament word never used for his apostles) or Church ministers. Francis *tried* to correct that by refusing ordination and also by his rush toward simplicity.

Once we saw the clerical state as a place of advancement instead of downward mobility, once ordination was not a form of initiation but a continuation of patriarchal patterns, the authentic preaching of the Gospel became the exception rather than the norm—whether Orthodox, Catholic, or Protestant. The first human demon that normally needs to be exposed is the human addiction to power, prestige, and possessions. These tend to pollute everything.

Once we preach the true Gospel, I doubt we are going to fill the churches.

+Adapted from *A Lever and a Place to Stand: The Contemplative Stance, the Active Prayer*, pp. 95–96

A NECESSARY PENDULUM

If we look at history, I think we can see a constant swinging back and forth between two poles, right and left, representing two necessary values. Those two necessary values have something to do with the first task of life (building the container) and the second task of life (filling it with contents), but they also need and feed one another. One emphasizes continuity and authority in a culture (conservatives) and the other emphasizes change and reform in that same culture (progressives).

The first task seeks order, certitude, clarity, and control. It is the best way to start. But whenever that pattern is in place for too long or is too overbearing, what will eventually emerge is a critical alternate consciousness. Whenever the law-and-order thing is overdone, another group of people will react against it. Once you have an establishment, you will eventually have a *dis*-establishment. When some have all the power, those who don't have power ask very different questions, and the pendulum swings back again—eventually. That has been the story of most of history and the sequencing of most revolutions. It is understandable and predictable, although the extremism on both sides could be avoided if we had more initiated elders who held the middle.

+Adapted from *A Lever and a Place to Stand: The Contemplative Stance, the Active Prayer*, pp. 96–97

RIGHT AND LEFT

It is interesting that these two different powers took the words *right* and *left* from the *Estates-General* in France. On the right sat the nobility and the clergy (what were the clergy doing over there?) and on the left sat the peasants and 90 percent of the population. Those are now commonly used terms in the global political world. The right is normally concerned with maintaining some status quo, stability, continuity, and authority; that is a legitimate need, and without it, you have chaos. Those on the right, however, are normally considered innocent until proven guilty.

Those on the left are presumed, for some reason, to be guilty until proven innocent, at least in the minds of many. (Note how the Vatican goes to great length to reconcile heretics on the right, but never the opposite.) The powers that have tended to write history have usually been from the side of authority and power, and those who protect power and authority. Once we see this, we wonder why we never saw it before. Without some form of right, we have chaos in society, and without some form of left, there is no truth and reform in a culture. Thomas Jefferson said, "God forbid we should ever be twenty years without a rebellion," or the American experiment would become its own new tyranny. And thus the pendulum swings, and I guess we all hope we are living at the appropriate time when it is swinging toward our preferred side, or there are at least a few elders around.

+Adapted from *A Lever and a Place to Stand: The Contemplative Stance, the Active Prayer*, p. 97

THE KINGLY VERSUS THE PROPHETIC

In the biblical tradition, the power on the right and the power on the left are symbolized by the kings and the prophets, respectively. There is almost a necessary tension and even opposition between them. There is only one time in all the Hebrew Scriptures that those two ever made friends, and then only barely. That is when David the king accepted the critique of Nathan the prophet after Nathan accused him of his sinfulness, and David had the humility to say that he was correct: "I have sinned against the Lord" (see 2 Samuel 12).

The right always considers itself the product of rationality, experience, and civilization. The people on the left are always the product of these silly people's movements arising out of high-minded ideology, unbearable injustices, or both. Neither of these currents is totally rational (even the Supreme Court disagrees on what is rational). Movements from the left are normally not well-planned at the beginning. They are intuitive and come from what is suffered by the little people, who at that point are of no account and have no press or status. Thus, they rely on symbols, songs, slogans, and momentary charismatic leaders to get off the ground. Remember when white people laughed at black people for singing "We Shall Overcome"? Remember also those naïve English colonists on the east coast of America who said, "No taxation without representation." The pattern is always the same: kings (power) versus prophets (truth).

+Adapted from *A Lever and a Place to Stand: The Contemplative Stance, the Active Prayer*, pp. 97–98

BIBLE BREAKS THE PATTERN

The point that must be remembered is that most of political and Church history has been controlled and written by people on the right because they are normally the people in control. *One of the few subversive texts in history, believe it or not, is the Bible.* The Bible is a most extraordinary text because, again and again, it legitimates not the people on the top, but invariably the people on the bottom or those who move toward those on the bottom—from Abraham to Moses to Jeremiah to Job to John the Baptist to Jesus. It has taken an amazing degree of denial and selective attention to miss this quite obvious alternative pattern.

After a while you might get tired of the rejected son, the younger son, the barren woman, the sinner, the outsider always being the chosen one of God! It is *the* biblical pattern—which we prefer *not* to see. It takes away our power to exclude "the least of the brothers and sisters" because that is precisely where Jesus says he is to be found (Matthew 25:40)! If indeed women, blacks, other religions, gays, and other outsiders are least in our definition, it seems that gives them, in fact, a privileged and revelatory position! They are not to be excluded but honored. Jesus takes away from us any possibility of creating any class system or any punitive notion from religion. Unfortunately, thus far, it has not worked very well.

+Adapted from *A Lever and a Place to Stand: The Contemplative Stance, the Active Prayer*, pp. 98–99

HOW FOOLISHLY WE GUARD OUR NOTHING

Less than a block from where I used to live in downtown Albuquerque, there is a sidewalk where the homeless often sit against the wall to catch the winter sun. Once I saw fresh graffiti chalked clearly on the pavement in front of the homeless. It said, "I watch how foolishly man guards his nothing—thereby keeping us out. Truly God is hated here." (I returned to copy the quote exactly because it felt both prophetic and poetic at the same time.)

I can only imagine what kind of life experience enabled some person to write in such a cutting but truthful way. I understood anew why Jesus seemed to think that the expelled ones had a head start in understanding his message. Usually they have been expelled from what was unreal anyway—the imperial systems of culture, which always create those who are in and those who are out, victors and victims.

In God's reign, everything belongs, even the broken and poor parts. Until we have admitted this in our own souls, we will usually perpetuate exclusionary systems and dualistic thinking in the outer world of politics and class, sometimes even in the Church.

+Adapted from *Everything Belongs: The Gift of Contemplative Prayer*, p.16

EMOTION

We must go through the stages of feeling, not only in the last death of anything but all the earlier little deaths. If we abort these emotional stages by easy answers, all they do is take a deeper form of disguise and come out in another way. So many people learn that the hard way—by suffering from ulcers or depression, finding themselves victim to chronic irritability or misdirected anger, or by succumbing to all sorts of psychosomatic illnesses—because they refuse to let their emotions run their course, honor them consciously, or find some appropriate place to share them.

Emotions are not right or wrong, good or bad. They are merely indicators of what is happening, and must be listened to, usually in the body. *People who do not feel deeply finally do not know or love deeply either.* It is the price we pay for loving. Like Job, we must be willing to feel our emotions and come to grips with the mystery in our heads, our hearts and, yes, our bodies, too. To be honest, that takes an entire lifetime. My emotions are still a mystery to me; without contemplation, they would control me.

+Adapted from *Job and the Mystery of Suffering: Spiritual Reflections*, pp. 54–55

EMOTIONAL FREEDOM

All great spirituality teaches about letting go of what you don't need and who you are not. Often these are addictive feelings—and they are addictive. Then, when you can get little enough, naked enough, and poor enough, you'll find that the little place where you *really are* is ironically more than enough and is all that you need. At that place, you will have nothing to prove to anybody and nothing to protect from other people.

That place is called emotional freedom. It's the freedom of the children of God (Galatians 5:1). Such people can connect with everybody because they are not so attached to themselves, their hurts, memories, and neediness. To live from this place cuts the roots of violence at their very foundation, for now there is no irrational basis for fear or anger or self-protection or hatred. Negativity must be nipped in the bud—that is to say, *in the mind and in the emotions, or it will invariably lead to negative actions and behaviors*

+Adapted from *Healing Our Violence Through the Journey of
Centering Prayer* (CD)

REAL TRANSFORMATION

Bernard McGinn says that mysticism is "a consciousness of the presence of God that by definition exceeds description and...*deeply transforms the subject who has experienced it.*" If it does not deeply change the lifestyle of the person—world view, economics, politics, and ability to form community—you have no reason to believe it is genuine mystical experience. It is often just people with an addiction to religion itself, which is not that uncommon.

Mysticism is not just a change in some religious ideas or affirmations, but it is *an encounter of such immensity that everything else shifts in position.* Mystics have no need to exclude or eliminate others precisely because they have experienced radical inclusivity of themselves into something much bigger. They do not need to define themselves as enlightened or superior, whereas a mere transfer of religious assertions often makes people even more elitist and more exclusionary.

True mystics are glad to be common, ordinary, servants of all, and just like everybody else, because any need for specialness has been met once and for all.

+Adapted from *Following the Mystics through the Narrow Gate....
Seeing God in All Things* (CD, DVD, MP3)

TO WHICH SYSTEM AM I INDEBTED?

When we demand satisfaction of one another, when we demand any completion to history on our terms, when we demand that our anxiety or any dissatisfaction be taken away, saying as it were, "Why weren't you this for me?" or "Why didn't life do that for me?" we are refusing to say, "Come, Lord Jesus." We are refusing to hold out for the *full picture* that is always given in time by God.

When we set out to seek our private happiness, we often create an idol that is sure to topple. Any attempts to protect any full and private happiness in the midst of so much public suffering have to be based on illusion about the nature of the world in which we live. We can only do that if we block ourselves from a certain degree of reality and refuse solidarity with the other side of everything, even the other side of ourselves.

+Adapted from *Preparing for Christmas with Richard Rohr*, pp. 5, 7

THERE ARE MANY WAYS TO EXPERIENCE GOD

A very little bit of God goes an awfully long way. When another's experience of God isn't exactly the way I would describe it, it doesn't mean that they haven't had an experience of God or that their experience is completely wrong. We have to remain with Francis's prayer: "Who are you, God, and who am I?" Isn't there at least 10 percent of that person's experience of God that I can agree with? Can't I at least say, "I wish I could experience God in that way"?

What characterizes anyone who has had just a little bit of God is that they always want more of that experience! Could it not be that this Hindu, this Sufi, this charismatic, this Jewish woman has, in fact, touched upon the same eternal Mystery that I am seeking? Can't we at least give one another the benefit of the doubt? I can be somewhat patient with people who think they have the truth. The problem for me is when they think they have the *whole* truth.

The mystic probably represents the old shibboleth, "Those who really know don't speak too quickly. Those who speak too quickly don't really know."

+Adapted from *Following the Mystics through the Narrow Gate....*
Seeing God in All Things (CD, DVD, MP3)

CHRISTMAS IS ALREADY EASTER

Easter, not Christmas, was the big celebration for the first twelve hundred years of Christianity.

It was the Franciscans who popularized (and sentimentalized) Christmas. For Francis, if the Incarnation was true, then Easter took care of itself. He taught us to celebrate Jesus's birth and probably created the custom of the *crèche* or nativity scene. To his normally fasting friars, he said "Even the walls should eat meat on Christmas Day!" Incarnation was already redemption for him. Once God became a human being, then nothing human or worldly was abhorrent to God. The problem of distance or separation was resolved forever.

Resurrection is incarnation coming to its logical conclusion. If God is already in everything, then everything is *from* glory and *unto* glory. We're all saved by mercy, without exception. We're all saved by grace, so there's no point in distinguishing degrees of worthiness because God alone is all good, and everything else in creation participates in that one, universal goodness to varying degrees. There is no absolute dividing line between worthy and unworthy people in the eyes of God, because all our worthiness is merely participation in God's.

+For more on Franciscan mysticism, consider
The Great Chain of Being (CD, DVD, MP3)

GOD DOES JUSTICE BY RESTORING THINGS
INSTEAD OF PUNISHING THEM

The Spirit of the Lord God is upon me…he has sent me to bring good
news to the oppressed, to bind up the brokenhearted, to proclaim
liberty to the captives, and release to the prisoners.
— Isaiah 61:1

In this reading from Isaiah, the prophet describes the coming Servant of
Yahweh. It is precisely this quote that Jesus first uses to announce the exact
nature of his own ministry (Luke 4:18–19). In each case, Jesus describes his
work as reuniting things that have in any way lost their divine state, or been
marginalized or demeaned by society.

Jesus's ministry is not to gather the so-called good into a private country
club and punish the outsiders, but to reach out to those on the edge and
on the bottom, those who are last, to tell them they might just be first!
That is almost the very job description of the Holy Spirit and, therefore, of
Jesus. Some call it God's unique kind of justice or "restorative justice." God
justifies things *by restoring them to their true and full identity in himself*, as
opposed to retributive justice, which seeks only reward and punishment.
To receive unearned love is their only punishment.

+Adapted from *Preparing for Christmas with Richard Rohr*, pp. 36–37

WAS THE CROSS A CAPITULATION TO EVIL?

Darkness will never totally go away. I've worked long enough in ministry to know that moral evil isn't going to disappear, but the Gospel offers something much more subtle and helpful: "The light shines on the inside of the darkness, and the darkness will not overcome it" (John 1:5).

Such is the Christian form of yin and yang, our own belief in paradox and mystery.

We must all hope and work to eliminate darkness, especially in many of the great social issues of our time: We wish we could eliminate world hunger. We wish we could stop wasting the earth's resources on armaments. We wish we could stop killing people from womb to tomb.

But at a certain point, we have to surrender to the fact that the darkness is part of reality, and my logical mind does not know why. But the only real question becomes how to trust the light, receive the light, and spread the light. That is not a capitulation to evil any more than the cross was a capitulation to evil. It is real transformation into the unique program of the crucified and Risen Christ. This is the "reproducing of the pattern of his death" (Philippians 3:10) that redeems and transforms evil instead of punishing evil or even thinking we can eliminate it entirely. Our main job is to face it in ourselves and then absorb and reveal its tragic effects instead of inflicting it on others—redemptive sacrifice instead of the usual story line of redemptive violence.

+Adapted from *Preparing for Christmas with Richard Rohr*, p. 22

A WARNING TO RELIGION
FROM THE GARDEN OF EDEN

The sin warned against at the very beginning of the Bible is "to eat of the tree of the knowledge of good and evil" (Genesis 2:17). It does not sound like that should be a sin at all, does it? But the moment I sit on my throne, where I *know with certitude* who the good guys and the bad guys are, then I'm capable of great evil—while not thinking of it as evil! I have eaten of a dangerous tree, according to the Bible. Don't judge, don't label, don't rush to judgment. You *don't* usually know other people's real motives or intentions. You hardly know your own.

The author of the classic book *The Cloud of Unknowing* says that first you have to enter into "the cloud of forgetting." Forget all your certitudes, all your labels, all your explanations, whereby you've put this person in this box, this group is going to heaven, this race is superior to that race. Just forget it. It's largely a waste of time. It's usually your ego projecting itself, announcing itself, and protecting itself. It has little to do with objective reality or real love of the truth.

If the world and the world's religions do not learn this kind of humility and patience very soon, I think we're in historical trouble.

+Adapted from *Beginner's Mind* (CD, DVD, MP3)

"PEACE OF MIND" IS A CONTRADICTION IN TERMS

"Beginner's mind" is actually someone who's *not* in their mind at all! They are people who can immediately experience the naked moment apart from filtering it through any mental categories. Such women and men are capable of simple presence to what is right in front of them without "thinking" about it too much. This must be what Jesus means by little children already being in the kingdom of God (Matthew 18:3–4). They don't think much, they just experience the moment—good and bad. That teaching alone should have told us that Christianity was not supposed to be about believing doctrines and moralities. Children do not believe theologies or strive for moral certitudes. They respond vulnerably and openly to what is offered them moment by moment. This is pure presence, and is frankly much more demanding than securing ourselves with our judgments.

Presence cannot be easily defined. Presence can only be experienced. But I know this: *True presence to someone or something allows them or it to change me and influence me—before I try to change them or it!*

Beginner's mind is pure presence to each moment before I label it, critique it, categorize it, exclude it, or judge it up or down. That is a whole new way of thinking and living. It is the only mind that has the power to actually reform religion.

+Adapted from *Beginner's Mind* (CD, DVD, MP3)

PARACHURCH AS A NEW KIND OF REFORMATION

What some call "Emerging Christianity" has four common elements, in my opinion, even if they might be described in different ways:

There is a new honest, broad, and ecumenical Jesus scholarship. We are reading what theologians of all denominations are saying. And the amazing thing is that, at this level of scholarship at least, there is a strong consensus emerging about what Jesus really taught and emphasized.

There is a reemergence of a contemplative mind in all of the churches. It's not content with the dualistic mind that has dominated for the last five hundred years. Contemplation receives the whole field of the moment and lets such an open lens teach us—what we understand along with what we don't understand. Finally there is room for mystery and the acceptance of even being wrong or just partially right.

This consensus (both at the scholarly and experiential levels) is revealing that Jesus tended to emphasize very different things than present organized Christianity tends to emphasize. Present organized Christianity (in all denominations) tends to be preoccupied with things that Jesus never talked about *ever*, and sometimes even disagreed with.

New community structures and *new parallel church organizations* are often emerging and flourishing to make this possible. (The CAC would be an example of such a parachurch group, as well as hospice, Habitat for Humanity, various social service ministries, contemplative prayer groups, and volunteer and mission work.) None of these are in competition with Sunday religion, but they give us ways to actually do what we are told to do on Sunday. The emphasis is often orthopraxy (practice) instead of just repeating the orthodox creeds every Sunday.

+Adapted from the webcast *What Is the Emerging Church?* (CD, DVD, MP3)

A BROADENING GROUP OF
APOSTLES AND DISCIPLES

Much of Christian experience, from all of our groups, is acknowledging that it's mostly at the energetic level, the lifestyle level, the love level, that the mystery of Jesus is passed on; and not just getting the words right—or belonging to the correct group. I personally believe this is the deepest and truest meaning of apostolic succession, or how the Christ mystery is really passed from generation to generation. There is slight evidence that this is primarily done by bishops laying their hands on young men's heads.

Up to now, the hegemony on Christian teaching and theology was held by a very small and exclusive group: males, the educated, the Northern Hemisphere, those with a vested interest in organized religion, those who went to their own denominational seminaries, and nothing else.

Finally the neglected perspectives are having their day—the feminine lens, the lens of those on the bottom instead of just those on the top, the lens of blacks, Latinos, and Asians, the lens of sexual minorities and all minorities, the honest Jewish lens, the lens of the incarcerated, and even the lens of sincere secular seekers.

Truth, like beauty, is in the eye of the beholder. And we have a lot of new *beholders*.

+Adapted from the webcast *What Is the Emerging Church?* (CD, DVD, MP3)

SOME CONTEMPLATIVE HISTORY

The contemplative mind is really just the mind that emerges when you pray first instead of think first. Praying opens the field and moves beyond fear and judgment and agenda and analysis, and just lets the moment be what it is—as it is.

We really have to be taught that mind now. It was systematically taught—mostly in the monasteries—as late as the thirteenth and even into the fourteenth century. Plus agrarian, suffering, uneducated, and non–media-saturated people probably learned contemplation much more naturally. But once we got into the oppositional mind of the Reformation and the rational mind of the Enlightenment, the contemplative mind pretty much fell by the wayside. The wonderful thing is that it is now being rediscovered across the Christian spectrum, and there is no select group that holds it or that teaches it, although we Catholics have easier historical access to it, as do the Orthodox if they were influenced by the *Philokalia*.

Contemplation also links us with the Native and Eastern religions, which often held on to the contemplative mind much better than we did in the Western world, which was formed by Greek logic, Roman upward mobility, and a whole bunch of technological advantages that left us enthralled with our ability to perform and achieve.

+Adapted from the webcast *What Is the Emerging Church?* (CD, DVD, MP3)

DO CONSUMER LIFESTYLES
AND MILITARISM GO TOGETHER?

Many things that Christians feel are nonnegotiable today are at major variance with what Jesus actually taught and emphasized. How can you read the Eight Beatitudes and the Sermon on the Mount, for example, and not know that Jesus clearly taught nonviolence and simplicity of life?

Wouldn't you think the clear nonnegotiable item in Jesus's teaching is forgiveness and love of enemies? But we didn't emphasize that at all. That could've changed history. But we weren't interested in changing this world. We were more interested in the next world, and we ended up acting pretty much like everybody else *in this world*. None of the Christian nations have a record for peacemaking. We have to honor our Mennonite, Amish, and Quaker brothers and sisters who, thank God, retained the peace witness of the church and in many cases, also a nonconsumer, simple lifestyle. I have a feeling they go together!

Emerging Christianity is necessarily ecumenical, and not trapped inside of any one denomination and its historical biases, accidents, and limits. We Roman Catholics now recognize that our church, aligned in most of its history with the Roman Empire, had no freedom or ability to hear Jesus's clear teaching on love of enemies or nonviolence.

+Adapted from the webcast *What Is the Emerging Church?* (CD, DVD, MP3)

EUCHARIST AS NEW SOCIAL ORDER

Jesus was consistently inclusive. *You* try to find an example where Jesus intentionally excludes anyone. He will name their relationships honestly and correctly, but he never creates in groups and out groups and, in fact, moves in the very opposite direction.

Yet the common image of most Christian denominations is that they are largely exclusionary institutions. How did we ever get to this point? I think it is because most church people, and their leaders, have never transcended the early egocentric level of life.

Even the Eucharist itself is still used, at least in my Catholic Church, to define the worthy, the pure, and the true members, or as a reward for good behavior. Where did this come from? And we do it right after piously mumbling at Catholic Mass "Lord I am not worthy." But I guess we think we still really are! Almost every time Jesus eats, he seems to be eating with the wrong people, at the wrong table, saying the wrong things, or not washing his hands ahead of time. By doing so, Jesus potentially rearranged the social order, because *meal etiquette defined and maintained the social order and social class*, and this is surely what upset both religion and state. Eucharist still could and will redefine social relationships, but we have not had a lot of success up to now. When I was growing up we had white churches, Mexican churches, and black churches, all proclaiming their fervent belief in the Real Presence of Jesus—in their safe, separate groups. And some dare to say we did not need the reforms of Vatican II.

+Adapted from the webcast *What Is the Emerging Church?* (CD, DVD, MP3)

THE PRACTICE OF THE BETTER

Any new structures of emerging Christianity cannot be *in opposition* to any existing church structures or anybody at all. Any antagonistic action merely creates an equal and opposite reaction. "The best criticism of the bad is the practice of the better" is one of our core principles at the CAC. Just do it better yourself, and don't waste any time criticizing others or the past! This, in fact, purifies your own commitment and motivation.

Don't bother being against anybody, anything, any group, or any institution. That will only keep you at a low level of ego, while falsely feeling superior. It is a most common mistake. You can, however, practice simple avoidance or quiet noncooperation with immature organizations, but don't waste time or energy being oppositional to anything. We need positive energy now over negative criticism of anything. It is almost as if consciousness has now grown up to see this—and do this!

+Adapted from the webcast *What Is the Emerging Church?* (CD, DVD, MP3)

OUR RELIGIOUS ORDERS WERE ALWAYS "PARACHURCH" ORGANIZATIONS

The new structures for any "emerging church" have to be parallel and symbiotic with the existing church structures, not in opposition to or in competition with anything or any other group!

Let me name just a few of these mediating institutions:

Prayer groups and contemplative prayer groups

Bible study groups and book study groups

Service groups and volunteerism of every type

Mission groups

*Just*Faith groups and social service agencies

The New Monastics and the New Friars

This is quite new and amazing. Most of these people have *not* left their historic moorings. They just *pay attention to different things*. They have found a symbiotic relationship between their mother churches and their own specific calling, just as religious orders always did in the Catholic Church. As a Franciscan, I have been a part of such a parachurch group for most of my life.

+Adapted from the webcast *What Is the Emerging Church?* (CD, DVD, MP3)

MANY GIFTS AND MANY MINISTRIES

Another exciting piece of the emerging church is that, for the first time perhaps, we've stopped emphasizing and idealizing the top. We are beginning to recognize actual operative gifts and real ministry to God's world as in the early church (Ephesians 4:11–13; 1 Corinthians 12:4–30), instead of just being preoccupied with getting formally ordained or academic certification—not that there isn't a place for such things. I probably would never have had the access I did if I had not been ordained and "certified," especially in my young years.

But the first question is not just, "Is she trained in theology?" or "Is he ordained?" The first question can also be "Can she do the job?" or "Is he changing lives?" or "Is it working?" Most of us were ordained without ever having led a single person to conversion, transformation, or even spiritual health. What evidence did any bishop have that we were gifted for ministry? It was too often a decision for security and status, a sincere career move, but not really a recognition of any actual gift for service.

We are beginning to support lay leadership—competence itself being more important than role, office, costume, or title. In that light, the very terms *layman* or *laywoman* begin to be a real misperception and misnomer of what is happening.

+Adapted from the webcast *What Is the Emerging Church?* (CD, DVD, MP3)

AN INCLUSIVE RELIGION

The standing, structural proof that Christianity was intended to be *an inclusive religion* is that two thirds of our Christian Bible is, in fact, the Jewish Bible! Why don't more people see this obvious message?

Further, our entire Bible is filled with stories, metaphors, images, and even names for God that were taken from pre-Jewish religions, pagan sources, secular history, and Greek philosophy. We are more exclusionary than the biblical writers were! As Paul says to the Athenians "You already worshiped God without knowing it" (Acts 17:23).

Any myth of a pure, single, and unadulterated source for divine revelation is a pure myth itself! Yet naïve Christians still want to make their recent version of Christianity totally exclusionary and elitist in relationship to all other revelations of God. This is untrue to their declared history, sources, and theology.

When we are true to our Jewish sources, Jesus himself is easily seen as an *inclusive* Son of God (inviting us to join him there!), and not the exclusive Son of God that we made him into. It seems we found it much easier to worship him than to imitate him.

TRANSFORMATION

The separate self is the problem, whereas most religion and most people make the shadow self the problem. This leads to denying, pretending, and projecting instead of real transformation into the Divine.

INTRODUCTION

The problem of ego is so recurring in different religions, through successive periods of history and under various disguises, that we know we are dealing with some foundational and core issue, and one that must be almost unconscious. It is an issue that cannot be dealt with by simply being moral about this or that, or joining the right group; but by a fundamental dying, which almost all of us are afraid to do. As Jesus himself says in any number of ways: "Unless the grain of wheat dies, it remains just a single grain, but if it dies, it bears much fruit" (John 12:24). This is why I continue to say that moralism is always the cheap substitute for mysticism (or mature religion).

Since the twentieth century we have used the word *ego* (Latin for "I") to describe this rather total identification with one's own single grain as the reference point for life and perception. All great spiritual teachers will tell you that your small self is not the reference point for anything lasting or substantial at all, but only for a small memory bank of experiences, *my* feelings, and *my* temporary self-image—all too small and not a fitting reference point for big truth or reality. Paul, in an unfortunate choice of words called it "the flesh," and much of Hinduism and Buddhism would have called it "illusion" or even "emptiness." Thomas Merton and many of us call it the "false self."

Until this autonomous self is somehow dismantled as a worthy receiver station, one cannot get very far in spiritual seeing. You are too small at this point, and the God you will find will be made to fit inside of that smallness. Your own issues, your personal hurts, and your self-image will, on the other hand, be far too big, too exaggerated, and too grandiose—trying to overcompensate for such lack of perspective and substance. Your feeling world will be all about you, because it has no other center of gravity except what you feel moment by moment, and year by year—all of which is shifting sand.

So what happens at the early levels, which is where we all have to start, is that we look for something else to die instead of ourselves! We normally choose a specific behavior, an action, a place, a substitute sacrifice, or a body part to eliminate instead of our false self, which ironically is going to die anyway. This area, defined differently by each person and group, is what we mean by one's *shadow*. Your shadow self becomes your enemy, and is usually plausible things like sex, drugs, and rock and roll. There are often, of course, good reasons for tackling these concerns. But "the issue" is not really the issue! Tackling them does not of itself lead you to love of God, love of neighbor, the Gospel, love in general, or even truth.

Yet we persist in attacking the shadow because, frankly, it is a bit easier than dying to who we think we are, or who we need to be, or who we just want to be! And it gives one a false sense of moral high ground. In other words, *religion at the early levels largely substitutes superficial shadow boxing for significant death to the false self.* It can continue for much of your life and never achieve anything except more and more ego control of the shadow—which makes you more and more anal retentive—and in a most disguised kind of way only strengthens your egocentricity. You are trying to drive out the devil in a most devilish way. This is the garden-variety religion that much of the world dislikes and mistrusts. And it should.

This, in a word, is why immature religion creates such immature, but highly defended people. To use Jesus's brilliant metaphor, "You clean the outside of the cup, and not the inside...whereas if you clean the inside—the outside takes care of itself" (Matthew 23:25–26).

AN INCONVENIENT TRUTH FOR MUCH RELIGION

It is really shocking how little Jesus is shocked by human failure and sin. In fact, it never appears that he is upset at sinners at all. He is only and consistently upset at people *who do not think they are sinners*. This momentous insight puts him centuries ahead of modern psychology and right at the center of rare but authentic religion. So much so, that most Christianity itself never notices or addresses this pattern. It is an inconvenient truth.

Early stage religion is largely driven by ego needs: the need to be right, the need to feel morally superior, the need to be safe, and the need to project a positive image to others. At that point, religion has little to do with any real search for God; it is almost entirely a search for oneself, which is necessary—and which God surely understands. But we do this by trying to repress and deny our actual motivations and goals. These are pushed into the unconscious and called *the shadow self.* The shadow is not the bad self, but simply the denied or rejected self, which is totally operative but allowed to work in secret—and never called to accountability from that hidden place.

In my forty-two years as a priest, it has been clear to me that most people (not just religious people) focus on denying their shadow self—to keep feeling good about themselves—and their ego then enjoys a perpetual holiday. It is a massive misplacement of spiritual attention. You can be a prelate or priest in the Church with a totally inflated ego, while all your energy goes into denying and covering up your shadow—which then gets projected everywhere else. What you don't transform, you will transmit.

JESUS AS PSYCHOLOGIST

Jesus, particularly in Matthew's Gospel, shows himself to precede the psychologists Jung and Freud by hundreds of years, with several of his extremely insightful teachings on shadow work: (1) the metaphors of "log in your own eye and seeing the splinter in your neighbor's eye" (Matthew 7:3–5), (2) the teaching that "the eye is the lamp of the body" (Matthew 6:22–23), and (3) coming to terms with your [inner] opponent before he can "take you to court and make you pay the last penny" (Matthew 5:25–26).

I would also like to point out a lesser-noted teaching that uses the imagery of Satan. It warns us against trying to cast out our demons, who find no place to occupy, and return to us "all swept and tidied" (Mark 12:44), and then bring with them "seven other demons," and we're worse than we were before. This to me is sheer psychological brilliance on Jesus's part, and people instead waste time arguing about whether demons really exist.

If you try to achieve a superior identity by projecting your demons onto other people or groups, and temporarily feel swept and tidied, you have only achieved a seeming and a very false victory. Your ego willfulness and your superiority complex are now even more disguised—from yourself. But they are still there, and now well-defended by a sense of purity. As Jesus's says in another place, you cannot "drive out Satan by Satan" for such a "divided house cannot stand" (Luke 11:17–18). We can only be reconciled to our shadow by honest admissions, and must never think we can dismiss it, deny it, or punish it. We cannot deny our ego, or it will only return in different forms.

CHANGE IS GOOD

Turn around and believe the good news!
—Jesus's first preached words, Mark 1:15

The authentic religious life is a matter of *becoming who we already are*, and *all* that we truly are! Can you imagine that? Is the seed already within you— of all that God wants you to be? Do you already know at some level who you authentically are? Are you willing to pay the price, even the mistrust of others? Could that be what we mean by having a unique soul? Most saints thus described the path as much more *unlearning* than learning. There are so many illusions and lies that we must all unlearn. And one of the last illusions to die is that we are that different or that separate. Finally we are all one and amazingly the same. Differentiation seems to precede union and communion for some strange reason.

This growing illumination is not just one "decision for Jesus." It is a whole journey of letting go and developing an ongoing practice of letting go, and turning around one more time, until it becomes a way of life. As the old Shakers use to sing and dance, "… turn, turn / will be our delight, / 'Till by turning / we come round right." To be authentically human is to change, and to be a whole human is to change many times—away from my smallness and toward an Unspeakable Greatness—which itself is never fully attained.

TRANSCEND AND INCLUDE

Bill Plotkin speaks of the first half of life as doing our "survival dance." The second half of life can then become our "sacred dance." Most of us never get beyond our survival dance to ask the deep concerns of the soul (we are too busy saving our souls, whatever that means!) and to do our sacred dance. Money, status symbols, group identity, and security are of limited value; but to the soul they are a distraction, and finally they become the very problem itself.

However, don't misunderstand me—and I say this as strongly as I can— you've got to go through this first half of life and its concerns. Every level of growth builds on the previous ones. The principle is this: *transcendence means including the previous stages.* Then you can see the limited— but real—value of the early stages. But you will no longer put too much energy into just looking good, making money, feeling secure at all costs, and making sure you are right and others are wrong. That's what it means to grow up; and Jews, Muslims, and Christians need to grow up just like everybody else.

+Adapted from *Loving the Two Halves of Life: The Further Journey*
(CD, DVD, MP3)

THE RENT YOU PAY FOR BEING HERE

Only the great self, the True Self, the God Self, can carry our anxieties. The little self cannot do it. People who don't pray basically cannot live the Gospel, because the self is not strong enough to contain and reveal our delusions and our fear. I am most quoted for this line: "If you do not transform your pain, you will always transmit it."

Always someone else has to suffer because I don't know how to suffer; that is what it comes down to. Jesus, you could say, came to show us how to suffer, how to carry "the legitimate pain of being human," as Jung called it. Beware of running from yourself and your own legitimate suffering, which is the price of being a human being in a limited world.

+Adapted from *A Lever and a Place to Stand: The Contemplative Stance, the Active Prayer*, pp. 79–80

CULTURE'S HABITUAL WORLD IS MERITOCRACY

The key to entering into the Divine Exchange is never our worthiness but always God's graciousness. Any attempt to measure or increase our worthiness will always fall short, or it will force us into the position of denial and pretend, which produces the constant perception of hypocrisy in religious people.

To switch to an economy of grace is a switch that is very hard for humans to make. We base almost everything in human culture on achievement, performance, accomplishment, an equal exchange value, or some kind of worthiness gauge. I call it meritocracy. Unless one personally experiences a dramatic and personal breaking of the rules of merit (forgiveness or undeserved goodness), it is almost impossible to disbelieve or operate outside of its rigid logic. This cannot happen theoretically or abstractly. It cannot happen "out there" but must be known personally "in here."

+Adapted from *A Lever and a Place to Stand: The Contemplative Stance, the Active Prayer*, p. 45

A PRAYER

Loving God, we love how you love us. We love how you free us. We love what you have given and created to surround us. Help us to recognize, and to rejoice in, what has been given, even in the midst of what is not given. Help us not to doubt all that you have given us, even when we feel our very real shortcomings. We thank you for the promise and sign of your love in the Eternally Risen Christ, pervading all things in the universe, unbound by any of our categories of logic or theology.

We offer you ourselves back in return. We offer you our bodies, our little lives, our racing minds, and our restless hearts into this one wondrous circle of Love that is You. My life is no longer just about me, but it is all about *you*.

+Adapted from *Radical Grace: Daily Meditations*, p. 155

REST VERSUS ACHIEVEMENT

After an optimistic explosion that we call hope and an ensuing sense of deep safety, comes an experience of deep *rest*. It's the verb, I'm told, most used by the mystics of all religions: some kind of resting in God. All of our striving and our need to perform, climb, and achieve becomes, on some very real level, unnecessary. The gift, the presence, the fullness is already here, now. I can stop all this overproduction and over-proving of myself. That's Western and American culture. It's not the Gospel, and yet we have made the Gospel conform to the meritocracy of most cultures.

One thing that got me into men's work is that I found that males are especially driven by the performance principle. Most males just cannot believe that we could be respected, admired, received, or loved without some level of achievement. So many of us are performers and overachievers to some degree, and we think that only then will we be lovable or acceptable. Even when we achieve something with a good day of performing, as I often do myself as a type A personality, it is never enough, because it is inherently self-advancing and therefore self-defeating. We might call it "spiritual capitalism."

+Adapted from *Following the Mystics through the Narrow Gate....*
Seeing God in All Things (CD, DVD, MP3)

SLAMMING DOORS

We don't teach meditation to the young monks. They are not ready for it
until they stop slamming doors.
—Thich Nhat Hanh to Thomas Merton in 1966

The piercing truth of this statement struck me as a perfect way to communicate the endless disguises and devices of the false self. There is no more
clever way for the false self to hide than behind the mask of spirituality.
The human ego will always try to name, categorize, fix, control, and insure
all its experiences. For the ego, everything is a commodity. It lives inside of
self-manufactured boundaries instead of inside the boundaries of the Godself. It lives out of its own self-image instead of mirroring the image of God.
It is that superior self-image which must die.

The ego is constantly searching for any solid and superior identity. A
spiritual self-image gives us status, stability, and security. There is no better
way to remain unconscious than to baptize and bless the forms of religion,
even prayer itself. As long as I am going to church, it is really meaningless
whether I close the door quietly or slam the door. A spiritual master would
say, "First stop slamming doors, and then you can begin in the kinder-
garten of spirituality." Too many priests, bishops, and ministers are still
slamming doors, so how can we expect the laity to be any better?

In the name of seeking God, the ego pads and protects itself from self-
discovery, which is an almost perfect cover for its inherent narcissism. I
know this because I have done it all myself.

+Adapted from *Contemplation in Action*, pp. 79–80

AVAILABLE ABUNDANCE

You might ask, "How can I be more holy?" We don't have to make ourselves holy. We already are, and we just don't know it yet. In Christian terminology this inherent holiness is called the Divine Indwelling or the gift of the Holy Spirit. The awakening of the True Self in God is the essential, foundational, and primary task of all religion. Thus authentic religion is more about subtraction than addition, more letting go of the false self than any attempt at engineering our own True Self. You can't create what you already have.

We become the One we gaze upon. We are, eventually, just like the God we worship. This reciprocal gaze *is* the True Self, perfectly given to us, and always waiting to be perfectly received. It is so dear and so precious that it needs no external payoffs whatsoever. The True Self is abundantly content as it is.

+Adapted from *Contemplation in Action*, pp. 84–85

NOT AS WE IMAGINED

Jesus didn't move from Jesus to the eternal Cosmic Christ except through death and resurrection to a larger space and time. We don't move from our independent, historical body to the Christ consciousness without dying to our false self, either. As Stephen Levine says, death is the "imaginary loss of an imaginary self"—imaginary because it thinks it is separate.

We, like Jesus himself, have to let go of who we think we are, and who we think we need to be. "Dying at thirty? I am just getting started!" he must have thought. We have to let go of the passing names by which we have tried to name ourselves and become the "naked self before the naked God." That will always feel like dying, because we are so attached to our passing names and identities. Your bare, undecorated self is already and forever the beloved child of God. When you can rest there, you will begin to share in the universal Christ consciousness, the very "mind of Christ" (1 Corinthians 2:16).

+Adapted from *The Cosmic Christ* (CD, MP3)

MAKE SURE YOU ARE HUNGRY

Christ is the bread, awaiting hunger.
— St. Augustine

Eucharist is presence encountering presence—mutuality, vulnerability. There is nothing to prove, to protect, or to sell. It feels so empty, simple, and harmless that all you can do is be present. In most of Christian history we instead tried to understand and explain presence. As if we could.

The Eucharist is telling us that God is the food and all we have to do is provide the hunger. Somehow we have to make sure that each day we are hungry, that there's room inside of us for another presence. If you are filled with your own opinions, ideas, righteousness, superiority, or sufficiency, you are a world unto yourself and there is no room for another. Despite all our attempts to define who is worthy and who is not worthy to receive Communion, our only ticket or prerequisite for coming to Eucharist is hunger. And, most often, sinners are much hungrier than the so-called saints.

+Adapted from *Eucharist as Touchstone* (CD, MP3)

EATING YOUR TRUE SELF

Jesus says, "If you eat this bread you will live forever" (John 6:51). It is so interesting that he chooses taste, flavor, and nutrition as the symbol of how life is transferred and not intellectual cognition. If you live by the momentary identity that others give you, that's what dies when you die, and you're left with nothing. Your relative identity passes away, but it is like the painful erasing of an unwanted tattoo. When Jesus says he's giving himself to you as the bread of life, he's saying, as it were, "Find yourself in me, and this will not pass or change or die. Eat this food as your primary nutrition, and you are indestructible." This is your absolute and indestructible identity.

We all slowly learn how to live in what Thomas Merton would call the True Self—who you are and always have been, in God. Who you are in God is who you forever are. In fact, that's all you are, and it is more than enough. Everything else is passing away. Reputations, titles, possessions, and roles do not determine our identity. When I hand out the Eucharistic bread I love to say to the assembly, "You become what you eat. Come and eat who you are—forever!" You access Great Truth by absorption and digestion, almost never by analysis or argumentation.

+Adapted from *Eucharist as Touchstone* (CD, MP3)

THE PRICE OF INDIVIDUALISM

The West has made an art form of the individual person; it is one of our gifts to civilization, but we have paid a big price for this gift. Because of our over-identification with this autonomous self, we have overemphasized our separateness and uniqueness, leaving us trapped and alone. (Christians, who should know better, usually seek an entirely private notion of salvation instead of their *communion with everybody else*—which would be heaven here and now.)

What mature religion does is give us an experience of what Owen Barfield calls "full and final participation" in the mystery of God and creation. This means that *before* you identify with your separateness, *you identify with your union and participation in something larger than yourself.* This no longer comes naturally to us in the overdeveloped world; now we crawl back to our primal union with great difficulty. Some form of contemplative awareness will facilitate the process immensely. The private self we are overly conscious of, the self we are absorbed in, is the one that mystics say does not even *exist* as separate—at all! Buddhists would call this passing form "emptiness." Jesus would call it "the self that must die"—and it is going to die anyway in its illusion of separateness. So Jesus would say, "Go ahead and let it die now and then you will be free!"

+Adapted from *Jesus and Buddha: Paths to Awakening* (CD, DVD, MP3)

RELATIVE AND ABSOLUTE IDENTITY

Moving to the level of participative knowing is first of all a cellular experience, a full-body knowing. It is nothing you can prove merely with the mental ego. It is something you know by inner experience—by prayer, by love, and by suffering. Paul's line, quoted even by Buddhists, is "I live no longer, not 'I'; but I live with the life of Christ, who lives in me" (Galatians 2:20). Our little self that appears to be visible here and takes itself so seriously is merely a *relative identity* (whether good or bad); it is not our *absolute identity* that we are eternally in God.

The Buddhist idea of letting go of our attachment to our relative identity is almost identical to Jesus's teaching of *dying to our self* (or even "renouncing the self" as in Mark 8:34). Christians got themselves off of a necessary hook by thinking Jesus was talking about various forms of mortifications and little sacrifices, which were usually nothing more than rearranging the deck chairs on a Titanic that must and will sink. I must say it that strongly in hopes that you will hold out for a full-body knowing, and not just a minor knowing of yourself as sacrificial, generous, and therefore holy. Holiness is wholeness in God and not any private perfection. Psychological wholeness is never fully possible anyway.

+Adapted from *Jesus and Buddha: Paths to Awakening* (CD, DVD, MP3)

AT LEAST BUDDHISTS UNDERSTOOD
THE INDIVIDUAL DEATH

There are so many parallel quotes from Buddha and Jesus that it is clear they are coming from a similar level of consciousness. Their diagnosis of the human dilemma is also very similar. For example, humans are ignorant more than malicious, blind more than evil. As Jesus said on the cross, "Father, forgive them. They don't know what they are doing" (Luke 23:34). The vast majority of humanity lives in blindness about who it is, where it came from, and where it is going.

Both Buddha and Jesus were trying to give us a kind of cosmic shock about what is real and what is unreal—about what lasts and what doesn't last. Marcus Borg says he believes the only real difference in their teaching is the strong social and political undercutting that you find in Jesus. The Buddha is so insightful in recognizing the games that the ego (separate self) is playing and puts most of his emphasis there. The sad thing is that most of the social implications of Jesus's teaching have been consistently ignored because we didn't want to move transformation to the political and economic levels. Christians kept salvation very private and personal, but largely without the Buddha's amazing insight and critique at that very level.

+Adapted from *Jesus and Buddha: Paths to Awakening* (CD, DVD, MP3)

THE SUPREME ART OF LETTING GO

What does letting go on the practical level tell us? Letting go is different than denying or repressing. To let go of something is to admit it. You have to own it. Letting go is different than turning it against yourself; different than projecting it onto others. Letting go means that the denied, repressed, rejected parts of yourself, which are nonetheless true, are seen for what they are; but you refuse to turn them against yourself or against others. This is not denial or pretend, but actual transformation.

The religious word for this letting go is some form of *forgiveness*. You see the imperfect moment for what it is, and you hand it over to God. You refuse to let any negative story line or self-serving agenda define your life. This is a very, very different way of living; it implies that you see your mistakes, your dark side, but *you do not identify with either your superiority or your inferiority*. Both are equally a problem.

Forgiveness is of one piece. Those who give it can also receive it. Those who receive it can pass forgiveness on. You are a conduit, and your only job is not to stop the flow. What comes around will also go around. The art of letting go is really the secret of happiness and freedom.

+Adapted from *The Art of Letting Go: Living the Wisdom of St. Francis* (CD)

WHAT IS IT THAT HAS TO DIE?

All religions in their own way talk about dying before you die! They are all indeed saying that something has to die. We all know this, but often religions have chosen the wrong thing to kill, which has given us a very negative image. In almost all history it was always the other, the heretic, the sinner, the foreigner that had to die. Seldom was it us.

In most ancient cultures it was the virgin daughters and eldest sons that had to be sacrificed; in biblical times it was an animal, as we see in the Jewish Temple. By the Christian Middle Ages, it was our desires, our intellects, our bodies, and our will that had to die, which made many people think that God had created something wrong in us. Religion then became purity or separation codes instead of transformational systems.

Jesus did say very clearly that we had to lose our self to find our self in several different settings. For much of Christian history this was interpreted as the body self that had to die, and for some miraculous reason this was supposed to make the spiritual self arise! It did not work, and it allowed us to avoid the real problem. What really has to die is *our false self* created by our own mind, ego, and culture. It is a pretense, a bogus identity, a passing fad, a psychological construct *that gets in the way of who we are and always were—in God.* This is our objective and metaphysically True Self.

It seems we all live with a tragic case of mistaken identity. Christianity's most important job is to tell you that *you indeed and already have a True Self* "hidden with Christ in God" (Colossians 3:3–4).

> +Adapted from *On Transformation: Collected Talks, Volume I:*
> *Dying, We Need It for Life* (CD)

DO YOU WANT HAPPINESS NOW OR LATER?

Early spiritual life is always about letting go of unnecessary baggage so that we're prepared for death's final letting go and also prepared to enjoy a bit of heaven now. That can only happen if we're willing to know that our protected self and projected self-image is not the deepest or real us. Our passing personas are important and a good part of the journey and they even help us to taste moments of the Great *I Am* (Exodus 3:14) that is God. But they are merely warm-up acts for the grand finale.

My deepest me is always God.

+Adapted from *Hope Against Darkness: The Transforming Vision of Saint Francis of Assisi in an Age of Anxiety*, p. 133

JESUS IS SMALLER THAN CHRIST

To understand Jesus in a whole new way, you must first know that *Christ* is not his last name, but the preexistent Christ Consciousness that existed from all eternity (Colossians 1:15–20) and his omnipresent identity after the resurrection—which now includes humanity and all of creation along with it (Ephesians 1:9–11). Jesus *became* the Christ (Acts 2:36) by his own process of transformation, and now wonderfully includes us in this sweeping, historical, and victorious identity!

That's why Paul then created a new shocking term: "the body of Christ," which clearly now includes all of us (1 Corinthians 12:12–30) and all of creation, too (Romans 8:18–21). What hope this offers everything!

So think of the good Jesus, who has to die *to what seems like him*—so that he can rise as the larger Christ. It is not a bad man who must die on the cross, but a good man (false self)—so that he can be a much larger man (True Self) or Christ. Jesus dies, Christ rises. The false self is not a bad self; it is just not the true self. It is inadequate and small, symbolized by Jesus's human body, of which he readily lets go.

+Adapted from *Things Hidden: Scripture as Spirituality*, p. 191

THE SACRED WOUND

Pain teaches a most counterintuitive thing—that we must go down before we even know what up is. It is first an ordinary wound before it can become a sacred wound. Suffering of some sort seems to be the only thing strong enough to destabilize our arrogance and our ignorance. I would define suffering very simply as whenever you are not in control.

All healthy religion shows you what to do with your pain. *If we do not transform our pain, we will most assuredly transmit it.* If your religion is not showing you how to transform your pain, it is junk religion. It is no surprise that a crucified man became the central symbol of Christianity.

If we cannot find a way to make our wounds into sacred wounds, we invariably become negative or bitter—because *we will be wounded.* That is a given. All suffering is potentially redemptive, all wounds are potentially sacred wounds. It depends on what you do with them. Can you find God in them or not?

If there isn't some way to find some deeper meaning to our suffering, to find that God is *somehow in it* and can even use it for good, we will normally close up and close down, and the second half of our lives will, quite frankly, be small and silly.

+Adapted from *Things Hidden: Scripture as Spirituality*, p. 25

TWO KINDS OF DARKNESS
CAN BOTH LEAD TO LIGHT

There is a darkness that we are all led into by our own stupidity, selfishness, blindness, or by just living out of our false self. I guess that is what most of us call "sin," which is often an opening to grace and mercy. There is also a darkness that God leads us through for our own enlightenment and deepening. In either case, we have to walk through these dark periods by simple honesty, apology of some sort, surrender, letting go, forgiveness, and often by some necessary restitution or healing ritual. (I still hear of Vietnam, Afghan, or Iraq vets who feel they must go back and help some children in those countries to themselves be healed—of whatever!) Eastern religions might call it "karmic restitution."

Others might call these acts of repentance, making amends, doing penance, or stripping of the ego. By any account, it is often major surgery and surely feels like dying (although it feels like immense liberation, too). We need help, companioning, and comfort during these times. We must let ourselves be led by God and also by others. But how can we know and value the light if we've never walked through some darkness first? To hope, you first have to feel hopeless.

+Adapted from *Hope Against Darkness: The Transforming Vision of Saint Francis in an Age of Anxiety,* pp. 165, 173

NECESSITY OF FALLING

In order to construct our life's container we all need some help from the Perennial Tradition that has held up over time. We cannot each start at zero, entirely on our own. Life is far too short, and there are plenty of mistakes we do *not* need to make—and some that we *need* to make. We are parts of social and family ecosystems that are rightly structured to keep us from falling, but also, more importantly, to show us *how* to fall and also *how to learn* from that very falling.

We are not helping our children by always preventing them from what might be necessary falling, because we learn how to recover from falling by falling! It is precisely by falling off the bike many times that you eventually learn what the balance feels like. Those who have never allowed themselves to fall are actually off balance, while not realizing it at all. That is why they are so hard to live with. Please think about that for a while.

+Adapted from *Falling Upward: A Spirituality for the Two Halves of Life*, p. 28

FIRST HALF OF LIFE DONE POORLY

When we are *not* able to do the task of the first half of life well, we go back and try to do it again—and then often overdo it! This pattern is usually an inconsistent mix of old-fashioned styles and symbols with very contemporary ideologies: of consumerism, technology, militarism, and individualism. These tend to be our blind spots, which make us not true conservatives at all. In fact, today's neoconservatives are usually intense devotees of modern progress, war, and upward mobility in the system, while loving the Latin Mass!

If you did the first half of life with some respect for law, tradition, and order, you do not need to go back on this early path, not because it was bad, but *precisely because you already did it, and learned from it.* You internalized its values and now know their real meaning and purpose. (See Jesus's words on this in Matthew 5:17–48.) Unfortunately, we have an entire generation of educators, bishops, and political leaders who grew up without much structure or a worship of structure—and are building their personal towers of success and therefore have little ability to mentor the young or challenge the beginners into maturity. They are still beginners themselves. This does not bode well for the future of any church or society.

+Adapted from *Falling Upward: A Spirituality for the Two Halves of Life*, pp. vii–viii

HE EXEMPLIFIES THE FULL PASSOVER

The clarification and rediscovery of what I am going to call the True Self lays a solid foundation—and a clear initial goal—for all religion. You cannot build any serious spiritual house if you do not first find something solid and foundational to build on—inside yourself. Like knows like is the principle. God in you already knows, loves, and serves God in everything else. All you can do is fully jump on board.

I would call that jump *consciousness*, and I believe the Risen Christ is the icon of full consciousness. In the human mind of Christ, every part of creation knows itself as (1) divinely conceived, (2) beloved of God, (3) crucified, and (4) finally reborn. He carries us across with him, assures us we are okay, and, thus, models the full journey and final direction of consciousness. That is my major thesis about how Jesus saves us.

+Adapted from *Immortal Diamond: The Search for Our True Self*, pp. xii

GOD IN YOU SEEKS GOD

The Perennial Tradition, the mystical tradition that I love to build on, says that there is a capacity, a similarity, and a desire for divine reality inside all humans; and all world religions recognize this in their own way. It also states that *what we seek is what we are*, which is exactly why Jesus says that we *will* find it (see Matthew 7:7–8), because, as it were, it first found us!

The Perennial Tradition invariably concludes that you initially cannot see what you are looking for because what you are looking for is doing the looking! God is never an object to be found or possessed as we find other objects, but *the One who shares your own deepest subjectivity*—or your self. We normally call it our soul. Religion calls it "the Divine Indwelling." Meister Eckhart put it best, perhaps when he said, "The eye with which I see God is the same eye with which God sees me."

+Adapted from *Immortal Diamond: The Search for Our True Self*, pp. xii–xiii

"TO CREATE ONE SINGLE NEW PERSON"
(Ephesians 2:15)

I believe the Risen Christ is the Symbolic True Self, a Corporate Personality that is offered to history, where matter and spirit finally operate as one, where divine and human are held in one container, where "there are no more distinctions between Jew and Greek, slave and free, male and female, but all of you are one in Christ Jesus" (Galatians 3:28). He is the icon of the whole.

Some will think I am arrogantly talking about being personally divine and eagerly dismiss this way of talking about resurrection as heresy, arrogance, or pantheism. The Gospel is much more subtle than that. Jesus's life and his risen body say instead that the discovery of our own divine DNA is the only, full, and final meaning of being human. The True Self is neither God nor human. *The True Self is both at the same time, and both are a total gift*—and it takes an essential dying to know that, which Jesus also dramatically exemplified.

+Adapted from *Immortal Diamond: The Search for Our True Self*, pp. xiii, xiv

THE GATE OF HEAVEN

I promise you that the discovery of your True Self will feel like a thousand pounds of weight have fallen from your back. You will no longer have to build, protect, or promote any idealized self-image. Living in the True Self is quite simply a much happier existence, even though we never live there a full twenty-four hours a day. But you henceforth have it as a place to always go back to. You have finally discovered the alternative to your False Self.

You are like Jacob awakening from sleep and joining the chorus of mystics in every age. "You were here all along, and I never knew it!" he says (Genesis 28:16). He "anoints the stone pillow where this happened, and names it *Bethel* or the house of God and gate of heaven" (28:17–18). Jacob then carries the presence with him wherever he goes. What was first only there is soon everywhere. The gate of heaven is first of all in one concrete place, better if carried with you and best when found everywhere. That is the progression of the spiritual life.

+Adapted from *Immortal Diamond: The Search for Our True Self*, pp. 7–8

THE FACE YOU HAD BEFORE YOU WERE BORN

Most spirituality, in one way or another, has taught that we have all indeed begun to forget, if not fully forgotten, who we are. Universal amnesia seems to be the problem. Religion's job is purely and simply one thing: to tell us and keep reminding us who we objectively are. Thus, Catholics keep eating the Body of Christ until they know that they *are* what they eat—a human body that is still the eternal Christ.

Is it possible that we do know our True Self at some level? Could we all know from the beginning? Does some part of us know from the beginning? Does some part of us know—with a kind of certitude—who we really are? Is the truth hidden within us? Could human life's central task be a matter of consciously discovering and becoming who we already are and what we somehow unconsciously know? I believe so. Life is not a matter of creating a special name for ourselves, but of uncovering the name we have always had.

+Adapted from *Immortal Diamond: The Search for Our True Self,* pp. 11–12

THE BIG DISCOVERY

Our True Self is surely the "treasure hidden in the field" that Jesus speaks of. It is your own chunk of the immortal diamond. He says that we should be "happily willing to sell everything to buy that field" (Matthew 13:44)—or that diamond mine! Could any one thing be that valuable that we would sell everything for it? In all the Gospels, Jesus is quoted as saying, "What will it profit you if you gain the whole world and lose your own soul?" (Matthew 16:26). The context invariably implies he is talking about something happening in *this* world. If you find the treasure hidden in your own field, then everything else comes along with it. It is indeed the "pearl of great price" (Matthew 13:46) to continue our precious gem metaphor.

The early Christian writers tell us that this discovery of our True Self is also at the same time a discovery of God. *The two encounters with a True God and a True Self are largely experienced simultaneously and grow in parallel fashion.*

+Adapted from *Immortal Diamond: The Search for Our True Self*, pp. 12–14

HORSE FIRST, CART FOLLOWS

One of Jesus's most revealing one-liners is, "Rejoice only that your name is written in heaven!" (Luke 10:20). If we could fully trust this, it would change our whole life agenda. This discovery will not create overstated or presumptuous individualists, as religion usually fears, but instead makes all posturing and pretending largely unnecessary. Our core anxiety that we are not good enough is resolved from the beginning, and we can stop all our climbing, contending, criticizing, and competing. All accessorizing of any small, fragile self henceforth shows itself to be a massive waste of time and energy. Costume jewelry is just that: a small part of an already unnecessary costume.

Most of Christian history has largely put the cart of *requirements* before the horsepower itself, thinking that loads of carts or the best cart will eventually produce the horse. It never does. *The horsepower is precisely our experience of primal union with God.* Find God, the primary source, and the springwater will forever keep flowing naturally (Ezekiel 47:1–12; John 7:38). Once you know that, the problem of inferiority, unworthiness, or low self-esteem is resolved from the beginning and at the core. You can then spend your time much more positively, marching in the "triumphal parade" (2 Corinthians 2:14), as Paul so playfully calls it.

+Adapted from *Immortal Diamond: The Search for Our True Self*, pp. 14–15

THISNESS

Your True Self is who you are in God and who God is in you. You can never really lose your soul; you can only fail to realize it, which is indeed the greatest of losses: to have it but not have it (Matthew 16:26). Your essence, your exact "thisness," will never appear again in another incarnation.

You (and every other created thing) begin with a divine DNA, an inner destiny, as it were, an absolute core that knows the truth about you, a blueprint tucked away in the cellar of your being, an *imago Dei* that begs to be allowed, to be fulfilled, and to show itself. As it says in Romans 5:5, "It is the Holy Spirit poured into your heart, and it has been given to you."

Franciscan philosopher John Duns Scotus (1265–1308) called each soul a unique "thisness" *(haecceity)*, and he said it was to be found in every act of creation in its singularity. For him, God did not create universals, genera, and species, or anything that needed to come back again and again to get it right (reincarnation), but only specific and unique incarnations of the Eternal Mystery—each one chosen, loved, and preserved in existence as itself—*by being itself.* And this is the glory of God!

+Adapted from *Immortal Diamond: The Search for Our True Self*, pp. 16–18

INTIMACY

So how do you communicate to others what is inherently a secret? Or can you? How can the secret become unhidden? It becomes unhidden when people stop hiding—from God, themselves, and at least one other person. The emergence of our True Self is actually the big disclosure of the secret. Such risky self-disclosure is what I mean by intimacy, and intimacy is the way love is transmitted. Some say the word comes from the Latin *intimus*, referring to that which is interior or inside. Some say its older meaning is found by *in timor*, or "into fear."

In either case, the point is clear: intimacy happens when we reveal and expose our insides, and this is always scary. One never knows if the other will receive what is exposed, will respect it, or will run fast in the other direction. One must be prepared to be rejected. It is always a risk. The pain of rejection after self-disclosure is so great that it often takes a lifetime for people to risk it again.

+Adapted from *Immortal Diamond: The Search for Our True Self*, pp. 168–169

TO CARE AND NOT TO CARE

The greatest gift of centered and surrendered people is that they know themselves as part of a larger history, a larger Self. Their lives are not about them! They are just one lovely instance of a Much Larger and More Wonderful Life, the very life of God.

Holy people are in one sense profoundly conservative, knowing that they merely stand on the shoulders of their ancestors and will be shoulders to support generations to come. They are only a part of the Eternal Mystery of God unfolding in time, *and yet they are a part!*

Yet these same people are often quite liberal and reforming because they have no private agendas or self-interest to protect. They are unattached to any superior self-image or inferior self-image or any career or promotion. Such freedom! It is all about God for them, and they are just along for the ride. Such seeming contradictions held inside of the same person usually make it into a very wild ride. Contemplatives are often the most daring and wonderful combination of radical traditionalists and go-for-broke progressives at the very same time.

+For more on this theme, please consider *The Art of Letting Go: Living the Wisdom of St. Francis* with Fr. Richard Rohr (CD)

MARY AS CORPORATE PERSONALITY

We see that Mary is the archetype, the personification, of the one who represents and sums up the entire mystery of *how salvation is received*, and this has many dimensions. Like Jesus, I believe she is a Corporate Personality, a stand-in and exemplar for all of us. This is why the older churches so honored her and were fascinated by her. She is us!

The immaculate conception refers to her identity before she had done anything right or anything wrong (perhaps implied in Romans 8:30).

Her free election at the annunciation makes no mention of merit (Luke 1:38), as it is for us.

Her virgin motherhood is shrouded in mystery even for her (Luke 2:19, 51), as it is for us.

She has a quiet, ordinary life (no statements for thirty years), as most of ours are.

She shows heroic standing in dignity and solidarity with the pain and despair at the end (John 19:25).

She demonstrates receptivity to the shared life of the Holy Spirit along with everybody else at Pentecost (Acts 1:14).

All of these dimensions point to the full meaning of how God is born into the world! It is never about us, and always about God. We, like Mary, are merely handmaids, instruments, and it took such a woman as this to make the whole pattern glaringly clear.

+Adapted from *Things Hidden: Scripture as Spirituality*, pp. 177–178

THE PROBLEM IS ALREADY RESOLVED

One of the major problems in the spiritual life is our attachment to our own self-image—either positively or negatively created. We confuse this *idea* of ourselves with who we actually *are* in God. Our ideas about things are not the things in themselves. Concepts are not immediate contact with reality. Deep religion is deep contact with full reality, and Jesus seems to be saying that full reality is nothing to be afraid of. In fact, it is quite the contrary.

Who we are, and forever will be, in God, is the only real, enduring, and solid foundation for our identity. *God always sees his son, Jesus, in me, and cannot* not *love him* (see John 17:22–23). What the Gospel promises us is that *we are objectively and inherently children of God* (see 1 John 3:2). This is full reality.

It is not a moral worthiness that we attain; it is ontological, metaphysical, and substantial worthiness, and we have it from the beginning, our own private "immaculate conception," as it were. When this given God image becomes our self-image, we are home free, and the Gospel is just about the best good news we can hope for!

+Adapted from *Preparing for Christmas with Richard Rohr*, pp. 43–44

WE SURRENDER TO FIND

G.K. Chesterton wrote, "When a person has found something which he prefers to life itself, he [sic] for the first time has begun to live."

Jesus in his proclamation of the kingdom told us what we could prefer to life itself. The Bible ends by telling us we are called to be a people who could say, "Come, Lord Jesus" (Revelation 22:20), who could welcome something more than business as usual and live in God's Big Picture. We all have to ask for the grace to prefer something to our small lives because we have been offered the Shared Life, the One Life, the Eternal Life, God's Life, which became visible for us in this world as Jesus.

What we are all searching for is Someone to surrender to, something we can prefer to life itself. Well here is the wonderful surprise: *God is the only one we can surrender to without losing ourselves!* The irony is that we actually *find* ourselves, but now in a whole new and much larger field of meaning.

+Adapted from *Preparing for Christmas with Richard Rohr*, pp. 45, 71–73

YOU HAVE TO BE A BELOVED TO KNOW

Think of the many, many stories about God choosing people. There are Moses, Abraham, and Sarah; there are David, Jeremiah, Gideon, Samuel, Jonah, and Isaiah. There is Israel itself. Much later there are Peter and Paul, and, most especially Mary.

God is always choosing people. First impressions aside, God is not primarily choosing them for a role or a task, although it might appear that way. God is really choosing them *to be God's self in this world, each in a unique situation.* If they allow themselves to experience being chosen, being a beloved, being somehow God's presence in the world, they invariably communicate that same chosenness to others. And thus the Mystery passes on from age to age. Yes, we do have roles and tasks in this world, but finally they are all the same—to uniquely be divine love in a way that no one else can or will.

+Adapted from *Things Hidden: Scripture as Spirituality*, pp. 42–43

SELF-EMPTYING AS REVERSING
THE ENGINE OF CULTURE

Have this mind in yourselves, which is in Christ Jesus, who though he
was in the form of God, did not count equality with God a thing to be
grasped at, but emptied himself, taking the form of a servant, being born
in the likeness of the human.

—Philippians 2:5–7

It's a gift to joyfully recognize and accept your own smallness and ordinariness. Then you are free with nothing to live up to, nothing to prove,
and nothing to protect. Such freedom is my best description of Christian
maturity, because once you know that your "I" is great and one with God,
you can, ironically, be quite content with a small and ordinary "I."

No grandstanding is henceforth necessary. Any question of your own
importance or dignity has already been resolved from the inside out—once
and for all. Such salvation is experienced now in small tastes, whetting our
appetite for eternity.

+Adapted from *Radical Grace: Daily Meditations,* pp. 255–256

THE PROBLEM OF GOODNESS

We are not so at home with the resurrected form of things, despite a yearly springtime, healings in our bodies, the ten thousand forms of newness in every event and every life. The death side of things grabs our imaginations and fascinates us as fear and negativity always do, I am sad to say. We have to be taught how to look for anything infinite, positive, or good, which for some reason is much more difficult.

We have spent centuries of philosophy trying to solve the problem of evil, yet I believe the much more confounding and astounding issue is the problem of good. How do we account for so much gratuitous and sheer goodness in this world? Tackling this problem would achieve much better results.

+Adapted from *Immortal Diamond: The Search for Our True Self*, pp. x–xi

PROCESS

The path of descent is the path of transformation.
Darkness, failure, relapse, death, and woundedness are
our primary teachers, rather than ideas or doctrines.

INTRODUCTION

There are three serious misperceptions—really heresies by official church statements—which deeply distorted the reading of the Scriptures and much spirituality: Pelagianism, Jansenism, and perfectionism. They overlap and reveal the same problem, which I would call "spiritual capitalism." "I can do it, and I must do it, and I will do it" might be its common philosophy.

This is the early stage ego speaking. It puts all the emphasis on me and my effort and my spiritual accomplishments, and has little active trust in one's total reliance upon grace and mercy. The driving energy is, unfortunately, fear and more effort instead of quiet confidence and gratitude—which moves spirituality into an entirely different ballpark. It is now about climbing instead of surrendering. The first feels good, the second feels like falling or failing, or even like dying. Who likes that? Certainly not the false self or the ego. The ego always wants to feel that it has achieved salvation somehow. Grace and forgiveness are always a humiliation for the ego.

Pelagianism, surely attributed wrongly to the Irish monk Pelagius (early fifth century), seemed to suggest that we could achieve salvation by our own will power and effort. It underplayed the importance and universal availability of grace and God's choice and guidance. Although condemned as heresy early on by the Church and later by the Council of Trent, much of the church has still continued to operate in a Pelagian way itself. We assumed because we condemned it, we were not doing it. It is an ecclesiastical form of reaction formation (meaning to overcoming your own anxiety about something characteristic of yourself by exaggerating the opposite as if it were true: A deeply angry person saying, "I have little patience with angry people," which allows them to think that they are not one of those people!)

Most mainline Christians pay sincere lip service to grace and mercy, but in the practical order it is almost entirely about performance and moral achievement. It is just the moral issues that change, or the precise *techniques* of salvation where the imperial and individual "I" must push the right spiritual buttons. Paul and Luther were right on, although most Lutherans and Evangelicals fell right back into a much more disguised form of "works righteousness," as they called it. They were indeed "saved by grace" but it sure had to be their form of grace and inside their categories of meaning. Catholics, early Anabaptists, and gays were clearly not in on the deal of salvation by grace.

Jansenism was named after a Dutch theologian and bishop, Cornelius Jansen (d. 1638), who emphasized moral austerity and a fear of God's justice more than any trust in God's mercy. God was wrathful, vindictive, and punitive, and all the appropriate Scriptures were found to make these very points. It is hard to find a Western Christian—Catholic or Protestant—who has not been formed by this Christian form of Pharisaism, which is really pagan Stoicism. It strongly influenced most seventeenth- and eighteenth-century Catholicism in France, Belgium, Holland, Italy, and Germany, and it still lingers on in much pre–Vatican II Catholicism all over the world. Although it was officially condemned as a heresy by Rome in 1715, it is still quite common, especially, it seems to me, among people who had punitive and angry parenting patterns. This is the way they comfortably shape their universe and their God. They actually prefer such a God—things are very clear, and you know where you stand with such a deity—even though this perspective leaves almost all people condemned and is a very pessimistic and fearful world view.

The common manifestation of these ever-recurring patterns might simply be called *perfectionism*. The word itself is taken from a single passage in Matthew 5:48, where Jesus tells us "to be perfect as your heavenly Father is perfect." Of course, perfection as such is a divine or a mathematical concept and has never been a human one. Jesus offers it as guidance for how we can love our enemies, of which he has just spoken (5:43–47), and is surely saying that we cannot obey this humanly impossible commandment by willpower but only by surrendering to the Divine Perfection that can and will flow through us. In other words, of ourselves, we cannot be perfect, but God is. Yet we used this one passage to give people the exact opposite impression that they could indeed be perfect in themselves! This did untold damage in convents and monasteries all over the world, leading many to leave or, more commonly, split their personality, when they could not, in fact, be perfect. The *New Jerusalem Bible* wisely translates this verse as, "You must set no bounds to your love, just as your heavenly Father sets none to his." Not setting bounds is another way of trusting in grace and guidance. It is not saying, "If you would just try harder, you could do it."

In his proclamation of St. Thérèse of Lisieux as a Doctor of the Church, Pope John Paul II said, "She has made the Gospel shine appealingly in our time...she helped to heal souls of the rigors and fears of Jansenism, which tended to stress God's justice rather than God's mercy. In God's mercy she contemplated and adored all the divine perfections, because as in her own words *'even his justice seems to me to be clothed in love.'*"

Thérèse rightly named this spirituality her "Little Way." It was nothing more than a simple and clear recovery of the pure Gospel message! It was she (and Francis of Assisi!) who gave me the courage as a young man to read the Scriptures through this primary lens of littleness instead of some possible bigness. This changed everything. The true Gospel is a path of descent, and not ascent. It is totally amazing we could miss this message given the rejection, betrayal, passion, and crucifixion of Jesus as our primary and central template for redemption. We piously thanked Jesus for doing this instead of following Jesus on the same inevitable and holy path.

NO ONE WOULD HAVE THOUGHT!

How does transformation actually and concretely happen?

Ladder-climbing Western culture, and the clinging human ego, made the Gospel into a message of spiritual advancement—ascent rather than descent. We hopefully do advance in wisdom, age, and grace (Luke 2:40), but not at all in the way we thought. Jesus got it right! He brilliantly and personally taught the way of the cross and not the way of climbing.

We come to God much more by doing things wrong than by doing things right. God absolutely leveled the human playing field by using our sins and failures to bring us to divine union. This is surely the most counterintuitive message of the Gospels—so counterintuitive that it largely remains hidden to this day—in plain sight.

GREAT LOVE AND GREAT SUFFERING

We must learn to be able to think and behave like Jesus, who is the arche-typal human being. This becomes a journey of great love and great suffer-ing. *These are the two normal and primary paths of transformation into God, preceding all organized religion.* This journey leads us to a universal love where we don't love just those who love us. We must learn to participate in a larger love—divine love.

In this, God utterly leveled the playing field and made grace available from the first moment of creation when "God's Spirit overshadowed the chaos" (Genesis 1:2). Surely the God who created all things was thus avail-able to all creation, starting with the natives of all continents, and, yes, even the barbarians. I can only assume that they loved and suffered too and thus met God "who is love" (1 John 4:7–8).

Any journey of great love or great suffering makes us go deeper into our faith and eventually into what can only be called universal truth. Love and suffering are finally the same, because those who love deeply are commit-ting themselves to eventual suffering, as we see in Jesus. And those who suffer often become the greatest lovers.

+Adapted from the webcasts *Exploring and Experiencing the Naked Now: A Compilation* (CD, DVD, MP3)

IT'S ALWAYS PAYBACK TIME

Living in the second half of life, I no longer have to prove that I or my group is the best, that my ethnicity is superior, that my religion is the only one that God loves, or that my role and place in society deserve superior treatment. I am not preoccupied with collecting more goods and services; quite simply, my desire and effort—every day—is to pay back, to give back to the world a bit of what I have received. I now realize that I have been gratuitously given *to*—from the universe, from society, and from God. I try now, as Elizabeth Seton said, "to live simply so that others can simply live."

+Adapted from *Falling Upward: A Spirituality for the Two Halves of Life*, p. 121

IT IS HARD TO FALL WHEN YOU ARE AT THE TOP

All that is hidden, all that is plain I have come to know, instructed by
Wisdom who designed all things.
—Wisdom 7:21–22

The irony of ego consciousness is that it always excludes and eliminates the unconscious—so it is actually not conscious at all! It insists on knowing, on being certain, and it refuses all unknowing. So most people who think they are fully conscious (read "smart") have a big leaden manhole cover over their unconscious. It gives them control but seldom compassion or *wisdom*.

That is exactly why politicians, priests, CEOs of anything, and know-it-alls, *must* continue to fail and fall (spiritually speaking), or they never come to any real wisdom. The trouble is that we have to put up with them in the meantime and wait for another growth spurt. Sometimes that very power position makes failing and falling quite rare and even impossible for them.

+Adapted from *A Lever and a Place To Stand:*
The Contemplative Stance, the Active Prayer, p. x

FALLING

How does one transition from the survival dance to the sacred dance? Let me tell you how it starts. Did you know the first half of life *has* to fail you? In fact, if you do not recognize an eventual and necessary dissatisfaction (in the form of sadness, restlessness, emptiness, intellectual conflict, spiritual boredom, or even loss of faith), you will not move on to maturity. You see, faith really is about moving outside your comfort zone, trusting God's lead, instead of just forever shoring up home base. Too often, early religious conditioning largely substitutes for any real faith.

Usually, without growth being forced on us, few of us go willingly on the spiritual journey. Why would we? The rug has to be pulled out from beneath our game so we redefine what balance really is. More than anything else, this falling/rising cycle is what moves us into the second half of our own lives. There is a necessary suffering to human life, and if we avoid its cycles we remain immature forever. It can take the form of failed relationships, facing our own shadow self, conflicts and contradictions, disappointments, moral lapses, or depression in any number of forms.

All of these have the potential to either edge us forward in life or to make us dig in our heels even deeper, producing narcissistic and adolescent responses that everybody can see except us. We either fall upward, or we just keep falling.

+Adapted from *Loving the Two Halves of Life: The Further Journey*
(CD, DVD, MP3)

THE INCURABLE WOUND
AT THE HEART OF EVERTHING

In order to arrive at the second half of life, one has to realize there is an incurable wound at the heart of everything. Much of the conflict from the age of twenty-five to sixty-five is just trying to figure this out and then to truly accept it. Swiss theologian Hans Urs Von Balthasar said toward the end of his life: "All great thought springs from a conflict between two eventual insights: (1) The wound which we find at the heart of everything is finally incurable, (2) Yet we are necessarily and still driven to try!" (Think about that for an hour or so!)

Our largely unsuccessful efforts of the first half of life are themselves the training ground for all virtue and growth in holiness. This wound at the heart of life shows itself in many ways, but *your holding and suffering of this tragic wound, your persistent but failed attempts to heal it, your final surrender to it, will ironically make you into a wise and holy person.* It will make you patient, loving, hopeful, expansive, faithful, and compassionate—which is precisely second-half-of-life wisdom.

+Adapted from *Loving the Two Halves of Life: The Further Journey*
(CD, DVD, MP3)

THE HEART OF THE MATTER

Until we walk with despair, and still have hope, we will not know that our hope was not just hope in ourselves, in our own successes, in our power to make a difference, in our image of what perfection should be. We need hope from a much deeper Source. We need a hope larger than ourselves.

Until we walk with personal issues of despair, we will never uncover the Real Hope on the other side of that despair. Until we allow the crash and crush of our images, we will never discover the Real Life beyond what only seems like death. Remember, *death is an imaginary loss of an imaginary self*, which is going to pass anyway.

This very journey is probably the heart of what Jesus came to reveal.

+Adapted from *Near Occasions of Grace*, p. 100

SIMPLICITY AS CENTRAL

We are all complicit in and benefitting from what Dorothy Day called "the dirty rotten system." That's not condemning anybody; it's condemning everybody because we are all complicit and enjoying the fruits of domination and injustice. (Where were your shirts and underwear made? What wars allow us to have cheap food and gas?) Usually the only way to be really non-complicit in the system is *to choose to live a very simple life*. That's the only way out of the system!

Thus most of the great wisdom teachers like Gandhi, Saints Francis and Clare, Simone Weil, Dorothy Day, Jesus and Buddha—lived voluntarily simple lives. That's almost the only way to stop bending the knee before the system. This is a truly transfigured life in cultures that today are almost always based on climbing, consumption, and competition (1 John 2:15–17).

Once we idealize social climbing, domination of others, status symbols, power, prestige and possessions, we are part of a never-ending game that is almost impossible to escape. It has its own inner logic that is self-maintaining, self-perpetuating, and self-congratulating as well as elitist and exclusionary. It will never create a just or happy world, yet most Christians never call it into question. Jesus came to free us from this lie, which will never make us happy anyway, because it's never enough, and we never completely win.

+Adapted from *Spiral of Violence: The World, the Flesh, and the Devil* (CD, MP3)

RELIGION IS NOT FOR THE SAKE
OF SOCIAL ORDER

In the divine economy of grace, sin and failure become the base metal and raw material for the redemption experience itself. Much of organized religion, however, tends to be peopled by folks who have a mania for some ideal order, which is never the case, so they are seldom happy or content. Religion is for the sake of divine union, not social order, yet the powers that be always want to use it for maintaining social order. This pollutes much of religion's goal and purpose.

In fact, it makes you anal retentive after a while, to use Freud's rude phrase, because you can never be happy with life as it is, which is always filled with handicapped people, mentally unstable people, people of other and so-called false religions, irritable people, gay people, and people of totally different customs and traditions. Not to speak of *wild* nature, which we have not loved very well up to now. Organized religion has not been known for its inclusiveness or for being very comfortable with diversity. Yet pluriformity, multiplicity, and diversity are representative of the only world there is! It is rather amazing that we can miss, deny, or ignore what is in plain sight everywhere.

Salvation is not sin perfectly avoided, as the ego would prefer; but in fact *salvation is sin turned on its head and used in our favor.* That is how transformative divine love is.

+Adapted from *Falling Upward: A Spirituality for the Two Halves of Life*, p. 60

GRACE

Our word for God's dramatic breaking beyond our ironclad rules is *grace*. Grace is God's magnificent release from our self-made prisons, and the only way that God's economy can triumph over our deeply internalized merit-badge system. Grace is the secret key whereby God offers to be the Divine Locksmith for every life and for all of history. Life, when lived fully, tends to tool and retool us until we eventually find some form of grace is necessary for our very survival and sanity. *Without grace, almost everything human declines and devolves into smallness, hurt, and blame.*

Grace humiliates our attempts at private virtue. Grace makes us feel powerless, where before, we knew that if we did *this*, then we would earn *that*. Accepting grace can make us feel poor and empty and even useless. Who wants grace? Only sinners and almost no one else!

+From *A Lever and a Place to Stand: The Contemplative Stance, the Active Prayer*, pp. 45–46

WILLFULLNESS VERSUS WILLINGNESS

A common saying is, "God helps those who help themselves." I think the phrase can be understood wisely, but in most spiritual situations it is not completely true. Scripture clearly says, in many ways, that God helps those who *trust in God*, not those who help themselves.

We need to be told that very strongly because of our do–it–yourself orientation. As educated people, as Americans, as middle class people who have practiced climbing, we are accustomed to doing things ourselves. It takes applying the brakes, letting go of our own plans, allowing Another, and experiencing power from a Larger Source to really move to higher awareness. Otherwise, there is no real transformation, but only increased willpower. As if the one with the most will power wins! *Willfulness is quite different than willingness.* They are two different energetic styles and normally yield very different fruit.

+Adapted from *Radical Grace: Daily Meditations*, p. 77

SPIRITUAL CAPITALISM

The phrase "spirituality of subtraction" was inspired by Meister Eckhart (c. 1260 –1327), the medieval Dominican mystic. He said the spiritual life has much more to do with subtraction than it does with addition. Yet I think most Christians today are involved in great part in a spirituality of *addition*, and in that, they are not very traditional or conservative at all.

The capitalist world view is the only one most of us have ever known. We see reality, experiences, events, other people, and things—in fact, everything—as objects for our personal consumption. Even religion, Scripture, sacraments, worship services, and meritorious deeds become ways to advance ourselves—not necessarily ways to love God or neighbor.

The nature of the capitalist mind is that things (and often people!) are there for *me*. Finally, even God becomes an object for my consumption. Religion looks good on my resume, and anything deemed spiritual is a check on my private worthiness list. Some call it spiritual consumerism. It is not the Gospel.

+Adapted from *Radical Grace: Daily Meditations*, p. 114

WILL ANYONE SECOND THE MOTION?

Risk all for love, Jesus tells us, even your own life. Give that to me and let me save it. The healthy religious person is the one who allows *God* to do the saving and the leading, while I do my little part to bring up the rear. It always feels like a loss of power and certitude at the beginning, which is why it is called faith, and why true Biblical faith is probably somewhat rare. God is always the initiator and mover. All we do is *second the motion*.

Mary, the Mother of Jesus, sums up in herself the attitude of the "little poor ones" whom God is able to save because they are not self-entitled or able to climb (the *anawim* of Zephaniah 2:3, 3:12). She is deeply aware of her own emptiness without God (Luke 1:52). She longs for the fulfillment of God's promise (Luke 1:54); she has left herself open, available for God's work (Luke 1:45, 49). And when the call comes, she makes her full personal surrender of: "Let it be!" (Luke 1:38).

+Adapted from *Radical Grace: Daily Meditations*, p. 322

YOU CAN'T MAKE LOVE ALL DRESSED UP

We fear nothingness. That's why we fear death, of course, which feels like nothingness. Death is the shocking realization that everything I thought was me, everything I held onto so desperately, was finally nothing (read Kathleen Dowling Singh's *The Grace in Dying: How We Are Transformed Spiritually as We Die*).

The nothingness we fear so much is, in fact, the treasure and freedom that we long for, which is revealed in the joy and glory of the Risen Christ. We long for the space where there is nothing to prove and nothing to protect; where I am who I am, in the mind and heart of God, and that is more than enough.

Spirituality teaches us how to get naked ahead of time, so God can make love to us as we really are.

+Adapted from *Radical Grace: Daily Meditations*, p. 333

GETTING TO YES

Real holiness doesn't feel like holiness; it just feels like you're dying. It feels like you're losing it. And you are! Every time you love someone, you have agreed for a part of you to die. You will soon be asked to let go of some part of your false self, which you foolishly thought was permanent, important, and essential!

You know God is doing this in you and with you, when you can somehow smile, and trust that what you lost was something you did not need anyway. In fact, it got in the way of what was real.

Many of us were taught to say No without the deep joy of Yes. We were trained to put up with all dying and just take it on the chin. Saying No to the self does not necessarily please God or please anybody. There is too much resentment and self-pity involved. When God, by love and freedom, can create a joyous Yes inside of you—so much so that you can absorb the usual noes—then it is God's full work. The first might be resentful dieting; the second is a spiritual banquet.

+Adapted from *Radical Grace: Daily Meditations*, p. 334

THE GOSPEL OF PROSPERITY

Soul knowledge sends you in the opposite direction from consumerism. It's not addition that makes one holy, but subtraction: stripping the illusions, letting go of the pretense, exposing the false self, breaking open the heart and the understanding, not taking my private self too seriously. Conversion is more about unlearning than learning.

In a certain sense we are on the utterly wrong track. We are climbing while Jesus is descending, and in that we reflect the pride and the arrogance of Western civilization, usually trying to accomplish, perform, and achieve. This is our real operative religion. Success is holy! We transferred much of that to our version of Christianity and made the Gospel into spiritual consumerism. The ego is still in charge. There is not much room left for God when the false self takes itself and its private self-development that seriously.

All we can really do is get ourselves out of the way, and honestly *we* can't even do that. It is done to us through this terrible thing called suffering.

+Adapted from *Radical Grace: Daily Meditations*, p. 46

EXODUS IS THE FIRST BIBLICAL METAPHOR

The Hebrew people entered the desert feeling themselves as a united and strong people, and you'd think that perhaps they would have experienced greater strength as they continued, but not so: they experienced fragmentation and weariness; they experienced divisions among their people. They were not the people they thought they were. The Jewish exodus is a rather perfect metaphor for spirituality.

When all of our idols are taken away, all our securities and defense mechanisms, we find out who we really are. We're so little, so poor, so empty—and a shock to ourselves. But the biblical God takes away our shame, and we are eventually able to present ourselves in an honest and humble form. Then we find out who we really are and who God is for us—and it is more than enough. That is how an enslaved people became God's people, Israel.

+Adapted from *Radical Grace: Daily Meditations*, p. 130

LEPERS AND WOLVES

Isn't it wonderful news, brothers and sisters, that we come to God not by our perfection but by our imperfection! That gives all of us an equal chance and utterly levels the human playing field. No pretending or denying is helpful any longer. Deep within each of us lives both a leper and a wolf, both of which we are ashamed and afraid of. In Franciscan lore, they are our inner imperfections.

Francis embraced the leper below Assisi and called it his conversion; later Francis tamed the wolf that was ravaging the countryside of Gubbio. The stories did happen historically, but first of all they must have happened in his soul. Our inner life, our emotional life, our prayer life, is where we first do our battles, and then we are prepared for our outer life conflicts.

It is on the inside of us that lepers and wolves first live. If we haven't been able to kiss many lepers, if we haven't been able to tame many wolves in the outer world, it's probably because we haven't first of all made friends with our own leprosy and the ferocious wolf within each of us. They are always there in some form, waiting to be tamed and needing to be forgiven.

+Adapted from *Radical Grace: Daily Meditations*, p. 276

FINDING OUR REAL POWER

The spirituality behind the Twelve-Step Program of Alcoholics Anonymous is a "low Church" approach to evangelization and healing that is probably our only hope in a pluralistic world of over seven billion people. Most of these people are not going to become Christian or join our Church, which even the Vatican now admits.

Our suffering in developed countries is primarily psychological, relational, and addictive: the suffering of people who are comfortable on the outside but oppressed and empty within. It is a crisis of meaninglessness that leads us to try to find meaning in possessions, perks, prestige and power, which are always *outside* of the self. It doesn't finally work. So we turn to ingesting food, drink, or drugs, and we become addictive consumers to fill the empty hole within us.

The Twelve-Step Program walks us back out of our addictive society. Like all steps toward truth and Spirit, they also lead downward, which they call *sobriety*. Bill Wilson and his A.A. movement have *shown* us that the real power is when we no longer seek, need, or abuse outer power because we have found real power within. They rightly call it our "Higher Power."

+Adapted from *Radical Grace: Daily Meditations*, p. 315

THE TWO HALVES OF LIFE

The soul has many secrets. They are only revealed to those who want them, and are never completely forced upon us. One of the best-kept secrets, and yet one hidden in plain sight, is that *the way up is the way down*. Or, if you prefer, *the way down is the way up*.

In Scripture, we see that the wrestling and wounding of Jacob are necessary for Jacob to become Israel (Genesis 32:26–32), and the death and resurrection of Jesus are necessary to create Christianity. The loss and renewal pattern is so constant and ubiquitous that it should hardly be called a secret at all.

Yet it is still a secret, probably because we do not *want* to see it. We do not want to embark on a further journey (the second half of life) if it feels like going down, especially after having put so much sound and fury into going up (the first half of life). This is surely the first and primary reason why many people never get to the fullness of their own lives.

+Adapted from *Falling Upward: A Spirituality for the Two Halves of Life*,
pp. xviii–xix

YOU WILL FAIL

Some kind of falling, what I call "necessary suffering," is programmed into the full journey. All the sources seem to say it, starting with Adam and Eve and all they represent. Yes, they sinned and were cast out of the Garden of Eden, but from those very acts came consciousness itself, development of conscience, and their own further journey.

It is not that suffering or failure *might* happen, or that it will only happen to you if you are bad (which is what many religious people often think), or that it will happen to the unfortunate, or to a few in other places, or that you can somehow by cleverness or righteousness avoid it. No, it *will* happen, and to you!

Losing, failing, falling, sin, and the suffering that comes from those experiences—all of this is a necessary and even good part of the human journey. As my favorite mystic, Lady Julian of Norwich put it in her Middle English, "Sin is behovely!"

+Adapted from *Falling Upward: A Spirituality for the Two Halves of Life*, p. xx

ONE INSULT AFTER ANOTHER!

You cannot avoid sin or mistakes anyway (Romans 5:12), but if you try too fervently, it often creates even worse problems. Jesus loves to tell stories like that of the publican and the Pharisee (Luke 18:9–14) and the famous one about the prodigal son (Luke 15:11–32), in which one character does his life totally right and is, in fact, wrong; and the other who does it totally wrong ends up God's beloved! Now deal with that!

Jesus also tells us that there are two groups who are very good at trying to deny or avoid this humiliating surprise: *those who are very rich and those who are very religious.* These two groups have very different plans for themselves, as they try to totally steer their own ships with well-chosen itineraries. They follow two different ways of going up and avoiding down.

Such a down-and-then-up perspective does not fit into our Western philosophy of progress, nor into our desire for upward mobility, nor into our religious notions of perfection or holiness. "Let's hope it is *not* true, at least for me," we all say! Yet the perennial tradition, sometimes called the wisdom tradition, says that it is and will always be true. St. Augustine called it the passing over mystery (or the "paschal mystery" from the Hebrew word for Passover, *pesach*).

+Adapted from *Falling Upward: A Spirituality for the Two Halves of Life*,
pp. xx–xxi

THE DEMAND FOR THE PERFECT
IS THE ENEMY OF THE GOOD

We grow spiritually much more by doing it wrong than by doing it right. That might just be the central message of how spiritual growth happens; yet nothing in us wants to believe it.

If there is such a thing as human perfection, it seems to emerge precisely from how we handle the imperfection that is everywhere, especially our own. What a clever place for God to hide holiness, so that only the humble and earnest will find it! A so-called perfect person ends up being one who can consciously forgive and include imperfection rather than one who thinks he or she is totally above and beyond imperfection.

It becomes sort of obvious once you say it out loud. In fact, I would say that *the demand for the perfect is the greatest enemy of the good.* Perfection is a mathematical or divine concept; goodness is a beautiful human concept that includes us all. People whom we call "good people" are always people who have learned how *to include contradictions and others,* even at risk to their own proper self-image or their social standing. This is quite obvious in Jesus.

+Adapted from *Falling Upward: A Spirituality for the Two Halves of Life*,
pp. xxii–xxiii

BEYOND BOY SCOUT SPIRITUALITY

By denying their pain, avoiding the necessary falling, many have kept themselves from their own spiritual depths—and therefore have been kept from their own spiritual heights. First-half-of-life religion is almost always about various types of purity codes or "thou shalt nots" to keep us *up, clear, clean, and together*, like good Boy and Girl Scouts. A certain kind of purity and self-discipline is "behovely," at least for a while in the first half of life, as the Jewish Torah brilliantly presents. (I was a Star Scout and a Catholic altar boy myself, and did them both quite well, but it made me love me, not God.)

Because none of us desires a downward path to growth through imperfection, seeks it, or even suspects it, we have to get the message with the authority of a divine revelation. So Jesus makes it into a central axiom: the last really do have a head start in moving toward first, and those who spend too much time trying to be first will never get there. Jesus says this clearly in several places and in numerous parables, although those of us still on the first journey just cannot hear it. It is far too counterintuitive and paradoxical.

Our resistance to the message is so great that it could be called outright denial, even among sincere Christians. *The human ego prefers anything, just about anything, to falling or changing or dying.* The ego is that part of you that loves the status quo, even when it is not working.

+From *Falling Upward: A Spirituality for the Two Halves of Life*,
pp. xxiii–xxiv

FALLING UPWARD

Some have called this principle of going down to go up a "spiritual-ity of imperfection" or "the way of the wound." It has been affirmed in Christianity by St. Therese of Lisieux as her Little Way, by St. Francis as the way of poverty, and by Alcoholics Anonymous as the necessary First Step. St. Paul taught this unwelcome message with his enigmatic "It is when I am weak that I am strong" (2 Corinthians 12:10). Of course, in saying that, he was merely building on what he called the folly of the crucifixion of Jesus—a tragic and absurd dying that became resurrection itself.

You will not know for sure that this message is true until you are on the upside. You will never imagine it to be true until you have gone through the downside yourself and come out on the other side in larger form. You must be pressured from on high, by fate, circumstance, love, or God, because nothing in you wants to believe it or wants to go through it.

Falling upward is a secret of the soul, known not by thinking about it or proving it but only by risking it—at least once. And by allowing yourself to be led—at least once. Those who have allowed it know it is true, but only after the fact.

+Adapted from *Falling Upward: A Spirituality for the Two Halves of Life*,
pp. xxiv, xxvi

THE SIGN OF JONAH

No sign will be given you except the sign of Jonah.
—Luke 11:29

This clear one-liner of Jesus feels rather amazing and largely unheard. Especially since our logo became the sign of the cross. Maybe they are the same sign? Indeed it is not a sign at all, but more an anti-sign. It seems to demand that we must release ourselves into a belly of darkness before we can know what is essential. It insists that the spiritual journey is more like giving up control than taking control. It might even be saying that others will often throw us overboard, as was the case with Jonah, and that will get us to the right shore—and even by God's grace more than any right action on our part.

Jonah knew what God was doing and how God does it and how right God is—only *after* emerging from the belly of the whale. He has no message whatsoever to give until he has first endured the journey, the darkness, the spitting up on the right shore—all in spite of his best efforts to avoid these very things. Jonah indeed is our Judeo-Christian symbol of transformation. Jesus had found the Jonah story inspiring, no doubt, because it described almost perfectly what was happening to him!

+Adapted from *Wondrous Encounters: Scripture for Lent*, pp. 31–32

PAIN AS A WAY OF KNOWING

Suffering is the necessary *deep feeling* of the human situation. If we don't feel pain, suffering, human failure and weakness, we stand antiseptically apart from it and remain numb and small. We can't fully understand such things by thinking about them. The superficiality of much of our world is that it tries to buy its way out of such necessary knowing.

Jesus did not numb himself or withhold himself from human pain, as we see even in his refusal of the numbing wine on the cross (Matthew 27:34). Some forms of suffering are necessary so that we can more fully *know* the human dilemma, so that we can even name our shadow self and confront it. Maybe evil itself has to be *felt* to understand its monstrosity and to empathize with its victims.

Brothers and sisters, the irony is not that God should feel so fiercely; it's that his creatures feel so feebly. If there is nothing in your life to cry about, if there is nothing in your life to yell about, you must be out of touch. We must all feel and know the immense pain of this global humanity. Then we are no longer isolated, but a true member of the universal Body of Christ. Then we know God not from the outside but from the inside!

+Adapted from *Radical Grace: Daily Meditations*, p. 209

GRIEFWORK

We live a long time in order to become lovers. God is like a good parent, refusing to do our homework for us. We must learn through trial and error. We have to do our homework ourselves, the homework of suffering, desiring, loving, winning and losing, hundreds of times.

Grief is one of the greatest occasions of deep and sad feeling, and it's one that is socially acceptable. Most understand and want to walk with you in your grief. When we lose a beloved friend, wife, husband, child, parent, or maybe a possession or a job, we feel it is okay to feel deeply. But we must broaden that. We've got to find a passion that is also experienced when we *have* it, not just when we're losing it. And we have it all the time. Don't wait for loss to feel, suffer, or enjoy deeply. But the grief process is still a marvelous teacher and awakener, for many men in particular, it is the only emotion that shakes them to their core.

+Adapted from *Radical Grace: Daily Meditations*, p. 282

A SISTERHOOD AND BROTHERHOOD OF PAIN

Something very special is happening here at Lourdes. And God wants to give us the eyes to see it and the ground to receive it. What are all these disabled people telling us? What is the witness of all these nurses and litter-bearers? It seems God wants us to live a vulnerable life, a life dependent on other people, a life that is unafraid to cry, a life that puts the obviously wounded ones at the very center—so we can bare our own less obvious wounds too.

The little ones here are unable to numb themselves. The numb do not notice. The sophisticated will not suffer. The comfortable need not complain. But Jesus teaches us, in effect, how to suffer graciously. He actually *increases*, it seems, our capacity for holding sadness and pain. This might be the central message of the eight Beatitudes (Matthew 5:3–12).

What kind of God is this? Could it be a God who actually allows deformities, sickness, and handicaps so we can all be bound together in a sisterhood of need and a brotherhood of compassion? I do not know how else to understand it all and we surely see it acted out right here. That is the primary miracle of Lourdes.

+Adapted from a recording at Lourdes, France

FIRST WORLD LIBERATION THEOLOGY

Do you realize with what difficulty surrender will come to a fixing, managing mentality? There's nothing in that psyche prepared to understand the spiritual wisdom of surrender. All of the great world religions teach surrender. Yet most of us, until we go through the hole in our soul, don't think surrender is really necessary. At least that's how it is for those of us in developed countries. The poor, on the other hand, seem to understand limitation at a very early age. They cannot avoid or deny the big hole in much of reality and even in their own soul.

The developing world faces its limitation through a breakdown in the social-economic system, and any access to basic justice. But we, in the so-called developed world, have to face our limitations; it seems, on the inside. That's our liberation theology. We must recognize our own poor man, our own abused woman, the oppressed part of ourselves that we hate, that we deny, that we're afraid of. That's the hole in our soul. This is our way *through*, maybe the only way, says the crucified Jesus.

+Adapted from *Radical Grace: Daily Meditations*, p. 66

WHAT IS SUFFERING?

Pain teaches a most counterintuitive thing—that we must go down before we even know what up is. In terms of the ego, most religions teach in some way that all of us must die before we die, and then we will not be afraid of dying. Suffering of some sort seems to be the only thing strong enough to destabilize our arrogance and our ignorance. I would define suffering very simply as whenever you are not in control.

If religion cannot find a meaning for human suffering, humanity is in major trouble. All healthy religion shows you what to do with your pain. Great religion shows you what to do with the absurd, the tragic, the nonsensical, the unjust. *If we do not transform this pain, we will most assuredly transmit it to others, and it will slowly destroy us in one way or another.*

If there isn't some way to find some deeper meaning to our suffering, to find that *God is somewhere in it,* and can even use it for good, we will normally close up and close down. The natural movement of the ego is to protect itself so as not to be hurt again. The soul does not need answers, it just wants meaning, and then it can live. Surprisingly, suffering itself often brings deep meaning to the surface to those who are suffering and also to those who love them.

+Adapted from *Things Hidden: Scripture as Spirituality*, p. 25

A DIFFERENT MODEL OF AUTHORITY

"The greatest among you must behave as if he were the youngest, the
leader as if he were the one who serves"
—Luke 22:26

That statement is probably the simplest and most powerful definition of
spiritual authority to be found in all four Gospels.

For who is the greater, the one at table or the one who serves? Most of
us would say immediately, "The one at table." Yet Jesus says, "Yet here I
am among you as one who serves" (Luke 22:27). Jesus says, in effect, "I'm
telling you that the way of domination will not build a new world. I have
come to model for you the way to be fully human which is to be divine and
exercise authority as God does." Often the church has not even understood
or even agreed with this. In much of our history we have pretty much exer-
cised authority and imposed laws and punishments in the same way as
secular society. This is surely not Jesus's servant leadership.

+Adapted from *The Good News According to Luke: Spiritual Reflections*, p. 185

THE CRUCIFORM PATTERN TO REALITY

The Gospel of Mark is likely the oldest gospel and the shortest. In many ways it is the simplest and clearest, and it cuts the hardest because it is so utterly without frills. The more that commentators have studied this gospel, the more they find that the way in which Mark put events together is trying to say a lot about the centrality of suffering and the cross.

By the end, it is as if the entire gospel is an extended introduction to an extended passion, death, and resurrection account. Mark is telling us that this is how a life of truth and faith culminates in this world. Rather bad news more than good news. There is a cruciform pattern to reality. Life is filled with contradictions, tragedies, and paradoxes, and to reconcile them you invariably pay a big price.

It eventually becomes evident that you're going to get nailed for any life of real depth or love, because this upsets the world's agenda of progress. This is not what the world wants and not what the world understands. Any life of authenticity will lead to its own forms of crucifixion—from others or often leading to various forms of self-denial. Mark constantly brings us back to the central importance of suffering. There's no other way we're going to break through to the ultimate reality that we call resurrection without going through the mystery of transformation, which is dramatically symbolized by the cross.

+Adapted from *The Four Gospels* (CD, MP3)

MODELS FOR MINISTRY

Mark begins his Gospel with the preaching of John the Baptist, a new religious voice from the riverside instead of the temple, and from there calling for change (which is the real meaning of the poorly translated word *repent*). Big Truth invariably comes from the edges of society, or those who have been to the edges or the "wilderness" as it is here called (Mark 1:3).

Jesus's new reality is affirmed and announced on the margins, where people are ready to understand and to ask new questions. The establishment at the center is seldom ready for the truth because it has too much to protect; it has bought into the system and will invariably protect the status quo. As Walter Brueggeman says, "The home of hope is hurt," and it is seldom comfort or security.

John wore a garment of camel hair, and he lived on locusts and wild honey—surely a non-establishment costume for a son of the priestly class. John is amazingly free from his own agenda, his own religious and cultural system, and also his own ego. "He must grow greater, I must grow smaller," he says (John 3:30). John is able to point beyond himself. He's not trying to gather people around himself—which is why he becomes the proto-evangelist. He sets the gold standard of pointing beyond himself and his own security or status—to the Mystery itself. Ministry cannot be a career decision but an urgent vocation.

One can only conclude that Mark began in this way, not just because it was historically true, but because it mirrored his own journey. Some scholars today, especially with new information from the Gnostic Gospels, think that the anonymous man who runs away naked in the Garden of

Gethsemane (Mark 14:50–52) is very likely Mark himself. He is quietly admitting that he also "deserted him" (verse 50) and ran from suffering and humiliation. His nakedness is not just his but ours too.

+Adapted from *The Four Gospels* (CD, MP3)

RELIGIOUS LEADERS CAN BE THE WORST ENEMIES OF THE ACTUAL MESSAGE

Three times in the Gospel of Mark Jesus prophesies his necessary rejection and persecution by "the chief priests, scribes, and teachers of the Law" (Mark 8:31). There should be a message there, somehow.

Then the first time Jesus tells the disciples that "The Human One"—as he deliberately calls himself—will suffer grievously and be rejected and put to death (Mark 8:31), Peter totally rejects this path. Jesus strongly rebukes him—and this is the only person that Jesus ever calls a devil (Mark 8:33). For some reason, Roman Catholics are never told that the first pope also got the strongest reprimand and directly rejected the necessary path and is the only one who later denies Jesus three times.

This is good news for the possibility of conversion, but bad news for those who think that religious authorities are always right. In Mark's account, they show themselves to be unbelievers until the very end of the Gospel, guardians of their own security and status more than any message of resurrection. Read the closing chapter of Mark, which is really rather disappointing.

+Adapted from *The Four Gospels* (CD, MP3)

THIRD TIME SHOULD BE A CHARM!

After their first opposition to the message (Mark 8:31–38), Jesus talks about necessary suffering again (Mark 9:30–37). He tells them that The Human One must be delivered into the hands of the people. They will put him to death, and three days later he will be raised up. But the disciples do not understand what he says, and this time they are afraid to ask him. Maybe they don't want to get bawled out a second time. And yet, they mutter amongst themselves about who is the greatest. It feels like a cartoon.

So Jesus sits down. He calls them to him. You can just feel his exasperation. He says, "Now listen, if anyone wants to be first, he's got to make himself last of all and servant of all" (Mark 9:35). He takes a little child in his arms and says, "Anyone who welcomes one of these little children in my name welcomes me" (Mark 9:37). He's turning the social order upside down. But they still miss the message! So Jesus speaks of necessary suffering a third time (Mark 10:32f). It is hard to believe but the disciples respond by asking "to be seated at Jesus's right and left hand when he comes in glory" (Mark 10:35–37)! It is as if they are on another planet. And these are the famous twelve apostles who founded our faith?

It would be laughable if it were not so tragic, and if it had not become a prediction of so much of church leadership down to our own time. In Mark's Gospel, and you can check it out for yourself, the blind man Bartimaeus (Mark 10:52), the pagan Roman centurion (Mark 15:39), and the sinner Mary Magdalene (Mark 16:9–13) are the only named believers. Again, I must say it: There is a message here!

+Adapted from *The Four Gospels* (CD, MP3)

THE REAL INSPIRATION IN THE BIBLE

Except for the Bible itself, it took until the second half of the twentieth century for the voices of reform and change to begin to have a wide, public, and legitimate voice. I do not think that is an overstatement. In any swing of the pendulum in the direction of justice, the masses, the bottom, were always considered subversive and traitorous, up until the 1960s! Why not, when even the churches were usually looking down from the top and the Bible had been made into establishment literature—which it clearly is not.

The Bible affirms law, authority, and tradition, as most writings in most of history have done, but then it also does something much more: it strongly affirms reform, change, and the voiceless, starting with the Exodus event itself. This is what makes the Bible a truly revolutionary and inspired book. It affirms the necessity of authority and continuity in a culture (tradition), but against the usual pattern it also affirms the currents of change, reform, poverty, inclusion, and justice for the marginalized groups—starting with the enslaved Jewish people themselves.

The Biblical bias toward the bottom has been called by some "the preferential option for the poor." But it is an option, an invitation: it is a grace, and it emerges from inner freedom—or else it would not be from God. In the last analysis, the Bible is biased; it takes the side of the rejected ones, the abandoned ones, the barren women, and the ones who have been excluded, tortured, and kept outside. This is all summed up in Jesus's own ministry: He clearly prefers, heals, and includes the foreigner, the non-Jew, the handicapped and the sinner—without rejecting the people of power, but very clearly critiquing them.

+Adapted from *A Lever and a Place to Stand: The Contemplative Stance, the Active Prayer*, pp. 99–100

GOD IS NOT A SPECTATOR

We live in a finite world where everything is dying, shedding its strength. This is hard to accept, and all our lives we look for exceptions to it. We look for something strong, undying, infinite. Religion tells us that something is God. Great, we say, we'll attach ourselves to this strong God. Then this God comes along and says, "Even I suffer. Even I participate in the finiteness of this world." Thus Clare and Francis's image of God was not an almighty and strong God, but in fact a poor, vulnerable, and humble one like Jesus. This is at the heart of the Biblical and Franciscan world view.

The enfleshment and suffering of Jesus is saying that God is not apart from the trials of humanity. God is not aloof. God is not a mere spectator. God is not merely tolerating or even healing all human suffering. Rather, God is participating with us—in *all* of it—the good and the bad! I wonder if people can avoid becoming sad and cynical about the tragedies of history if they do not know this.

+Adapted from *Job and the Mystery of Suffering*, p. 25

A CENTRAL POINT!

Why does the Bible, and why does Jesus, tell us to care for the poor and the outsider? *It is because we all need to stand in that position for our own conversion.* We each need to stand under the mercy of God, the forgiveness of God, and the grace of God—to understand the very nature of reality. When we are too smug and content, then grace and mercy have no meaning—and God has no meaning. Forgiveness is not even desired.

When we have pulled ourselves up by our own bootstraps, religion is always corrupted because it doesn't understand the mystery of how divine life is transferred, how people change, and how life flows. It has been said by others that religion is largely filled with people who are afraid of hell, and spirituality is for people who have gone through hell.

Jesus is always on the side of the crucified ones. He is not loyal to one religion or this or that group or the so-called worthy ones—*Jesus is loyal to suffering itself, wherever it is.* He is just as loyal to the suffering of Iraqis or Afghanis as he is to the suffering of Americans. He is just as loyal to an oppressed gay man as he is to an oppressed married woman. We do not like that! He grabs all of our self-created boundaries away from us, and suddenly all we have is a free fall into the arms of God, who is our only and solid security. This seems to be God's very surprising agenda, if I am to believe the Bible.

+Adapted from *A Lever and a Place to Stand: The Contemplative Stance,
the Active Prayer*, pp. 100–101

YOU NEED TO BE SHOVED

Creativity and newness of life have a cost, and the cost is what appears to look like death. But really it is not. It is just letting go of one thing to make room for another thing. Loss is always perceived as an enemy or affliction and looks like what we don't want. Somehow to embrace loss, spiritually speaking, is to achieve something more and something bigger. Some form of positive dying invariably allows us to be united with what is Larger Reality, but of course we never know that ahead of time.

So if you spend your whole life avoiding dying, the spiritual teachers would say you will never get there. Meditate on the phrase Jesus gave us, "Unless the grain of wheat dies, it remains just a grain of wheat; but if it dies, it bears much fruit" (John 12:24). That quotation is about as counterintuitive as you can get. Rationally I cannot prove that to you. You have to walk through it. You have to experience it to know that it is in fact true and *true for you*. Frankly, none of us go there until we are shoved.

+Adapted from *The Art of Letting Go: Living the Wisdom of Saint Francis* (CD)

JESUS AND BUDDHA

In many ways, Jesus and Buddha were talking about a very similar process of human transformation.

Pain is the foundational teacher of transformation for both of them, which led to compassion in Buddhist language and love in Christian language (I accept the common definition that our suffering is the degree of resistance we have toward our pain). Buddha taught us how to change our mind about what causes our suffering; Jesus taught us to change our very attitude toward necessary suffering, and we could make it into a redemptive experience for all concerned.

They both recognized that pain is the only thing strong enough to grab our attention and defeat the ego's dominance. Our suffering, in my definition, is *whenever we are not in control.* It is our opposition to the moment, our inner resistance that says, "I don't want it to be this way." Since the ego is always trying to control reality, it is invariably suffering, irritated, or unhappy, because reality is never exactly what we want. Isn't that true? So Buddha teaches us how to undercut the ego in a most radical way through mental attitude and discipline. Jesus teaches us how to undercut the imperial ego by always choosing love, dedication, and service. The final result is often the same, although Jesus's teaching had more social implications, which most Christians roundly ignored.

Jesus's suffering on the cross was a correct diagnosis and revelation of the human dilemma. It was an invitation to enter into solidarity with the pain of the world and our own pain instead of always resisting it, avoiding it, or denying it. Lady Julian of Norwich, my favorite Christian mystic, understood it so well, and she taught, in effect, that "there is only one suffering, and we all share in it." That is the way a higher consciousness eventually sees the so-called problem of evil. That is the way the Buddha saw it too. There is only one suffering, and for Christians Jesus personified a radical surrender to the cosmic mystery of human suffering—a non-resistance to reality until we learn its deepest lessons.

+Adapted from *Jesus and Buddha: Paths to Awakening* (CD, DVD, MP3)

FORGIVENESS OF REALITY

We don't come to God (or truth or love) by insisting on some ideal worldly order or so-called perfection, but in fact we come "to knowledge of salvation by the experience of forgiveness" (Luke 1:77)—forgiveness of reality itself, of others, of ourselves—for being so ordinary, imperfect, and often disappointing. Many also have to forgive God for not being what they wanted or expected. One reason why I am so attracted to Jesus and then to Francis is that they found God in disorder, in imperfection, in the ordinary, and in the real world—not in any idealized concepts. They were more into losing than winning. But the ego does not like that, so we rearranged much of Christianity to fit our egoistic pattern of achievement and climbing.

Isn't it strange that Christians worship a God figure, Jesus, who appears to be clearly losing by every criterion imaginable? And then we spend so much time trying to win, succeed, and perform. We even call Jesus's losing the very redemption of the world—yet we run from it. I think Christians have yet to learn the pattern of redemption. It is evil *undone* much more than evil ever perfectly avoided. It is *disorder reconfigured in our hearts and minds*—much more than demanding any perfect order to our universe.

Much of the Christian religion has largely become holding on instead of letting go. But God, it seems to me, does the holding on (to us!), and we must learn the letting go (of everything else).

+Adapted from *The Art of Letting Go: Living the Wisdom of Saint Francis* (CD)

THE SOUL

It is good to remember that a part of you has always loved God. There is a part of you that has always said Yes. There is a part of you that is Love itself, and that is what we must fall *into*. It is already there. Once you move your identity to that level of deep inner contentment, you will realize you are drawing upon a Life that is much larger than your own and from a deeper abundance. Once you learn this, why would you ever again settle for scarcity in your life? "I'm not enough! This is not enough! I do not have enough!" I am afraid this is the way culture trains you to think. It is a kind of learned helplessness. The Gospel message is just the opposite—inherent power.

Thomas Merton said the way we have structured our lives. We spend our whole life climbing up the ladder of supposed success, and when we get to the top of the ladder we realize it is leaning against the wrong wall—and there is nothing at the top anyway. To get back to the place of inherent abundance, you have to *let go* of all of the false agendas, unreal goals, and passing self-images. It is all about letting go. The spiritual life is more about unlearning than learning, because the deepest you *already knows and already enjoys* (1 John 2:21).

+Adapted from *The Art of Letting Go: Living the Wisdom of Saint Francis* (CD)

THE SUPREME SUNDAY SCHOOL

We must learn how to walk through the stages of dying. We have to grieve over lost friends, relatives, and loves. Death cannot be dealt with through quick answers, religious platitudes, or a stiff upper lip. Dying must be allowed to happen over time, in predictable and necessary stages, both in those who die graciously and in those who love them. Grief, believe it or not, is a liminal space where God can fill the tragic gap with something new and totally unexpected. Yet the process cannot be rushed. I would say that *being present at live birth and conscious death are probably the supreme catechism classes and Sunday schools that we have available to humanity. And yet we have turned them largely into medical events instead of the inherently spiritual events that they are.*

It is not only the loss of persons that leads to grief, but also the loss of ideals, visions, plans, places, relationships, and our youth itself. Elisabeth Kubler-Ross helped us name the necessary stages of grief as denial, anger, bargaining, depression, and finally acceptance (They are the same as the stages of dying itself). Grief work might be one of the most redemptive, and yet still unappreciated, ministries in the church. Some call it bereavement ministry. Thank God, it is being discovered as perhaps the paramount time of both spacious grace and painful gifts.

+Adapted from *Near Occasions of Grace*, p.99

WE LIVE IN THE SHADOWLANDS

All God appears to want from us is honesty and humility (and they are finally the same thing). If God is holding out for human perfection, God is going to have a long wait. There is no other way to read Jesus's stories of the prodigal son (Luke 15:11–32) or the publican and the Pharisee (Luke 18:9–14). In each story, the one who did wrong ends up being right—simply because he is honest and humble about it. The one who is formally right, ends up being terribly wrong because he is proud about his own performance.

How have we been able to miss that important point? I suspect it is because the ego wants to think well of itself and deny any shadow material. Only the soul knows we grow best in the *shadowlands*. We are blinded inside of either total light or total darkness, but "the light shines on inside the darkness, and it is a light that darkness cannot overcome" (John 1:5). Ironically, it is in darkness that we find and ever long for more light. Mystics such as John of the Cross recognized this to be true on the spiritual level first.

It seems the inner and outer worlds mirror one another.

+Adapted from *Breathing under Water: Spirituality and the Twelve Steps*, p. 33

HOLY TEARS

We only become enlightened as the ego dies to its pretenses, and we begin to be led more by soul and by Spirit. That dying is something we are led through by the awesome and quiet grace of God and by the hard work of confronting our own shadow. As we learn to live in Divine Space, we will almost naturally *weep* over our former mistakes, as we recognize that we ourselves are often the very thing that we hate and attack in other people. Weeping, by the way, is much more helpful and true than ever attacking, hating, or denying our sin—maybe not literally weeping, but sincere, non-self-hating *compunction* for our mistakes. (Compunction was the subtle word that the mystics often used to describe a regretful ownership of our sins, but without descending into abusive self-hatred.) Only grace can teach us how to do that. But only then can we begin to become and to live the Great Mystery of compassion, even toward ourselves. How you treat yourself, is how you will usually treat other people too. The person who was vindictive to you today has been vindictive in his own mind since early this morning. She is punitive toward you because she has been punitive toward herself for years—without even knowing it.

God's one-of-a-kind job description is that God actually uses our problems to lead us to the full solution. God is the perfect Recycler, and in the economy of grace, nothing is wasted, not even our worst sins nor our most stupid mistakes. God does not punish our sins, but uses them to soften our hearts toward everything.

+Adapted from *A Lever and a Place to Stand: The Contemplative Stance, the Active Prayer*, pp. 39, 42

JESUS PRAISES FAITH EVEN MORE THAN LOVE

Without the sign of Jonah—the pattern of new life *only* through death (in the belly of the whale)—Christianity remains largely an impotent ideology, another way to win instead of the transformative pain of faith. Or it becomes a language of ascent instead of the treacherous journey of descent that characterizes Jonah, Jeremiah, Job, John the Baptizer and Jesus. After Jesus, Christians used the metaphor the way of the cross. Unfortunately, it became what Jesus did to save us—or a negative theology of atonement—instead of *the necessary pattern that is redemptive for all of us.* Yes, love is always the final goal, but faith seems to be the way you get there. It is the only way to keep your mind, heart, and body open—when it wants to close down.

Faith is thus an end in itself. Faith is not what we do in order to get to heaven. Faith is not belonging to a group or believing a set of intellectual truths. Mutual perfect faith would be a bit of heaven now! To have faith is already to have come alive. "Your faith has saved you" (Luke 18:42) is the way Jesus put it to the blind man. Faith is the opposite of resentment, cynicism, and negativity. Faith is always, finally, a self-fulfilling prophecy. Faith actually begins to create what it desires. Faith always recreates the good world. Without faith, we will inevitably sink into various kinds of despair. Faith is a matter of having new eyes, seeing everything, even our most painful suffering, through and with the eyes of God. It is the only way to keep on the path toward love.

+Adapted from *The Good News According to Luke: Spiritual Reflections*,
pp. 152, 178

THE POWER OF SELF-DISCLOSURE

One's biggest secrets and deepest desires are usually revealed to others, and even discovered by ourselves, in the presence of sorrow, failure, or need—when we are very vulnerable and when one feels entirely safe in the arms of someone's love. That is why all little ones have a huge head start. When vulnerable exchange happens, there is always a *broadening of being* on both sides. We are bigger and better people afterward. Those who never go there always remain small and superficial and unconnected to themselves. You would normally experience it as a lack of substance or even reality in a person. People who have avoided all intimacy normally do not know who they are at any depth—and cannot tell others who *they* are.

What the saints discovered is that God was always disclosing himself to them, not ideas, nor formulas, not answers, but God's inner secrets or what St. Therese of Lisieux called the very "science of love." Such divine intimacy gives you a great big head start in knowing how to do human intimacy.

+Adapted from *Immortal Diamond: Searching for Our True Self*, p. 165

A SECOND GAZE AT ANYTHING IS GOOD

The almost embarrassingly common recurrence of barren—but favored—women in the Old Testament is a brilliant metaphor: "I can't do it, but God can—and will!" This is summed up and personified in the Virgin Mary, but it is still the same Jewish symbol. In Mary, and in us, we see our own incapacity to make spiritual things happen by our own devices, by our own intelligence, and with our own bodies, but I can receive, trust, and allow God to do it in me and through me.

Many translations of Luke's "Magnificat" (Luke 1:46–55) use the wonderful phrase "God has *regarded me* in my lowliness" (Luke 1:48). This French-based word *regardez* means to look at twice, or look at again, or look at deeply. Mary allows herself to be looked at with God's deeper and more considered gaze. When we do that, God's eyes always become more compassionate and merciful. And so do ours if we *regard* anything.

CHRISTMAS IS ALREADY EASTER

In Jesus, God achieved the perfect synthesis of the divine and the human. The incarnation of Jesus demonstrates that God meets us where we are as humans. God freely and fully overcomes the gap from God's side. The problem of redemption is already resolved once and for all, long before its dramatic illustration on the cross. Bethlehem already revealed that it was good to be a human being.

For the Christian, spiritual power is always hidden inside of powerlessness, just as God was hidden and yet revealed in a defenseless baby. If God is ever to be loved and shared, God had to risk both human embodiment and human vulnerability. This is the only thing that enchants and evokes the human heart. We do not properly fall in love with concepts or theological ideas, although some do try; persons fall in love with other persons.

In a weak little child, God is both perfectly hidden and perfectly revealed—and fully loveable.

A BIAS TOWARD THE BOTTOM

Another of Jesus's non-negotiables is the work of justice and generosity toward the poor and the outsider. That's quite clear, quite absolute—page after page of the Gospels. Yet Christian history, even at the highest levels of church, has shown the Church as thinking nothing of amassing fortunes and living grandly (while others starved), but rather totally identifying with power, war, and money (they tend to go together).

At this point in history, when most people can read Jesus's (and the Bible's) clear and consistent bias toward the poor, the foreigner, and the marginalized, it can only be ignored with a culpable blindness and ignorance. Most Christians have indeed been cafeteria Christians when it comes to this. Usually they will markedly emphasize something else (often a sexual issue) to divert attention from what Jesus did not divert attention. As Jesus himself put it, "You strain out gnats and you swallow camels!" (Matthew 23:24). The issues never change in any age, as long as the same old ego is in charge.

+From the webcast *What is the Emerging Church?* (CD, DVD, MP3)

WHO EVER TOLD YOU THAT YOU WERE NAKED?

Jesus was consistently and heroically concerned with the healing of human shame, fear, and guilt, leading to his final and full identification with all human shame on the cross—so we ourselves could become, as Paul says, "the very goodness of God" (2 Corinthians 5:21).

In a way, that is the whole message, starting with Yahweh "sewing tunics of skin" (Genesis 3:21) for Adam and Eve, because *they* felt so ashamed and inferior. Yahweh had just asked them "Who ever told you that you were naked?" (Genesis 3:10). "I surely didn't," he seems to imply.

Today many would say that Christians have become major purveyors of exclusion, guilt and shame for too many of their own people, and surely for the other religions, instead of absorbing shame, healing guilt, and living in solidarity with human suffering as Jesus did so clearly on the cross. No wonder so many no longer take us seriously. We are so unlike Jesus and the God he loved. Jesus was totally inclusive in his entire public life, and yet we created an exclusionary religion in his name. It makes no sense.

+From the webcast *What is the Emerging Church?* (CD, DVD, MP3)

GOAL

Reality is paradoxical and complementary. Non-dual thinking is the highest level of consciousness. Divine union, not private perfection, is the goal of all religion.

INTRODUCTION

One could easily say that what makes something spiritual is precisely that it is paradoxical. "Spiritual things," as we call them, always have a character of mystery, seeming contradiction, awesomeness, invisibility, or a kind of impossibility to them. That is exactly why we call them spiritual! Isn't that true for you?

Organized religion has tended to recognize this, but then tries to organize what is always Mystery so that it does not seem so impossible, invisible, or contradictory. This was probably good and inevitable and is much of the function of Scripture and Sacred Story. They take away some of the shock and impossibility of what we are actually saying. This made for a much more beautiful and engaging story than mere literal telling of bare theological facts. (Read the book or see the movie, *Life of Pi*, where this very point is made brilliantly. Both the literal and the symbolic story are in their own way true, and you can choose the one you prefer to believe at the end.) I really doubt if God cares, as long as you get inside of the Great Mystery of Life and Love.

Organized religion makes for a highly communicable message, one that is much more accessible and often more attractive, that allows us to take great things in necessarily small doses and creates a sharable and sacred language that we could all agree upon and talk about in a hushed or authoritative voice. It also creates a lot of backlash from those who hate or fear symbolism, because it all seems so fanciful to them. This has largely been the case since the seventeenth and eighteenth centuries in the countries that were influenced by what was called the Enlightenment and now the rest of the world, which they in great part colonized.

But organized religion also created *fast food religion* that did not make actual God experience needed or even available to most people. They just believed things or belonged to so-called special and superior groups. Transformation of self or transformation of consciousness was not deemed necessary, except at a few artificial behavioral levels. ("We fast on this day." "We don't drink alcohol or caffeine." "We attend this kind of service.") Such agreed upon practices were very good for creating a kind of social order in a country, but in and of themselves they did not lead people to any deep experience of union with God—or themselves. This, of course, is much of the point that St. Paul goes to great length to demonstrate in two of his most important letters: Romans and Galatians.

As many have said in varying ways, you can (1) Do the old thing with the old mind (conservatives), (2) Do a new thing with the old mind (liberals), or (3) *Do a new thing with a new mind.* Only the third way deserves to be called authentic religion. The other two stances often avoid the necessary dying to self, which is called transformation. The new mind could be called the contemplative mind. The new thing is always love—at ever-deeper levels.

What was originally just thought of as prayer was an attempt to change your thinking cap and look out at reality from a different pair of eyes. Because the word became *cheapened by ego usage*, many of us now use the word *contemplation* to describe this new mind or alternative consciousness. The single most precise way to describe this mind is that it sees things in a non-dual way, which is precisely why holy people can love enemies, overlook offenses, see things as paradoxical without giving up their reason, and believe in Jesus as both fully human and fully divine at the same time. Frankly, without the contemplative mind almost all major religious doctrines and dogmas are just silly nonsense, and worse, they are not even helpful to humanity—or God!

With the contemplative mind, things like forgiveness, love, embracing the outsider, surrender to Mystery, and the integration of contradictory ego and shadow all become possible and even attractive. Now the goal of all religion is in sight—actual union with what is. And what is is called God.

UNITIVE CONSCIOUSNESS

Reality is not totally one, but it is not totally two, either! All things, events, persons, and institutions, if looked at *contemplatively* (non-egocentrically), reveal contradictions, create dilemmas, and have their own shadow side. Wisdom knows how to hold and to grow from this creative tension; ego does not. Our ego splits reality into parts that *it* can manage, but then we pay a big price in regard to actual truth or understanding.

The contemplative mind will be at the heart and center of all teaching in our new Living School. Only the contemplative mind can honor the underlying unity (not two) of things, while also working with them in their distinctness (not totally one). The world almost always presents itself as a paradox, a contradiction, or a problem—like our themes of action and contemplation, Christian and non-Christian, or male and female first did. At the mature level, however, we learn to see all things in terms of *unitive consciousness*, while still respecting, protecting, and working with the very real differences. This is the great—perhaps the greatest—art form. It is the supreme task of all religion.

PRACTICE OVER THEORY

Unless you let the truth of life teach you on its own terms, unless you develop some concrete practices for recognizing and overcoming your dualistic mind, you will remain in the first half of life forever, as most humanity has up to now. In the first half of life, you cannot work with the imperfect, nor can you accept the magical sense of life, which finally means that you cannot love anything or anyone at any depth. Nothing is going to change in history as long as most people are merely dualistic, either-or thinkers. Such splitting and denying leaves us at the level of mere information.

Whole people see and create wholeness wherever they go; divided people see and create splits in everything and everybody. We are meant to see in wholes and no longer just in parts. Yet we get to the whole by falling *down* into the messy parts—so many times, in fact, that we long and thirst for the wholeness and fullness of all things, including ourselves. I promise you this unified field is the only and lasting meaning of *up*.

+Adapted from *Falling Upward: A Spirituality for the Two Halves of Life*,
pp. 150–151

WONDERMENT

"Wondering" is a word connoting at least three things:

Standing in disbelief

Standing in the question itself

Standing in awe before something

Try letting all three standings remain open inside of you. This is a very good way to grow spiritually, as long as the disbelief moves beyond mere skepticism or negativity.

When Scholastic philosophy was at its best (in the twelfth and thirteenth centuries), the development of an idea proceeded by what the great teachers called the *questio* (Latin for "to seek"). Our English word *quest* may come from that understanding. The systematic asking of questions opened up wonder and encouraged spiritual curiosity, ever refining the question itself instead of just looking for the perfect answer.

Scholastic philosophy quickly degenerated when people rushed to supposed easy answers instead of remaining in the brilliance and humility of the *questio* or quest itself. We ended up with Thomists instead of the fitting silence of Thomas Aquinas himself. We ended up with Scotists, who bored you beyond belief, instead of the joyful humility of John Duns Scotus.

+Adapted from *The Naked Now: Learning to See as the Mystics See*, pp. 46–47

YOU MUST START WITH YES

By teaching "Do not judge" (Matthew 7:1) the great teachers are saying that you cannot start seeing or understanding anything if you start with no. You have to start with a Yes of basic acceptance, which means not too quickly labeling, analyzing, or categorizing things as in or out, good or bad, up or down. You have to leave the field open, a field in which God and grace can move. Ego leads with no whereas soul leads with Yes.

The ego seems to strengthen itself by constriction, by being against things; and it feels loss or fear when it opens up. No always comes easier than Yes, and a deep, conscious Yes is the work of freedom and grace. So the soul lives by expansion instead of constriction. Spiritual teachers want you to live by positive action, open field, and studied understanding, and not by resistance, knee-jerk reactions, or defensiveness, and so they always say something like "Do not judge," which is merely a control mechanism.

Words and thoughts are invariably dualistic, but *pure experience is always non dualistic*. You cannot really experience reality with the judgmental mind, because you are dividing the moment before you give yourself to it. The judgmental mind prevents you from being present to the full moment by trying to divide and conquer. Instead, *you* end up dividing yourself and being conquered.

+Adapted from *The Naked Now*, pp. 46–47, 49–50, and
When Action Meets Contemplation (CD, DVD)

SMILING IS A FORM OF SALVATION

In the second half of life, you have begun to live and experience the joy of your inner purpose. The outer purpose and goals matter less and less and have less power over you. You are much more self-possessed and grounded. At one and the same time, you know what you do know (but now deeply and quietly), and you also know what you do not know. This is perhaps what Thomas Merton means by living in the "belly of a paradox." Many politicians and clergy know what they know, but they don't know what they don't know, and that's what makes them dangerous. Only people who are comfortable not knowing can usually smile. People who are preoccupied with knowing have little space for smiling.

A creative tension in the second half of life, knowing what you know *and* knowing what you don't know, is a necessary one. All you know is that it is foundationally all right, despite the seeming contradictions and conflict. That's why the holy old man can laugh and the holy old woman can smile. I heard recently that a typical small child smiles three hundred times a day and a typical old man smiles three times a day in our culture. What has happened between six and sixty? Whatever it is, it tells me that religion is not doing its job very well.

+Adapted from *Adult Christianity and How to Get There* (CD, MP3)

THE THIRD EYE

No man can say his eyes have had enough of seeing,
his ears their full of hearing.
—Ecclesiastes 1:8

Third-eye seeing is the way the mystics see. They do not reject the first eye (thought or sight); the senses matter to them, but they know there is more. Nor do they reject the second eye (the eye of reason, meditation and reflection), but they know not to confuse knowledge with depth or mere correct information with the transformation of consciousness itself. The mystical gaze builds upon the first two eyes—*and yet goes further*. This is third eye seeing.

Third eye seeing happens whenever, by some wondrous coincidence, our heart space, our mind space, and our body awareness are all simultaneously open and nonresistant. I like to call it *presence*. It is experienced as a moment of deep inner connection, and it always pulls you, intensely satisfied, into the naked and undefended now, which can involve both profound joy and profound sadness, and it will always include the first and second eyes at some level. So it is never irrational, but it is indeed transrational. Dionysius called it "super-essential knowing."

+Adapted from *The Naked Now: Learning to See as the Mystics See*, p. 28

LIGHT AND DARKNESS

Our Christian wisdom is to name the darkness as darkness, and the Light as light, and to learn how to live and work in the Light so that "the darkness does not overcome it" (John 1:5). But we can never deny that darkness exists, even in us.

If we have a pie-in-the-sky, everything-is-beautiful attitude, we are in fact going to be trapped by the darkness because we are not seeing clearly enough to allow both the wheat and the chaff of everything. Conversely, if we can only see the darkness and forget the more foundational Light, we will be destroyed by our own negativity and fanaticism, or we will naïvely think we are apart from and somehow above the darkness.

Instead, we must wait and work with hope inside of the darkness—while never doubting the Light that Jesus says he is (John 8:12)—and that we are too! Many people do not notice that he also says we are the light of the world too (Matthew 5:14). That is the narrow birth canal of God into the world—*through* the darkness and into an ever greater Light, but a light that we carry with us and in us.

+Adapted from *Preparing for Christmas with Richard Rohr*, pp. 23–24

THE NAKED NOW

From now on, we must look at nothing from the ordinary point of view. If anyone is in Christ, they have become a completely new construct, and the old construct must pass away!
—2 Corinthians 5:16

Today the unnecessary suffering on this earth is great for people who could have known better and should have been taught better by their religions. In the West, religion became preoccupied with *telling people what to know more than how to know, telling people what to see more than how to see.* We ended up seeing Holy Things faintly, trying to understand Great Things with a whittled-down mind, and trying to love God with our own small and divided heart. It has been like trying to view the galaxies with a five-dollar pair of binoculars.

Contemplation, my word for this larger seeing, keeps the whole field open; it remains vulnerable before the moment, the event, or the person—before it divides and tries to conquer or control it. Contemplatives refuse to create false dichotomies, dividing the field for the sake of the quick comfort of their ego. I call contemplation "full-access knowing"—not irrational, but pre-rational, non-rational, rational and transrational all at once. Contemplation is an exercise in keeping your heart and mind spaces open long enough for the mind to see other hidden material. It is content with the naked now and waits for futures given by God and grace.

+Adapted from *The Naked Now: Learning to See as the Mystics See,* pp. 33–34

PURE PRESENCE

"Wisdom is bright and does not grow dim...
and is found by those who look for her"
—Wisdom 6:12–13

Wisdom is not the gathering of more facts and information, as if that would eventually coalesce into truth. Wisdom is precisely a different way of seeing and knowing the ten thousand things in a new way. I suggest that wisdom *is precisely the freedom to be truly present to what is right in front of you*. Presence *is* wisdom! People who are fully present know how to see fully, rightly, and truthfully.

Presence is the one thing necessary for wisdom, and in many ways, it is the hardest thing of all. Just try to keep (1) your heart space open, (2) your mind without division or resistance, and (3) your body aware of where it is—and all at the same time! Most religions just decided it was easier to believe doctrines and obey often arbitrary laws than the truly converting work of being present. Those who can be present will know what they need to know, and in a wisdom way.

+From *The Naked Now: Learning to See as the Mystics See*, pp. 59–60

STAYING AWAKE

Wisdom is a spirit, a friend to all.

—Wisdom 1:6

It is usually over time and with patience that we come to see the wonderful patterns of grace, which is why it takes most of us a long time to be converted. Our focus slowly moves from an initial preoccupation with perfect actions (first half of life issues), to naked *presence itself*. The code word for that is simply *prayer*, but it became cheapened by misuse.

Jesus will often call prayer "vigilance," "seeing," or "being awake." When you are aware and awakened, you will know for yourself all that you need to know. In fact, "Stay awake" is the last thing Jesus says to the apostles—three or perhaps four times—before he is taken away to be killed (Matthew 26:38–45). Finally, continuing to find them asleep, he kindly but sadly says, "Sleep now and take your rest," which might have been his resigned, forgiving statement to the church itself.

It is not that we do not want to be awake, but very few teachers have actually told us how to do that in a very practical way. We call it the teaching of contemplation.

+Adapted from *Things Hidden: Scripture as Spirituality*, p. 16

THE BRILLIANT CLOUD OF UNKNOWING

And I chose to have Wisdom rather than the light, because the splendor
of her never yields to sleep.
—Wisdom 7:10

The beauty of the unconscious is that it knows a great deal, whether personal or collective, but it always knows that it does not know, cannot say, dare not try to prove or assert too strongly, because what it does know is that there is *always more—and all words will fall short.* The contemplative is precisely the person who agrees to live in that unique kind of brightness (a combination of light and dark that is brighter still!). The paradox, of course, is that it does not feel like brightness at all, but what John of the Cross calls a "luminous darkness," or others call "learned ignorance."

In summary, you cannot grow in the great art form, the integration of action and contemplation, without (1) a strong tolerance for ambiguity, (2) an ability to allow, forgive, and contain a certain degree of anxiety, and (3) a willingness to not know and not even need to know. This is how you allow and encounter mystery. All else is mere religion.

+Adapted from *A Lever and a Place to Stand*: *The Contemplative Stance,
the Active Prayer*, p. x

PARADOX

God is the only one we can surrender to without losing ourselves. In fact, we find our deepest, truest, and most loving self in God. Yet it is still a paradox. I am increasingly convinced that all true spirituality has the character of paradox to it, precisely because it is always holding together the Whole of Reality, which is always everything.

Everything in this world is both attractive and non-attractive, light and darkness, passing and eternal, life and death—at the same time. Don't just accept my statement here, but think about this philosophically, physically, biologically, or scientifically. Everything has different sides, levels, truths, perspectives and potential problems that it carries along with it.

A paradox is something that appears to be a contradiction, but from another perspective is not a contradiction at all. You and I are living paradoxes, and therefore most prepared to see ourselves in all outer reality. If you can hold and forgive the contradictions within yourself, you can normally do it everywhere else, too. If you cannot do it in yourself, you will actually create, project, and revel in dichotomies everywhere else.

+Adapted from *Holding the Tension: The Power of Paradox* (CD, DVD, MP3)

NOT TO BE A SAINT

What is the source of your spiritual power? It's radical union with God, not just doing good things or holding a role or function.

Often we make the basis for ministry professionalism, education, and up-to-date-ism, which are all good in themselves. But in the end, the only basis for fruitful Christianity is divine union. Such people change you and change the world. Leon Bloy said it well: "There is only one sadness in life, only one—*not* to be a saint."

+Adapted from *Radical Grace: Daily Meditations*, p. 382

ONE GREAT INCARNATION IN DIFFERENT FORMS

Two thousand years ago was the *human* incarnation of God in Jesus, but before that there was the first and original incarnation through light, water, land, sun, moon stars, plants, trees, fruit, birds, serpents, cattle, fish, and "every kind of wild beast" according to our own creation story (Genesis 1:3–25). This was the Cosmic Christ through which God has "let us know the mystery of his purpose, the hidden plan he so kindly made from the beginning in Christ" (Ephesians 1:9). Christ is Jesus's title for his life's purpose.

All of creation, it seems, has been obedient to its destiny, "each mortal thing does one thing and the same…myself it speaks and spells, crying *'What I do is me, for that I came'*" (Gerard Manley Hopkins, "As Kingfishers Catch Fire"). Wouldn't it be our last and greatest humiliation, if one day we realized that all other creatures have obeyed their destiny with a kind of humility and with trustful surrender? All, except us.

It is only humans who have resisted "the one great act of giving birth" (Romans 8:22) and in fact have frequently chosen death for themselves and for so many others. We have resisted and denied our own incarnation as one representation, just one, of the living and dying of God. We do not need to be everything to be *one good and true thing*! That is more than enough.

+Adapted from *Radical Grace* 23, no. 2, p. 3

PERFECTION IS PRECISELY THE ABILITY TO INCLUDE IMPERFECTION

In an authentic Navajo rug there is always one clear imperfection woven into the pattern. And interestingly enough, this is precisely where the Spirit moves in and out of the rug! The Semitic mind, the Native mind, the Eastern mind (which, by the way, Jesus would have been much closer to) understands perfection in precisely that way. The East is much more comfortable with paradox, mystery, and non-dual thinking than the Western mind which has been much more formed by Greek logic, which is very clear, very consistent, and very helpful by also being dualistic. It seems to me that you first have to succeed at good dualistic thinking before you can also experience its limitations. But most Western people just stop there and find that they are unable to deal with death, suffering, the illogic nature of love, any honest notion of God, Mystery, or infinity.

Perfection is not the elimination of imperfection, as we think. Divine perfection is, in fact, the ability to recognize, forgive, and include imperfection!—just as God does with all of us. Only in this way can we find *the beautiful and hidden wholeness of God* underneath the passing human show. This is the pearl of great price in my opinion. Non-dual thinking and seeing is the change that changes everything. It makes love, mercy, patience, and forgiveness possible.

UNION, NOT PERFECTION

On a first level I see mystical moments as moments of enlargement. Suddenly we're bigger. We don't feel a need to condemn, exclude, divide or separate. Secondarily, mysticism is a deep experience of connectedness or union. Maybe that is why we feel larger? Unfortunately, most of us were sent on private paths of perfection which none of us could ever achieve.

The path of union is different than the path of perfection. Perfection gives the impression that by effort or more knowing I can achieve wholeness separate from God, from anyone else, or from connection to the Whole. It appeals to our individualism and our ego. It's amazing how much of Christian history sent us on a self-defeating course toward private perfection. On the day of my first vows in 1962, the preacher glared at us little novices and quoted the line "Thou shalt be perfect as your heavenly Father is perfect!" Most of the honest guys left within the first few years when they could not achieve it. They were told they could achieve heaven in a most hellish way.

Many people gave up on the spiritual life or religion when they saw they could not be perfect. They ended up practical agnostics or practical atheists, and they refused to be hypocrites. Many of us kept up the forms and the words, we kept going to church, but there was no longer the inner desire, joy, or expectation that is possible on the path of union. Mysticism does not defeat the soul; moralism always does. Mysticism invites humanity forward,; moralism (read "perfectionism") excludes and condemns itself and most others.

+Adapted from *Following the Mystics through the Narrow Gate….*
Seeing God in All Things (CD, DVD, MP3)

CALLING EVIL GOOD AND GOOD EVIL

With the spiritual "gift of discernment" (1 Corinthians 12:10) you can understand on a whole new level what we mean when we say, "God saves you," because now you see with wisdom and truth. It is the birth of subtlety, discrimination, and compassionate seeing. You move beyond any notion that this or that correct action will get you to heaven. It means that when "your eye is *single* [or sound], your whole body will be filled with light" (Luke 11:34). When you see things non-dually, in their wholeness, and do not split between the false totally good and totally bad, you will grow up spiritually and begin to live honestly and wisely in this world.

Recognizing the world, the flesh, and the devil as the classic three sources of evil (and also the source of the spiral of violence): (1) the world's agreed upon systems of self-congratulation and self-protection; (2) our individual sin, which is then inevitable; (3) the demonic legitimization of oppressive and destructive power by governments and institutions—can be a primary tool to help you discern what is truly good and what is often evil. Without discernment, many of us end up calling good evil and evil good, just as Isaiah predicted (Isaiah 5:20) and the murder of Jesus revealed. The proper sequencing is very important: if you nip the disguise of evil in the first stage of socially agreed upon evil, the next two largely lose most of their power to fool you. The flesh and the devil are exposed for what they are.

+Adapted from *Spiral of Violence: The World, the Flesh, and the Devil* (CD, MP3)

LOOKING OVER ITS SHOULDER

Our practice of contemplation is not avoiding distractions, as was foolishly taught, but instead we use them to look over our shoulders for God! This was the brilliant insight of the author of the fourteenth-century book, *The Cloud of Unknowing* (Chapter 32). The persistence of the distraction can actually have the effect of steadying your gaze, deepening your decision, increasing your freedom, your choice, and your desire for God and for grace—over this or that passing phenomenon. The same can be true with any persistent temptation.

The shoulders of the distraction almost become your necessary vantage point and they create the crosshairs of your seeing. Who would have thought? It is an ideal example of how God uses everything to bring us to God. I wasted years on trying to deny, repress, or avoid distractions and dirty thoughts—which never worked very well. Many gave up on prayer and the spiritual life because of it.

It is not the avoidance of problems that makes you a contemplative, but a daily holding of the problem, straight on (while not letting it hold onto you)—and finding a resolution in the much deeper and more spacious "peace of Christ, which will guard your heart and your mind" (Philippians 4:7). I never knew it would take such hourly vigilance to *guard my heart and my mind* from anger, judgment, fear, jealousy, and negativity of any kind. Only the vast peace of Christ can do it. Now it is almost my only daily discipline, much, much harder than poverty, chastity, and obedience ever were!

+Adapted from *Contemplation in Action*, p. 18

THE SECOND GAZE

To reach the goal of compassion we must not stop with the first gaze. It is the second gaze that we struggle and wait for most of our lives. In the first half of life, we have a critical mind and a demanding heart and a lot of impatience. These characteristics are both gifts and curses, as you might expect. We cannot risk losing touch with either our angels or our demons. They are both good teachers. The trials of life invariably lead us to a second gaze. This is the gaze of compassion and patience. Now we look out at life from a place of Divine Intimacy where we are finally safe and at home.

Only the second gaze sees fully and truthfully. The final surprise is that one's supposed second gaze is actually God's Eternal Gaze at you, which you have finally received like a long awaited radio signal, and once you receive it, it just automatically bounces back to the Sender.

+Adapted from *Contemplation in Action*, pp. 19–20

LIBERALS VERSUS CONSERVATIVES

At this time in history, the contemporary choice offered most Americans is *between unstable correctness (liberals) and stable illusion (conservatives)!* What a choice! It has little to do with real transformation in either case. How different from the radical traditionalism of T.S. Eliot: "You are not here to verify, instruct yourself or inform curiosity or carry report. You are here to kneel." (*Little Gidding*).

There *is* a third way, and it probably is a way of kneeling. Most people would just call it wisdom. It demands a transformation of consciousness and a move beyond the dualistic win/lose mind of both liberals and conservatives. An authentic God encounter is the quickest and truest path to such wisdom, which is non-dual consciousness.

Neither expelling nor excluding (conservative temptation), nor perfect explaining (liberal temptation) is our task. True participation in God liberates us each *from* our control towers and *for* the compelling and overarching vision of the Reign of God—where there are no liberals or conservatives. Here, the paradoxes—life and death, success and failure, loyalty to what is and risk for what needs to be—do not fight with one another, but lie in an endless embrace. We must penetrate behind them both—into the Mystery that bears them both. This is contemplation in action.

+Adapted from *Contemplation in Action*, pp. 27–30

NON-DUAL CONSCIOUSNESS

Contemplation teaches a different mind which leaves itself open so when the biggies come along (love, suffering, death, infinity, contradictions, God, and probably sexuality), we still remain with an open field. We don't just close down when it doesn't make full sense, or we are not in full control of immediately feel validated. That calm and non-egocentric mind is called contemplative or non-dual thinking.

The lowest level of consciousness is entirely dualistic (win/lose)—me versus the world and basic survival. Many, I am afraid, never move beyond this. The higher levels of consciousness are more and more able to deal with contradictions, paradoxes, and all Mystery (win/win). This is spiritual maturity. At the higher levels, we can teach things like compassion, mercy, forgiveness, selflessness, even love of enemies. Any good contemplative practice quickly greases the wheels of the mind toward non-dual consciousness. This is exactly why saints can overlook offenses and love enemies! We must be honest enough to admit that this has not characterized most Christian clergy or laity up to now. It is not really their fault. No one taught them how to pray, even in seminaries or the typical parish.

+Adapted from *Contemplation AND Action* (CD, MP3)

TRINITY

Niels Bohr, the Danish physicist who was a major contributor to quantum physics and nuclear fission, said the universe is "not only stranger than we think, but stranger than we can think." Our supposed logic has to break down before we can comprehend the nature of the universe and the bare beginnings of the nature of God. I think the doctrine of the Trinity is saying the same thing. The principle of three breaks down all dualistic either-or thinking and sets us on a dynamic course of ongoing experience.

There are some things that can only be known experientially, and each generation must learn it for themselves. The prayer of quiet is a most simple and universal path. Of all the religious rituals and practices I know of, nothing will lead us to that place of nakedness and vulnerability more than regular experiences of solitude and silence, where our ego identity falls away, where our explanations don't mean anything, where our superiority doesn't matter and we have to sit there in our naked who-ness.

If God wants to get through to us, and the Trinitarian Flow wants to come alive in us, that's when God has the best chance. God is not only stranger than we think, but stranger than the logical mind can think. Perhaps much of the weakness of the first two thousand years of reflection on the Trinity, and many of our doctrines and dogmas, is that we've tried to do it with our logical minds instead of with prayer. The belief in God as a Trinity is saying God is more an active verb than a stable noun. You know it in the flow of life itself.

+Adapted from *The Shape of God: Deepening the Mystery of the Trinity*
(CD, DVD, MP3)

THE MYSTERY OF PRESENCE

The Eucharistic body and blood of Christ is a place we must come to again and again to find our own face, to find our deepest name, and to find our absolute identity in God. It takes years for this to sink in. It is too big a truth for any one moment, too grand and wonderful for our small hearts and minds.

So we keep *eating this mystery* that is simultaneously the joy of God and the suffering of God packed into one meal. (Some have seen the body (bread) as eating the joy and the blood (wine) as drinking the suffering.) All we can really do is to be present ourselves, because we cannot ever rationally understand this. Presence cannot really be explained.

Now when the two presences meet, Jesus and the soul, then we have what Catholics brilliantly call "the Real Presence." We did maintain the objective end of the presence from God's side rather well, but we seldom taught people the subjective way of *how to be present themselves!* Presence is a relational concept, and both sides must be there, or there is no real presence.

+Adapted from *Eucharist as Touchstone* (CD, MP3)

WHY ARE WE HERE?

The Perennial Tradition, which most world religions have stated in different ways, somehow says that a person's final end is union with God and all things. This is the simple goal of our existence. If your religion is not helping you to do that, then you better get a new religion.

Most people, particularly young people, have no knowledge that the purpose of their life is union with Divine Reality. They have been told that the purpose of life is to get a degree and make money and have kids and die. That's the narrowed down secular understanding of reality, which is followed exactly by many Christians. Most are no longer connected to the perennial philosophy and just waste time fighting their own religion. This is not wisdom at all—it is low level survival. We're now living in a largely survival mode in most Western cultures. No wonder so many of our kids turn to drugs, drink, and promiscuous sex, because there's nothing else that's very exciting or very *true*.

Question number three of *The New Baltimore Catechism* was "Why did God make us?" And the answer was exciting, true, and simple enough for a whole lifetime of meaning: "God made us to show forth his goodness and to share with us his everlasting happiness in heaven."

ONE, TRUE, GOOD

The Scholastic philosophers were in rather universal agreement that the character of being is that it is always one (this is the basis for non-dual consciousness), it is always true, and it is always good! These were called *the three Transcendentals*. Naked *is-ness* is the most foundational level of being. And this pure, naked being is always one (inherently connected). It's always at its foundation true and not false. And Being is not bad but always good.

So Reality starts with an original blessing and not "original sin"! As Genesis had said five times in a row about creation, "It was good" and ends with "Indeed it was very good" (Genesis 1:10–25). It is so sad and really culpable that we turned such a wonderful message from the first chapter of the Bible around and started with a negative—which then became very hard to turn positive again. This deeply distorted the Christian message and Christian history.

So if you were connected inherently with the nature of being, you would always be united and uniting, you would always do the inherently true thing, and you would always do the morally good thing. This is your deepest nature.

BEAUTY

Franciscan John Duns Scotus says that when the one and the true and the good are operating in harmony, that is beauty! *Beauty is the harmony between unity, truth, and goodness.* When you can see all three, or even one, you will always be expanded and delighted. Whenever naked Being, which is *always one*, *truth itself*, and *always good*, shows itself, I will have the ability to see there's something beautiful about it too, even though it might be broken, or poor, or sad, or suffering. It creates a positive foundation for all of creation and humanity, a basis for cosmic hope, and a prediction of our final goal. Alpha and Omega must somehow match! That Omega Point of history is called by Christians "Resurrection."

Scotus was merely making a grounding philosophy out of Jesus's and Francis's own love of lepers, the marginalized, and the poor—whom they both found beautiful! Beauty was not first of all an aesthetic concept but a fully ethical concept. Beauty is what we experience whenever the harmony of goodness, truth, and integrity show themselves, despite any contrary evidence (which is always there!).

CONSCIOUSNESS

The word *Buddha* means "I am awake." The last words of Jesus before his arrest in the garden were also "Stay awake" (Matthew 26:38). To be awake is to be fully conscious. The Buddhists sometimes call it "object-less consciousness"; I might just call it "undefended knowing." It is a consciousness where we are not conscious of anything in particular but everything in general. It is a panoramic receptive awareness—whereby you take in all that the moment offers without eliminating anything or attaching to anything. You just watch it pass.

This does not come naturally to us, surely not in our culture. We have to work at it. All forms of meditation and contemplation teach some form of *compartmentalizing or limiting the control of the mental ego*—or what some call the "monkey mind," which just keeps jumping from observation to observation, distraction to distraction, feeling to feeling, commentary to commentary. Most of this mental action means very little and is actually the opposite of consciousness. In fact, it is unconsciousness. It is even foolish to call it "thinking" at all, although educated people tend to think their self-referential commentaries are high-level thinking.

+Adapted from *Jesus and Buddha: Paths to Awakening* (CD, DVD, MP3)

PARADOXES NOT CONTRADICTIONS

Spiritual teachers teach in the language of paradox and mystery and what seems like contradiction, but then they show us that it is not contradiction at all. I know paradox is not a word that we use much in our everyday life. Let me define a paradox very simply: A paradox is seeming contradiction which is not really contradictory at all if looked at from another angle or through a larger frame. A paradox always demands a change on the side of the observer. If we look at almost all things honestly we see everything has a character of paradox to it. Everything, including ourselves, and most especially God, has some seeming contradictions, some mysterious parts that we cannot understand or explain. Can you think of an exception?

Institutions, countries, groups, religions, and persons have many inherent contradictions. Understanding a paradox is to look at something long enough so as to overcome the contradiction and see things at a different level of consciousness. This should be one of the primary and totally predictable effects of authentic God experience. God surely greases the wheels of awareness and even the evolution of humanity by growing people toward a much higher capacity. Wouldn't you expect God to have that effect?

+Adapted from *The Art of Letting Go: Living the Wisdom of Saint Francis* (CD)

ONE INSULT AFTER ANOTHER!

Struggling with one's own shadow self, facing interior conflicts and moral failures, undergoing rejections and abandonment, daily humiliations, experiencing any kind of abuse, or your own clear limitations, even accepting that some people hate you: All of these are gateways into deeper consciousness and the flowering of the soul. These experiences give us a privileged window into the naked (read "undefendable") now, because impossible contradictions are staring us in the face.

Much needed healing; forgiving what is, weeping over and accepting one's interior poverty and contradictions are normally necessary to invite a person into the contemplative mind. (Watch Paul do this in a classic way from the depths of Romans 7:14 to the heights of his mystic poetry in most of Romans 8.) As one Zen Master said, "Avoid the spiritual journey, it is one insult after another!"

Yet in facing the contradictions that we ourselves are, we become living icons of Yes/And. Once we can accept mercy, it is almost natural to hand it on to others. You become a conduit of what you yourself have received.

+Adapted from *The Naked Now: Learning to See as the Mystics See*, pp. 125–126

ACTING OR WAITING

At times we have to step into God's silence and patiently wait. We have to *put out the fleece* as Gideon did (Judges 6:37–40), and wait for the descent of the divine dew or some kind of confirmation from God that we are on the right course. That is a good way to keep our own ego drive out of the way.

Yet there are other times when we need to go ahead and act on our own best intuitions and presume that God is guiding us and will guide us. But even then we must finally wait for the divine backup. Sometimes that is even the greater act of faith and courage and takes even more patience. What if the divine dew does not fall? What do we do then?

When either waiting or moving forward is done out of a spirit of *union and surrender*, we can trust that God will make good out of it—even if we are mistaken! *It is not about being correct, it is about being connected.*

THE FREEDOM OF NOT KNOWING

Prayer is largely just being silent: holding the tension instead of even talking it through, offering the moment instead of fixing it by words and ideas, loving reality as it is instead of understanding it fully. Prayer is commonly a willingness to say "I don't know." We must not push the river, we must just trust that we are already in the river, and God is the certain flow and current.

That may be impractical, but the way of faith is not the way of efficiency. So much of life is just a matter of listening and waiting and enjoying the expansiveness that comes from such willingness to hold. It is like carrying and growing a baby: women wait and trust and hopefully eat good food, and the baby is born.

BOTH BETTER AND WORSE THAN WE THINK

I am increasingly convinced that all true spirituality has the character of paradox to it, precisely because it is always holding together the whole of reality (and not just parts), which is always a kind of Yes/And. Everything except God is both attractive and non-unattractive, light and darkness, passing and eternal, life and death. There are really no exceptions.

Paradox admits that every profound truth is countered by another, often less flattering, profound truth—although sometimes it is more flattering. People who have an inner life of prayer always find out that God is much, much better than mere religion could ever imagine.

You and I are living paradoxes, which everybody can see except us. Others see your denied faults, but a few golden ones also see what is special and good about you. I hope you have a people like that in your life!

+Adapted from *Holding the Tension: The Power of Paradox* (CD, DVD, MP3)

HOLD OUT FOR WIN-WIN

Jesus, heard correctly, gives us a wonderful win-win world view (which is why it is called Good News!), but what the ego invariably does with the Gospel is make it into a low level win-lose game. That's the only way the dualistic mind can think. You're either in or you're out. The ego defines itself largely by what it is not and what it is against. The mystical or non-dual mind alone is capable of win-win.

Yet we don't know how to include, how to forgive, how to pour mercy and compassion and patience upon events as God apparently does. Augustine of Hippo, a man filled with contradictions, was a master at holding those contradictions within himself and before God. In his *Confessions*, probably the first real autobiography in the West, he beautifully describes the power and simultaneously the deep powerlessness of true God experience. Faith absolutely knows and yet it does not know at all—and Augustine appears to understand and live this thoroughly biblical notion of faith!

Yet even Augustine had his blind spots, particularly in regard to sexuality and poor Pelagius whom he wrongly condemned. Here he was not content to not know but instead knew negatively or judgmentally. But that gives me hope too, because I do the same. And, yet, we still call St. Augustine a "Doctor of the Church."

+Adapted from *Holding the Tension: The Power of Paradox* (CD, DVD, MP3)

THE IRONY OF FAITH

When Christianity aligns itself with power (and the mindset of power, which is the need to be right and always in control) there's simply very little room for the darkness of faith; that spacious place where God is actually able to form us. We told individuals to have faith, but seldom modeled it at the corporate level, so very often the individual did not know how to do it either. (This became evident in the worldwide pedophilia scandal, where our leaders protected the institution over truth and mercy.)

Good powerlessness (because there is also a bad powerlessness) allows you to "fall into the hands of the living God" (Hebrews 10:31). You stop holding yourself up so you can be held. There, wonderfully, you are not in control and only God needs to be right. That is always the very special space of any positive powerlessness and vulnerability, but it is admittedly rare.

Faith can only happen in this very special threshold space. You don't really *do* faith, it happens to you when you give up control and all the steering of your ship. Frankly, we often do it when we have no other choice. Faith hardly ever happens when we rush to judgment or seek too quick of a resolution of anything. Thus, you see why faith will invariably be a minority and suspect position. And you also see why the saints always said that faith is a gift. You fall into it more than ever fully choosing it, and only then do you know how grace, love, and God can sustain you and strengthen you at very deep levels.

+Adapted from *Holding the Tension: The Power of Paradox* (CD, DVD, MP3)

A TRAPDOOR INTO HOLINESS

If God is crucified flesh, and that is what Paul has fallen in love with, then everything shows itself for him to also be a disguise: weakness is really strength, wisdom is really foolishness, death is really life, matter is really spirit, religion is often slavery, and sin itself is actually the trapdoor into salvation. People must recognize what a revolutionary thinker Paul was with such teachings as these; and we made him into a mere moralistic churchman. That totally misses Paul's gift and Paul's genius.

So the truth lies neither in the total affirmation nor in the total denial of either side of things for Paul, but precisely in the tug of war between the two. I am convinced that St. Paul is a brilliant non-dual mystic. Follow him in this direction, and you might become wise and even holy. But be prepared to displease those on either entrenched side.

+Adapted from *Great Themes of Paul: Life as Participation* (CD)

CRUCIFIED ON THE COLLISION OF OPPOSITES

He made the two into one, breaking down the barrier keeping them
apart…. He destroyed in his own person the hostility…to create one single
New Humanity…restoring peace through the cross, to unite them in a
single Body and reconcile all things into God.
— Ephesians 2:14–16

What an absolutely amazing passage this is! It is an utterly new agenda for
humanity, which has never largely been followed. It demands a rather high
level of consciousness and conscience.

In the mystery of paradox, if you try to rest on one side and forget the
other, you always lose the Bigger Truth. The "Four Square Gospel," revealed
on the cross, is always Yes/And. As many sages have said, the opposite of
every profound truth is normally another profound truth, and they must
listen to one another for wisdom to emerge.

We've seen, for example, Christian cultures, like much of Latin America,
Russia, and Europe that are entirely centered on a pious, individualistic
notion of the Cross, while losing any real sense of Resurrection for history
or others. Justice for the poor, for animals, or the earth was not even in the
conversation. In the USA, on the other hand, we created a convenient pros-
perity gospel,—trumped-up resurrection for a few and almost no reference to the pain and suffering of the world. Much of American evangelical
Christianity up to now has had little capacity for self-criticism and tries to
get to resurrection without any acknowledgment of the cross that most of
the world must carry. They limit Christ's salvation to a very individualistic
notion, and their Christ ends up being very small and stingy.

Jesus was hung on—and held together—the cosmic collision of opposites (revealed in the very geometric sign of the cross). He let it destroy him, as his two nailed hands held all the great opposites safely together as one: the good and the bad thief, heaven and earth, matter and spirit, both sinners and saints gathered at his feet, a traditional Jew revealing a very revolutionary message to his and all religion, a naked male body revealing an utterly feminine soul. On the cross, Jesus becomes the Cosmic Christ.

+Adapted from *Great Themes of Paul: Life as Participation* (CD)

SOMEWHERE BEFORE EVERYWHERE

What we're doing in contemplation is learning, quite simply, how to *be present*. That is the only way to encounter any other presence, including God in prayer, Jesus in the Eucharist, Jesus in others. The change is all and always on *our* side. God is present everywhere all the time. There really is not much point in arguing about if and how Jesus is present in the bread and wine. Simply be present yourself and you will know all that you need to know. It is an exercise in surrender and presence from your side alone.

We know that God is always given from God's side, but we have to learn how to receive such total givenness, which is a very vulnerable position for humans. So Jesus said "Eat it" and did not say "Think about it," which is our defensive control tower. The Christian strategy seems to be this: struggle with divine presence in one focused, determined, and *assured* place (bread and wine, which is just about as universal a symbol as you can get)—and from that moment of space and time move to all space and all time. That is the final and full goal.

+Adapted from *CAC Foundation Set: Gospel Call to Compassionate Action (Bias from the Bottom)* and *Contemplative Prayer* (CD)

THE NARROW ROAD

Contemplation is meeting as much reality as we can handle in its most simple and immediate form, without filters, judgments, and commentaries. Now you see why it is so rare and, in fact, "the narrow road that few walk on" (Matthew 7:14). The only way you can contemplate is by recognizing and relativizing your own compulsive mental grids—your practiced ways of judging, critiquing, blocking, and computing everything.

This is what we are trying to do by practicing contemplative prayer, and people addicted to their own mind will find contemplation most difficult, if not impossible. Much that is called thinking is simply the ego's stating of what it prefers and likes—and its resisting of what it does not like. Narcissistic reactions to the moment are not worthy of being called thinking. Yet that is much of our public and private discourse.

When your judgmental grid and all its commentaries are placed aside, God finally has a chance to get through to you, because your pettiness is at last out of the way. Then Truth stands revealed! You will begin to recognize that we all carry the Divine Indwelling within us, and we all carry it equally. That will change your theology, your politics, and your entire world view. In fact, it is the very birth of the soul.

+Adapted from *CAC Foundation Set: Gospel Call to Compassionate Action
(Bias from the Bottom)* and *Contemplative Prayer* (CD, MP3)

"THY KINGDOM COME" MEANS MY KINGDOM GO

I hope you've met at least one Kingdom person in your life. They are surrendered and trustful people. You sense that their life is okay at the core. They have given control to Another and are at peace, which paradoxically allows them to calmly be in control. A Kingdom person lives for what matters, for life in its deepest and lasting sense. There's a kind of gentle absolutism about their lifestyle, an inner freedom to do what they have to do—joyfully. Kingdom people feel like grounded yet spacious people at the same time, the best of the conservative and the best of the progressive types in the same body.

Kingdom people are anchored by their awareness of God's love deep within them and deep within everyone else, too. They happily live on a level playing field, where God has come to *pitch his tent* (the literal translation of John 1:14) among all of us. All games of classism, sexism, racism, and nationalism are henceforth seen to be a waste of valuable time and energy that could be used for positive good.

+Adapted from *Jesus' Plan for a New World: The Sermon on the Mount*, pp. 110–111

INTIMATE WITH EVERYTHING

As I studied accounts of the Resurrection, I came to see what is now completely obvious to me: these texts reveal both the Christ and the True Self as a deep capacity for intimacy with oneself and with everything, probably including life itself. Starting with Christ's "white as snow" robe and his "face like lightning" (Matthew 28:3), we have initial statements of perfect transparency, accessibility, and radiant visibility. The True Self is a shared and sharable self, or it is not the True Self.

In John's account...Mary Magdalene knows Jesus not by sight but when he pronounces her first name (John 20:16). She completes the exchange by calling him "Master" in return. Jesus's puzzling "Do not cling to me" (John 20:17) statement is what makes true intimacy possible. Intimacy is possible only between two calm identities and it is not the same as melding or fusing into one. As we say in non-dual teaching, "Not two, but not one either."

+Adapted from *Immortal Diamond: Searching for Our True Self,* pp. 160, 162

A NEW, BUT REALLY OLD, SOFTWARE

The early but learned pattern of dualistic thinking can get us only so far; so all religions at the more mature levels have discovered software for processing the really big questions, such as death, love, infinity, suffering, and God. Many of us call this access "contemplation." *It is a non-dualistic way of seeing the moment.* Originally, the word was simply *prayer.*

It is living in the naked now, the sacrament of the present moment, that will teach us how to actually experience our experiences, whether good, bad, or ugly, and how to let them transform us. Words by themselves invariably divide the moment; pure presence lets it be what it is, as it is.

When you can be present, you will know the Real Presence. I promise you this is true.

And it is almost that simple.

+Adapted from *The Naked Now: Learning to See as the Mystics See,* p. 12

THE LOSS OF ANY ALTERNATIVE CONSCIOUSNESS

Hugh of St. Victor (1078–1141) and Richard of St. Victor (1123–1173) wrote that humanity was given three sets of eyes, each building on the previous one. The first set of eyes were the eyes of the flesh (thought or sight), the second set of eyes were the eyes of reason (meditation or reflection), and the third set of eyes were the eyes of true understanding (contemplation). They represent the last era of broad or formal teaching of the contemplative mind in the West, although St. Bonaventure (1221–1274) and Francisco de Osuna (1492–1542) are some rare examples who carry it into the following centuries. But for the most part, the formal teaching of the contemplative mind, even in the monasteries, winds down by the beginning of the fourteenth century. No wonder we so badly needed some Reformations by the sixteenth century.

I cannot emphasize strongly enough that the loss of the contemplative mind is at the basis of much of the short-*sight*edness and religious crises of the Western world. Lacking such wisdom, it is very difficult for churches, governments, and leaders to move beyond ego, the desire for control, and public posturing. Everything divides into oppositions such as liberal vs. conservative, with vested interests pulling against one another. Truth is no longer possible at this level of conversation. Even theology becomes more a quest for power than a search for God and Mystery.

+Adapted from *The Naked Now: Learning to See as the Mystics See*, pp. 28–29

IMPLICATIONS OF ITS LOSS

One wonders how far spiritual leaders can genuinely lead us without some degree of mystical seeing and action. It is hardly an exaggeration to say that us-and-them seeing, and the dualistic thinking that results, is the foundation of almost all discontent and violence in the world. It allows heads of religion and state to avoid their own founders, their own national ideals, and their own better instincts. Lacking the contemplative gaze, such leaders will remain mere functionaries and technicians, without any big picture to guide them for the long term. The world and the churches are filled with such people, often using God language as a cover for their own lack of certainty or depth.

+Adapted from *The Naked Now: Learning to See as the Mystics See*, pp. 28, 29

IT'S ALL ABOUT SEEING WELL

One increasing consensus among scholars and spiritual observers is that conversion or enlightenment moves forward step by step from almost totally dualistic thinking to non-dual thinking at the highest levels. We call that higher way of seeing and being present *contemplation*. If this ancient gift could be clarified and recovered for Western Christians, Muslims, and Jews, religion would experience a monumental leap forward. We could start *being present to one another*. We could live in the naked now instead of hiding in the past or worrying about the future, as we mentally rehearse resentments and make our case for why we are right and someone else is wrong.

Good religion is always about *seeing* rightly: "The lamp of the body is the eye; if your eye is sound, your whole body will be filled with light," as Jesus says in Matthew 6:22. *How you see is what you see.* And to see rightly is to be able to be fully present—without fear, without bias, and without judgment. It is such hard work for the ego, for the emotions, and for the body that I think most of us would simply prefer to go to church services.

+Adapted from *The Naked Now: Learning to See as the Mystics See*, pp. 62, 63

WITHOUT WHICH WE CANNOT LIVE THE GOSPEL

Non-dual thinking is a way of seeing that refuses to eliminate the negative, the problematic, the threatening parts of everything. Non-dual thinking does not divide the field of the naked now, but receives it all. This demands some degree of real detachment from the self. The non-dual/contemplative mind holds truth humbly, knowing that if it is true, it is its own best argument.

Non-polar thinking (if you prefer that phrase) teaches you how to hold creative tensions, how to live with paradox and contradictions, how not to run from mystery, and therefore how to practice what all religions teach as necessary: compassion, mercy, loving kindness, patience, forgiveness, and humility.

+Adapted from *The Naked Now: Learning to See as the Mystics See*, pp. 131, 132

JESUS LIVED CONTEMPLATION
MORE THAN FORMALLY TEACHING IT

The non-dual paradox and mystery was for Christians a living person, an icon we could gaze upon and fall in love with. Jesus became "the pioneer and perfecter of our faith" (Hebrews 12:2), the Mediator, very God and very human at the same time, who consistently said, "Follow me." He is the living paradox, calling us to imitate him, as we realize that "[he] and the Father are one" (John 10:30). In him, the great gaps are all overcome; all cosmic opposites are reconciled in him, as the author of Colossians 1:15–20 so poetically says in an early Christian hymn.

The dualistic mind gives us sanity and safety, and that is good enough. But to address our religious and social problems in any creative or finally helpful way, we also need something more, something bigger, and something much better. We need "the mind of Christ" (1 Corinthians 2:16). Jesus in his life and ministry modeled and exemplified the non-dual or contemplative mind more than academically teaching it. The very fact that the disciples had to ask him for a prayer like the disciples of the Baptist had (Luke 11:1), probably reveals that spoken or recited prayers was not his practice. Why else would he go apart and alone for such long periods, except that his prayer was the prayer of quiet more than synagogue or temple services?

+Adapted from *The Naked Now: Learning to See as the Mystics See*, pp. 154, 133

REWIRING THE BRAIN

I try to teach people an entirely new way of knowing the world, a way of knowing that has the power to move them beyond mere ideology and dualistic thinking, we call it contemplation. Mature religion will always lead us to some form of prayer, meditation, or contemplation to balance out our daily calculating mind. Believe me, it is major surgery, and you must practice it for years to begin to rewire your egocentric responses. Contemplation is work, so much so that most give up after their first futile attempts. But the goal is not success at all, only the practice itself. The only people who pray well are those who keep trying to pray.

Such seeing—and that is what it is—gives us the capacity to be happy and happily alone, rooted in God, comfortable with paradox and mystery, and largely immune to mass consciousness and its false promises. It is called wisdom seeing, and it is the job of elders to pass this on to the next generation.

+Adapted from *Adam's Return*, p. xii

A UNIVERSAL CONTAGION

We are all initially created in the image of God, and Jesus is always re-creating and restoring that image in his public ministry. You could say that is all he is doing! We Christians believe that we cannot know the mind of God until we see what God was doing in, through, and with Jesus. Salvation is contagious, and passes around in just that way. Transformed people, like Jesus, naturally transform people.

The real meaning of apostolic succession is probably not bishops laying their hands on the next generation of priests, but Christians rubbing off on one another! I know we need a process for passing on leadership, but right now we need to pass on grace and healing much more. We clergy find it much easier to magically transform bread than to transform people, situations, and the suffering of our world. Jesus's transformations were immediately verifiable and visible. It was Jesus's nonstop ministry of healing and exorcism. The real message here is not a mere medical cure (although I have seen them!), or whether Jesus could do such a thing, but that (1) God cares about human pain, (2) God cares about it in this world now, (3) God's action actually changes people in ways that we can see, and (4) such people and such people alone, are equipped to pass on the real message.

OUR PRAYERS CREATE US

When we celebrate New Year's Day, maybe Easter too, we celebrate a symbolic rebirth of time. We somehow hope for God to do new things with us and for us. We wait for the coming of grace, for the unfolding of Mystery. We wait for the always bigger Truth.

Such humble waiting and open ended expecting allows us to fall into what Thomas Merton called "a hidden wholeness." One does not create or hold onto such wholeness (holiness?) consciously—it holds onto us! Our common code word for this hidden wholeness is quite appropriately "God"! When we agree to love God, we are precisely agreeing to love everything. When we decide to trust God, we are also deciding to trust reality at its deepest foundation.

But we cannot just wait. We must pray too, which is to expect help from Another Source. Our prayers then start both naming us and defining us. When we hear our own prayers in our own ears and our own heart, we start choosing our deepest identity, our biggest future, and our best selves. We fall into our own hidden wholeness.

+Adapted from *Everything Belongs: The Gift of Contemplative Prayer* p. 154

ONLY LOVE CAN HANDLE THE TRUTH

The contemplative mind does not need to prove anything or disprove anything. It's what the Benedictines called a *Lectio Divina*, a reading of the Scripture that looks for wisdom instead of quick answers. It first says, "What does this text ask of *me*? *How can I* change because of this story?" And not "How can I use this to prove that I am right and others are wrong or sinful?"

The contemplative mind is willing to hear from a beginner's mind yet also learn from Scripture, Tradition—and others. It has the humility to move toward Yes/And thinking and not all or nothing thinking. It leads to a Third Way, which is neither fight nor flight, but standing in between— where we can hold *what we do know together with what we don't know*. Holding such a creative tension with humility and patience leads us to wisdom instead of easy answers, which largely create opinionated and smug people instead of wise people. We surely need wise people now who hold their truth humbly and patiently.

+Adapted from the webcast *What is the Emerging Church?* (CD, DVD, MP3)

RICHARD, YOU DO NOT TELL ME
ANYTHING TOTALLY NEW!

Beginner's mind is using your mind, but then letting go of it a bit and for a while—not trusting it too much to be the whole picture, not grasping it too closely so there's room for a larger mind to get in. You only overdo it when you think it is *you* doing all the work and all the thinking. But spiritual knowledge is more like retrieving than discovering. The best compliment I ever get is when people tell me, "Richard, you did not tell me anything new. Somehow I always knew this would be the case, and you just gave me the courage to believe it." I love that!

Beginner's mind is an opening to what might just be—and surely is—the Spirit of God, the promised anointing that "teaches you everything" as St. John says (1 John 2:27). You objectively and already have that anointing, and now you must draw upon it and depend upon it. John has also said, "It is not because you do not know the truth that I write to you, but because you know it already" (1 John 2:21). Spiritual cognition is always a form of *re-cognition*, because the Divine Spirit knows it in you, and through you, and *as you*—already. That is why you do not need to be anxious or try too hard. It is more an allowing when the ego is off to the side. Beginner's mind is a non-grasping, patient, and compassionate holding of truth with the readiness for God and life to reveal even more of that Truth, and the meaning of that Truth, as your life goes on. Beginner's mind is always a humble mind, always knowing that it does not yet fully know.

+Adapted from *Beginner's Mind* (CD, DVD, MP3)

RESOURCES

Methodology

Richard Rohr, *Things Hidden: Scripture as Spirituality* (Cincinnati: Franciscan Media, 2008).

Ewert Cousins, *Christ of the 21ˢᵗ Century* (London: Continuum, 1994).

Brian D. McLaren, *A Generous Orthodoxy* (Grand Rapids: Zondervan/ Youth Specialties, 2006).

John S. Dunne, *The Way of All the Earth: Experiments in Truth and Religion* (Notre Dame, Ind.: University of Notre Dame Press, 1986).

Cynthia Bourgeault, *The Wisdom Way of Knowing: Reclaiming an Ancient Tradition to Awaken the Heart* (New York: Jossey-Bass, 2003).

Aldous Huxley, *The Perennial Philosophy: An Interpretation of the Great Mystics, East and West* (New York: Harper Perennial, 2009).

Foundation

Paul S. Fiddes, *Participating in God: A Pastoral Doctrine of the Trinity* (Louisville, Ky.: Westminister John Knox, 2000).

Marcus J. Borg, *Meeting Jesus Again for the First Time: The Historical Jesus and the Heart of Contemporary Faith* (New York: HarperOne, 1995).

Catherine LaCugna, *God for Us: The Trinity and Christian Life* (New York: HarperOne, 1993).

Rudolf Otto and John W. Harvey, *The Idea of the Holy* (London: Oxford University Press, 1958).

Garry Wills, *What Jesus Meant* (New York: Penguin, 2007).

Raimon Pannikar, *Christophany: The Fullness of Man* (Maryknoll, N.Y.: Orbis, 2004).

FRAME

Mircea Eliade, *The Sacred and the Profane: The Nature of Religion* (New York: Harcourt Brace Jovanovich, 1987).

Ilia Delio, *Christ in Evolution* (Maryknoll, N.Y.: Orbis, 2008).

Bill Plotkin, *Nature and the Human Soul: Cultivating Wholeness and Community in a Fragmented World* (Novato, Calif.: New World Library, 2007).

Louis M. Savary, *Teilhard de Chardin—The Divine Milieu Explained: A Spirituality for the 21ˢᵗ Century* (Mahwah, N.J.: Paulist, 2007).

Mary Oliver, *New and Selected Poems* (Boston: Beacon, 1992).

St. Bonaventure, *The Soul's Journey into God*, ed. Ewert Cousins (Mahwah, N.J.: Paulist, 2000).

ECUMENISM

Richard Rohr, *Everything Belongs: The Gift of Contemplative Prayer* (New York: Crossroad, 2003).

Richard Rohr, *A Lever and a Place to Stand: The Contemplative Stance, the Active Prayer* (Mahwah, N.J.: Hidden Spring, 2011).

Walter Brueggemann, *The Prophetic Imagination* (Minneapolis: Fortress, 1978).

Gil Bailie, *Violence Unveiled: Humanity at the Crossroads*, Gil Bailie (New York: Crossroad, 1996).

Rene Girard, *The Girard Reader* (New York: Crossroad, 1996).

TRANSFORMATION

Richard Rohr, *Immortal Diamond: The Search for Our True Self* (New York: Jossey-Bass, 2013).

Ken Wilber, *Integral Spirituality: A Startling New Role for Religion in the Modern and Postmodern World* (Boston: Shambhala, 2007).

Thomas Merton, *The Wisdom of the Desert* (New York: New Directions, 1970).

Carl Jung, *The Portable Jung,* ed. R.F.C. Hull (New York: Viking, 1976).

Michael J. Christensen and Jeffery A. Wittung, *Partakers of the Divine Nature: The History and Development of Deification in the Christian Traditions* (Ada, Mich.: Baker Academic, 2008).

St. Nikodimos and St. Makarios, *The Philokalia* (New York: Faber and Faber, 1999).

Thomas Merton, *New Seeds of Contemplation* (New York: New Directions, 1972).

James Finley, *Merton's Palace of Nowhere* (Notre Dame, Ind.: Ave Maria, 2003).

PROCESS

Richard Rohr, *Falling Upward: A Spirituality for the Two Halves of Life* (New York: Jossey-Bass, 2011).

David G. Benner, *Spirituality and the Awakening Self: The Sacred Journey of Transformation*, David Benner (Ada, Mich.: Brazos, 2012).

Ernest Becker, *The Denial of Death* (New York: The Free Press, 1973).

Kathleen Dowling-Singh, *The Grace in Dying: How We Are Transformed Spiritually as We Die* (New York: HarperOne, 1998).

St. Thérèse of Lisieux, *Story of a Soul: The Autobiography of Thérèse of Lisieux,* trans. John Clarke (Washington, D.C.: ICS, 1996).

St. John of the Cross, *John of the Cross: Selected Writings* (New York: Paulist, 1988).

Caroline Myss and James Finely, *Transforming Trauma* (audio) (Boulder, Colo.: Sounds True, 2009).

Rainer Maria Rilke, *Rilke's Book of Hours: Love Poems to God,* Anita Barrows and Joanna Macy, trans. (New York: Riverhead, 2005).

GOAL

Richard Rohr, *The Naked Now: Learning to See as the Mystics See* (New York: Crossroad, 2009).

Cynthia Bourgeault, *The Wisdom Jesus: Transforming Heart and Mind—A New Perspective on Christ and His Message* (Boston: Shambhala, 2008).

James Finley, *Christian Meditation: Experiencing the Presence of God* (New York: HarperOne, 2005).

Jon Kabat-Zinn, *Wherever You Go, There You Are: Mindfulness Meditation in Everyday Life* (New York: Hyperion, 1995).

Richard Sardello, *Silence* (Santa Barbara, Calif.: Goldenstone, 2006).

The Cloud of Unknowing (New York: HarperCollins, 2004).

Anthony de Mello, *Sadhana, a Way to God: Christian Exercises in Eastern Form* (New York: Image, 1984).

ABOUT THE AUTHOR

Richard Rohr is a Franciscan priest of the New Mexico Province. He founded the Center for Action and Contemplation in Albuquerque, New Mexico, in 1986, where he presently serves as founding director. Rohr is the author of more than twenty books, an internationally known speaker, and a regular contributing writer for *Sojourners* and *Tikkun* magazines, as well as the CAC's quarterly journal, *Oneing*, and its daily online posts.